The Asian American Achievement Paradox

The Asian American Achievement Paradox

Jennifer Lee and Min Zhou

Russell Sage Foundation
New York

The Russell Sage Foundation

Library of Congress Cataloging-in-Publication Data

Lee, Jennifer, 1968-
  The Asian American achievement paradox/Jennifer Lee and Min Zhou.
    pages cm
  Includes bibliographical references and index.
  ISBN 978-0-87154-547-3 (paperback: alk. paper)—ISBN 978-1-61044-850-5 (ebook)
  1. Asian Americans—Social conditions. 2. Asian Americans—Economic conditions.
  3. Asian Americans—Ethnic identity. 4. United States—Ethnic relations. I. Zhou, Min,
  1956- II. Title.
  E184.A75L443 2015
  305.895'073--dc23

                        2014048848

Text design by Suzanne Nichols

RUSSELL SAGE FOUNDATION
112 East 64th Street, New York, New York 10065
10 9 8 7 6 5 4 3 2 1

To Our Husbands—
Michael Zimmerman (Jennifer Lee's husband)
and Sam Nan Guo (Min Zhou's husband),
who provide unconditional love and support,
and also gently remind us when it is time to
put our laptops away.

~ Contents ~

~ List of Figures and Tables ~

~ About the Authors ~

JENNIFER LEE is professor of sociology in the School of Social Sciences at the University of California, Irvine.

MIN ZHOU is professor of sociology and Asian American studies, Walter and Shirley Wang Endowed Chair in U.S.-China Relations and Communications, and founding chair of the Asian American Studies Department at UCLA. She is also Tan Lark Sye Chair Professor of Sociology at Nanyang Technological University, Singapore.

~ Preface ~

Following a recent public lecture in her hometown of Philadelphia, Jennifer Lee was approached by a female member of the audience who asked where she had gone to high school. The woman said that she was curious because, as a retired high school teacher, she wanted to know about Jennifer's educational background. Jennifer answered, after which the woman promptly seized the opportunity to convey her opinion of Korean students:

> I was so happy whenever I had Korean students in my classes. They were my best students; they were so bright and worked so hard! And some of these kids, they have parents who don't even speak English.

The retired teacher's comment, unrelated to her original question, did not come as a surprise. Both authors had heard it many times before about Korean students and about Asian American students more generally. Positive comments such as these reflect a puzzle for many Americans about the academic achievement of the children of Asian immigrants (the 1.5 and second generation). How do the children of Asian immigrants and refugees—even those whose parents have only an elementary school education, do not speak English, and work in restaurants and factories—graduate as high school valedictorians, earn admission to prestigious universities, and hold high-status professional jobs? Vexed by Asian Americans' exceptional achievement outcomes, some pundits point to Asian culture: because Asian Americans possess the "right" cultural traits and place a high value on education, they claim, Asian American students outperform their non-Asian peers, including native-born whites.

Allow us to get personal for a moment and briefly reflect on our own experiences of growing up in a Korean immigrant family as a member of the 1.5 generation, and raising a child of the 1.5 generation as a Chinese immigrant parent, respectively. Jennifer's parents decided to immigrate to the United States because her father wanted to pursue his PhD at Temple University and work with a professor there whose research he admired. Her mother—who was a nurse in Korea—obtained an immigrant visa for her family, including three-year-old Jennifer and her one-year-old sister, Stephanie, which was possible because the change in U.S. immigration law had opened the doors to Asian immigrants and gave preference to highly skilled applicants.

Upon settling in Philadelphia, Jennifer's parents quickly realized that they could not adequately support a family of four based on a nurse's salary alone, so they took an economic detour and decided to open a business in a predominantly African American neighborhood in West Philadelphia selling sneakers. With no savings or wealth to speak of, her parents borrowed money from family members until they had accumulated enough to open a business. After seven years of running the sneaker store, her father returned to graduate school and earned his PhD, while her mother continued to support the family by running the business alone. Jennifer's parents earned enough to send both daughters to private high school and college, and both attained graduate degrees. Jennifer graduated from Columbia University and later earned her PhD there. Stephanie graduated from Boston University and the University of the Sciences in Philadelphia. Stephanie is now a pharmacist, and Jennifer is a professor.

While Jennifer's parents raised their daughters to "try your best" in school, neither was a "Tiger" parent who employed strict, relentless, demeaning parenting practices. They did believe, however, that trying your best should result in straight A's and admission to an Ivy League university. They supported their belief by providing their daughters with a wealth of class resources: a home in a middle-class suburb of Philadelphia, private school education, educational books, SAT prep courses, and extracurricular activities such as gymnastics and piano lessons (which lasted only a few years since neither daughter was interested enough in music to practice much before the weekly lesson). For Jennifer's immigrant parents, being able to provide their 1.5-generation daughters with these resources was meaningful because such resources had been unavailable to them when they were growing up in Korea. Furthermore, her parents felt that it was their obligation to fully support their daughters, especially because they had the class resources to do so.

While Jennifer is a member of the 1.5 generation, Min Zhou is the mother of a 1.5-generation Chinese and the mother-in-law of a second-generation Vietnamese. Min's parents, who still live in China, did not have the opportunity to go to college, but education for their children was always a priority and doing well in school was non-negotiable. Growing up in turbulent times during the Chinese Cultural Revolution, Min could not attend college after graduating from high school, so she worked in a factory for five years before an opportunity to attend college presented itself. She was among the fortunate few to gain admission to college when China reopened its higher education entrance examination. After college, she migrated to the United States, leaving behind her husband and ten-month-old son in China and having only a single $50 bill in her pocket, to pursue her PhD at SUNY–Albany. Because of her foreign student visa, Min worked odds jobs under the table as a babysitter, housekeeper, hotel maid, restaurant dishwasher, and seamstress to make ends meet while she was in graduate school. After she attained a job as an assistant professor at Louisiana State University, she, like Jennifer's mother, sponsored her family to migrate to the United States under the visa preference category favoring the highly skilled.

Raising her only child, Philip, who left China at age five, while supporting her husband's graduate studies was no easy feat as the primary breadwinner on an assistant professor's meager salary. Unable to afford a babysitter or extracurricular activities such as violin or piano lessons for Philip, Min took Philip to her Saturday classes and summer school classes that she taught to earn extra income to support her family. On weekends and school holidays, she also took him to bookstores and libraries, where Philip had unlimited access to books and other academic resources and where she could do her own research. Neither Min nor her husband is a Tiger parent; they did not push Philip into a pre-programmed pathway. Nevertheless, Philip graduated from MIT with a bachelor's degree and a master's degree in engineering and earned his PhD in computer science from Stanford University. He is now an assistant professor of computer science at the University of Rochester.

Min's daughter-in-law Lisa, Philip's high school sweetheart, has a similar experience. Lisa's parents arrived in the United States in 1975 as penniless refugees from war-torn Vietnam. Her father was able to finish his undergraduate and graduate education in the United States, and he currently works as an electrical engineer. While her mother could have gone to college, she opened up a beauty salon instead because she had to earn a living and provide for her family. Like Min and her husband, Lisa's parents never pushed their three U.S.-born children to pursue a particular career path, but they were adamant about doing well in school, which, for them, meant that their children should earn at least a B average. Lisa and her two brothers grew up spending a lot of time in their mother's beauty salon, where a desk was set up for them to do homework together. Lisa graduated from UCLA and then UC San Francisco's dental school, and she now works as a dentist.

No one would dispute these success stories. Some of our readers would adopt a narrative that attributes these educational and occupational outcomes to Asian cultural traits and values, but as we argue throughout the book, this narrative misses several critical elements, including "starting points" and "hyper-selectivity."

How would the narrative change if we considered starting points and measured success by how much progress a child of immigrants or refugees makes from the position already achieved by his or her parents? Measured this way, Jennifer, Stephanie, Philip, and Lisa are not extraordinarily successful. Jennifer and Philip achieved a level of education no higher than that of their parents. (Jennifer's father and Philip's mother have PhD degrees.) Moreover, Stephanie's and Lisa's level of education is actually lower, so should we consider them downwardly mobile—and therefore unsuccessful? Furthermore, that Jennifer and Philip both hold a PhD is unsurprising because, according to the status attainment model in sociology, the strongest predictor of a child's level of education is the parents' level of education. So whom should we consider more successful: a second-generation Asian American whose parents hold a PhD who also attains a PhD, or a second-generation Mexican whose parents have less than an elementary school education who graduates from high school?

As for hyper-selectivity, which reflects a dual type of positive selectivity—a higher percentage of college graduates among immigrants compared to non-migrants from their country of origin, and a higher percentage of college graduates compared to the host country—how would the narrative change if Asian immigrants had the socioeconomic profile of their counterparts who migrated at the turn of the twentieth century? Being members of hyper-selected immigrant groups today has affected the cultural frame that immigrant parents have constructed for themselves and their 1.5- and second-generation children, as well as the ethnic capital and resources that immigrant communities generate to help their children attain the success frame. Others' perceptions of Asian Americans, as well as of their skills, ability, and work ethic, have also been affected by their membership in hyper-selected immigrant groups. In short, hyper-selectivity has cultural, institutional, and social psychological consequences, which we detail in our book.

Rather than shying away from the thorny and contentious relationship between culture and achievement, we tackle it head on and address the question: what is cultural about Asian American academic achievement? In the process, we unveil the many paradoxes that accompany high achievement, high expectations, and positive stereotypes among 1.5- and second-generation Asian Americans. Combining the literature in sociology and social psychology in a novel way, we have aimed to write a book that is more than the sum of its disciplinary parts, in a style that will appeal to a wide audience.

Reflecting on the long process of conducting interviews, collecting and analyzing data, and writing the book, we find ourselves humbled by and grateful for the numerous people who have helped shepherd our study to completion. Our first order of gratitude goes to the Russell Sage Foundation for funding the research on which our book is based, and especially to Eric Wanner, then the president of the foundation. Eric had the foresight to support a project in which a team of researchers proposed to collect original survey data on the adult children of immigrants in Los Angeles, which would later become the Immigration and Intergenerational Mobility in Metropolitan Los Angeles (IIMMLA) survey. Without Eric's steadfast support, the continued support of the foundation's new president, Sheldon Danziger, and the support from the foundation's board of trustees, this book would not have been possible.

IIMMLA brought together an interdisciplinary team to design and implement the survey, including Frank Bean, Rubén Rumbaut, Susan Brown, Leo Chavez, Louis DeSipio, and both of us. While we have thanked the members of the IIMMLA team in person for this collaborative effort, we would like to publicly acknowledge our gratitude to each of these scholars, from whom we have learned so much. After the survey data were collected, the Russell Sage Foundation also supported the collection of in-depth, life-history interviews for a separate project that we spearheaded, on which much of our book is based. This allowed us to hire a stellar group of graduate research assistants to help collect and analyze the data: Jody Vallejo, Rosaura Tafoya-Estrada, Leisy Abrego, James Bany, Kris Noam, Ada Lingjun Peng, Yang Sao Xiong, and Chengwei Xu. We were fortunate to have had the opportunity to work with such a superb group of young scholars, most of whom have since graduated and are making a name for themselves in their careers.

There would have been no interviews to conduct had there not been willing respondents from the IIMMLA survey to agree to be reinterviewed. Our interviewees gave generously of their time and shared their multifaceted experiences of growing up American. Some of them shared narratives that were humorous and happy, while others shared experiences that had been profound and painful. For many, this was the first time they had openly shared such intimate accounts, and each gave us so much more than we had expected. Their unbridled candor inspired us to write a book that reflects their experiences by identifying patterns, acknowledging disconfirming evidence, and drawing from theory and previous research to help explain our findings. Because we must protect their privacy and identity, we used pseudonyms throughout the book. We acknowledge our gratitude to these young Asian Americans who let us draw on their personal life histories to enrich social science research. We hope that when they read the book, they will feel that we recounted their life histories accurately.

Another invaluable asset at the Russell Sage Foundation is senior program officer Aixa Cintrón-Vélez; she helped us develop the project from its initial inception and provided key theoretical, empirical, and analytical insights, resulting in a much richer book. Aixa also leads the Russell Sage Foundation's Working Group on Cultural Contact and Immigration, of which Jennifer is a part. Joining together researchers from sociology, political science, geography, and social psychology, the working group aims to produce novel, cross-disciplinary perspective approaches to studying the effects of immigration in the United States. It was her participation in the working group that sparked Jennifer's interest in social psychology, especially in the effects of stereotypes and mind-sets on achievement among the children of immigrants. Several of the book's chapters bear the intellectual imprint of the members of the working group.

Director of publications Suzanne Nichols is a superb editor who knows precisely how to motivate us with her judicious balance of fair and warranted criticism, staunch support, and keen advice, all of which she delivers with razor-sharp humor. All authors should be fortunate to work with an editor as incisive, candid, and patient as she. We also thank Suzanne for suggesting a gifted copyeditor, Cynthia Buck, who made our writing immeasurably clearer and more accessible yet managed to retain our voice in the process. And we are grateful to partner with David Haproff, the foundation's director of communications, whose commitment to reaching a wide and diverse audience for our work matches ours.

The Russell Sage Foundation also supported Jennifer Lee as a visiting scholar during the academic year 2011–2012, which provided unfettered time to begin writing the manuscript in a milieu that can only be described as "academic mecca." One of the advantages of spending a year at the foundation is being among a community of interdisciplinary scholars whose research and perspectives help sharpen one's own. While grateful to the entire 2011–2012 Visiting Scholar cohort for the stimulating exchange of ideas, Jennifer is especially indebted to Rucker Johnson and Karthick Ramakrishnan, who continue to inspire with their pathbreaking research and their collegiality.

All writing, even that which is published, is work in progress. Ideas continue to evolve through critical reflection and dialogue, and we have benefited immensely from the reflection and dialogue that unfolded while presenting our research at colloquia and conferences. We were fortunate to have been invited to present our research to diverse and multidisciplinary audiences in the United States and abroad, including at the Academia Sinica (Taiwan), the Center for Advanced Study in the Behavioral Sciences, Columbia University, the CUNY Graduate Center, Hong Kong Baptist University, Hong Kong Chinese University, Huazhong Agricultural University (China), Huazhong University of Science and Technology (China), National University of Singapore, Pennsylvania State University, Population Reference Bureau, Princeton University, Russell Sage Foundation, Stanford University, Stockholm University (Sweden), Sun Yat-sen University (China), Syracuse University, Tsinghua University (China), University of Amsterdam (Netherlands), UC Berkeley, UC Davis, UC Riverside, University of Chicago, University of Hong Kong, University of Notre Dame, University of Osnabrück (Germany), University of Saskatchewan (Canada), University of Toronto (Canada), and Weelock College (Singapore). We also benefited from lively exchanges with our colleagues within our institutions: UC Irvine, UCLA, and Nanyang Technological University (Singapore). The insightful and critical comments, questions, and critiques we received challenged us to make our work better. We are also grateful for our home institutions for providing invaluable financial support, including research grants from the School of Social Sciences at UC Irvine, the Walter and Shirley Endowed Chair's fund at UCLA, and a research grant from the School of Humanities and Social Sciences at Nanyang Technological University.

We also presented our ideas while teaching our classes at UC Irvine and UCLA and benefited from the insights and thoughtful questions from our students, both graduates and undergraduates, many of whom were fascinated by and vexed about the role of culture in explaining Asian American achievement. Teaching our ideas to our students forced us to be clearer about them. We thank our students for indulging us with their patience, inquisitiveness, and perceptiveness. For many of our students who are the children of immigrants, this is a story about their lives of growing up American. We hope that they too feel that we have told it accurately.

Several colleagues read the full manuscript and offered discerning comments that strengthened it beyond measure: Philip Kasinitz, Van Tran, and Mark Vanlandingham. We are grateful for their close reading and candid assessment of an earlier draft, as well as for their astute suggestions about how we might improve it. Comparing the first and final drafts provides indisputable evidence of their intellectual imprint, for which we are deeply indebted. We are also fortunate to have a cadre of smart, critical, and supportive colleagues who were gracious enough to read portions of the manuscript and discuss our ideas at various stages of the book's development, all of which helped strengthen the final product. We thank Richard Alba, Jacob Avery, Carl Bankston, David Card, Prudence Carter, Margaret Chin, Yoonsun Choi, Maurice Crul, Michael Dawson, Kay Deaux, Sean Drake, Patricia Fernandez-Kelly, Nancy Foner, Eric Fong, Herbert Gans, Douglas Hartmann, Amy Hsin, Tomás Jiménez, Grace Kao, Vivian Louie, John Mollenkopf, Letta Page, Giovanni Peri, Alejandro Portes, Andreas Pott, Steven Raphael, Cecilia Ridgeway, Sarah Rothbard, Jens Schneider, John Skrentny, Mario Small, Robert Smith, Edward Telles, Christopher Uggen, Jody Vallejo, Roger Waldinger, and Harriet Zuckerman. A mere thank you seems inadequate to express our gratitude for their role in helping the book come to fruition.

We end on a personal note by extending our gratitude to our families, who provide unconditional love and support. Jennifer thanks her mother and father, Wonja and Sangrin Lee; her sister, Stephanie Lee; and her brother-in-law, Chris Larson, for providing a bedrock of security, cheering her on enthusiastically, and fueling her with incessant laughter. Min thanks her father, Leiming Zhou; her mother, Yaoping Yao; her brother, Jining; and sister, Sujuan, who live on different continents but continue to serve as her source of inspiration and emotional support and remain the backbone of her life and career. Min also thanks Philip and Lisa for offering their nuanced insight into the complex world of our study's subjects and Lisa's parents, Liem and Phuong Mai, for being always ready to lend a helping hand.

As the saying goes, one does not get to choose one's family, but if we had the choice, we would have chosen ours. We did, however, have a choice of husbands, and in this regard we chose wisely. Our life partners, Michael Zimmerman (Jennifer's husband) and Sam Nan Guo (Min's husband), provide immeasurable and unfailing support in all of our professional and personal endeavors. The patience, care, and humor with which they encourage us have allowed us to complete the book manuscript in a timely manner while also relishing the time apart from it. Because they give unconditionally to us, we dedicate this book to them, as a small and symbolic gesture of our love and appreciation. Michael and Sam, our deepest gratitude to you!

Jennifer Lee, Newport Beach, California, USA
Min Zhou, Singapore
February 2015

~ Chapter 1 ~

What Is Cultural About Asian American Achievement?

In 2012 the Pew Research Center, a nonpartisan think tank based in Washington, D.C., released a report entitled "The Rise of Asian Americans," based on a national survey of the largest Asian ethnic groups in the United States.[1] In part, the title refers to changing demographic trends: the number of Asian immigrants has surpassed the number of Latino immigrants, and Asian Americans are now the fastest-growing group in the country. The "rise" also refers to socioeconomic trends: Asian Americans have the highest median household income and highest level of education of all groups, including native-born whites. For example, half of Asian American adults age twenty-five and older have a bachelor's degree or higher, compared to 31 percent of whites, 18 percent of African Americans, and 13 percent of Latinos. The Pew Report also highlighted that Asian Americans place more value on hard work, career success, marriage, and parenthood than other Americans and are also more satisfied with their lives, their finances, and the direction of the country.

The release of the Pew Report immediately sparked controversy and generated criticism among Asian American scholars (including some of the study's external advisers), elected officials, community leaders, and Asian American organizations—all of whom criticized the way in which Pew presented its data.[2] By highlighting selective outcomes such as educational attainment and median household income and pairing these findings with data showing that Asian Americans place greater value on hard work for success than other Americans, Pew led readers to make a causal argument—that is, that Asian Americans' values about hard work and success drive their exceptional outcomes.

Pew's data are not problematic, but the way in which Pew led readers to interpret their findings is. In fact, Pew's findings of Asian Americans' outcomes are unsurprising because they are consistent with those based on analyses of the U.S. censuses since the 1980s.[3] The 2010 U.S. census shows that, on average, Asian Americans—a group that includes more than twenty nationalities from diverse socioeconomic backgrounds—fared better than the general U.S. population on many key socioeconomic measures. Most remarkable is their educational attainment: as mentioned, half of Asian American adults age twenty-five and older have a bachelor's degree or higher, a rate almost twice as high as the 28 percent of all American adults with a college education.

Recent admissions figures for the country's most competitive magnet high schools and elite universities point to the same trend. Among the students offered admission to New York City's famed Stuyvesant High School in the fall of 2013, more than 70 percent were Asian, 20 percent were white, and less than 10 percent were other ethnoracial groups. Among those offered admission to Bronx High School of Science, 60 percent were Asian, 30 percent were white, and less than 10 percent were other groups.[4] Asian Americans typically make up about one-fifth of the entering classes at Ivy League universities, including Harvard, Yale, and Princeton. And in prestigious public universities such as the flagship of the University of California (UC), Berkeley, they make up more than 40 percent of the undergraduate student body. At UC Irvine and UCLA, where we teach, respectively, they make up 54 percent and 40 percent of the student body.[5] At 13 percent of California's population and 5.5 percent of the U.S. population, Asian Americans are overrepresented as a proportion of their population in the country's most elite high schools and universities, making them highly visible in higher education.

While we applaud Pew for its initiative and its scientific approach to conducting a nationwide survey of the Asian American population, we remain critical of the way in which Pew and the media framed the findings.[6] It may not have been Pew's intent to advance a political agenda, but by framing Asian American achievement in this light, the report served to endorse a neoconservative political platform that propagates the belief that high socioeconomic outcomes result from adopting the "right" cultural values. Moreover, this framing reinforced the stereotype of Asian Americans as the "model minority" that has achieved success the right way.

Since the mid-1960s, when U.S. media images of Asian Americans as the model minority first became widespread, scholars and pundits have debated about how to explain the educational achievement of Asians Americans.[7] "Structuralists" emphasize the role of social structure; more specifically, they focus on the extent to which ethnoracial groups are constrained by or benefit from the broader stratification system and the networks of social relations within it.[8] However, even the most sophisticated regression models based on census and survey data consistently show significant ethnoracial effects: being Chinese, Korean, or Vietnamese positively affects educational outcomes (measured by grades and years of education), while being Mexican has a negative effect.

Furthermore, significant educational differences among ethnoracial groups persist even after controlling for all measurable demographic, socioeconomic, and contextual variables.[9] Largely owing to data limitations, structuralists have ceased their analyses at this point. A notable exception is the research by Amy Hsin and Xu Xie, who have advanced the debate with analyses of longitudinal data to explain the Asian-white achievement gap.[10] They find that while socioeconomic class and cognitive ability cannot explain the achievement gap, differences in effort can. Based on teachers' assessments, Hsin and Xie find that teachers consistently rate Asian students more highly in this regard vis-à-vis their white peers.

While data limitations are part of the problem, there are other reasons why social scientists have difficulty in explaining the persistent intergroup differences in educational outcomes. First, the differences may be the direct or spillover consequences of racism and ethnoracial discrimination, including implicit biases, which are not easily captured by structural variables or interaction terms. Second, many scholars have been reluctant to publicly engage in a substantive discussion about the relationship between ethnoracial status and culture because these tend to ignite controversy, stir tensions between and within groups, and lead to uncomfortable conclusions.[11]

The reluctance to critically engage in the debates about culture and achievement, however, has left the door wide open for pundits like David Brooks and Nicholas Kristof and scholars like Charles Murray, Amy Chua, and Jed Rubenfeld to advance culturally essential arguments.[12] Unlike structuralists, "culturalists" focus on the role of the cultural traits, values, attitudes, and behavioral patterns of successful ethnoracial and religious groups and argue that these explain the variation in intergroup outcomes. They have argued that Asian Americans exhibit certain traits and values in spades: they are more hardworking and more disciplined, and they have tight-knit families, respect their parents, delay gratification, make sacrifices, and value education more than other groups.[13]

They view cultural characteristics as fixed and essential to ethnoracial groups and ignore a host of structural factors that affect educational outcomes, including the educational selectivity of contemporary immigrants and differences in access to economic, ethnic, cultural, and public resources. Furthermore, culturalists overlook the effects of ethnoracial stereotypes, implicit biases, and micro-aggressions—the brief, commonplace verbal, behavioral, and institutional indignities imposed on marginalized ethnoracial groups.[14]

While structuralists underscore social structure and have largely avoided discussions about culture, culturalists flagrantly tout values, traits, and behavior and have ignored a host of structural factors that affect educational achievement. Although researchers from both perspectives have drawn on ample empirical data to develop sophisticated theoretical models to explain ethnoracial differences in educational outcomes, neither camp attempts to engage in a fruitful dialogue. As a result, the ideological divide that separates them grows even wider and efforts to bridge the divide remain woefully insufficient.

This is the point of departure for our study. We ask the central question: What is cultural about Asian American achievement, and how do we explain the Asian American achievement paradox? That is, how do we explain the exceptional academic achievement of the children of Asian immigrants, including those whose parents were penniless immigrants and refugees when they arrived in the United States, have only an elementary school education, do not speak English, and work in ethnic restaurants and factories? To address this question we place culture front and center in our analyses but do not lose sight of the structural circumstances that affect the formation of cultural institutions, frames, stereotypes, and mind-sets.

We adopt an "emergent" approach to culture, meaning that we argue that culture emerges from structure, but we caution that this is not a unidirectional relationship. Rather, we maintain that culture, being dynamic and dialectical, re-forms and adapts in order to best fit the host-society context.[15] More concretely, we maintain that an immigrant group's culture—which we delineate by its institutions, frames, and mind-sets—emerges and continually re-forms as a result of historical, legal, institutional, and social psychological processes. Hence, culture can act in parallel with structure and can also change structural opportunities for group members.[16] By shedding light on the dynamic interaction between structural and cultural processes, we show how the children of poor and working-class Asian immigrants are able to override their class disadvantage in ways that defy the status attainment model.

The Aim of the Study

We approach the Asian American achievement paradox by studying the adult children of Chinese immigrants and Vietnamese refugees. We systematically analyze their everyday experiences to identify discernible empirical patterns, construct theory, and draw practical and policy implications.

We chose to focus on these two Asian ethnic groups—Chinese and Vietnamese—for three reasons. First, the Chinese, a long-standing immigrant group in the United States, and the Vietnamese, a relatively recent refugee group, share certain cultural traditions, such as Confucianism, but differ enormously in the structural circumstances from which they emigrated. The economic and political contexts of their homelands differ radically, as does their premigration socioeconomic status (SES). While Chinese immigrants exhibit higher-than-average levels of education compared to the U.S. mean, Vietnamese immigrants exhibit lower-than-average levels of education. Second, their contexts of reception and patterns of settlement upon immigrating to the United States also differ. Third, despite the tremendous intergroup differences among the first generation in their immigration histories, socioeconomic backgrounds, and settlement patterns, the educational outcomes of the children of Chinese immigrants and Vietnamese refugees converge within one generation—a vexing pattern that we refer to as "second-generation convergence." Focusing on two diverse Asian immigrant groups whose U.S.-born and -raised children exhibit similarly high educational outcomes enables us to identify the structural and cultural mechanisms and processes that result in an Asian American achievement paradox.

Research Questions

We approach the Asian American achievement paradox by addressing three general research questions:

1. How do we explain second-generation convergence? That is, why do 1.5- and second-generation Chinese and Vietnamese converge in educational outcomes in spite of their immigrant parents' diverse origins, conditions of emigration, and family socioeconomic status?

2. How do the children of Chinese and Vietnamese immigrants from poor and working-class backgrounds override their disadvantaged class status and achieve exceptional academic outcomes?

3. Is there something exceptional about Asian culture or being Asian American that drives these outcomes?

Our analyses are mainly based on eighty-two in-depth interviews with 1.5- and second-generation Chinese and Vietnamese respondents who were randomly selected from the Immigration and Intergenerational Mobility in Metropolitan Los Angeles (IIMMLA) survey.[17] We also include in-depth interview data with fifty-six 1.5- and second-generation Mexicans, as well as twenty-four third-plus-generation native-born whites and blacks—all of whom were also randomly drawn from the IIMMLA survey—to offer fruitful points of comparison.[18] To place our findings from the qualitative data in context, we analyze quantitative patterns in the IIMMLA survey data, which include larger, representative samples of 1.5- and second-generation Chinese, Vietnamese, and Mexicans, as well as third-plus-generation Mexican, black, and white respondents. Finally, we also draw on findings from other relevant quantitative data sets, including the U.S. Census, to provide even broader context to our analyses.

The Central Argument

We bridge the literature in sociology and social psychology to explain how structural, cultural, and social psychological processes interact at the global and local levels in a way that provides 1.5- and second-generation Chinese and Vietnamese with a "toolkit" of resources that help them get ahead, even in spite of class disadvantages.[19] We highlight the roles of immigrant educational selectivity, ethnic community organization, and host-society reception—all of which provide access to public and ethnic resources that facilitate second-generation educational attainment and mobility. We illustrate how immigrant educational selectivity affects patterns of immigrant adaptation, especially the formation of cultural institutions and frames that influence the achievement mind-sets of the 1.5 and second generation. We caution, however, that the cultural frame and mind-set come at a heavy price, serving as a double-edged sword for the children of Asian immigrants.

We break down our central argument into seven main points. First, ethno-racial culture emerges and reproduces as a result of changes in U.S. immigration laws. The legal change in immigration policies following the passage of the 1965 Immigration and Nationality Act led to preferences for foreign-born applicants with high levels of education and skills. As a result, post-1965 Asian immigrants are highly educated and highly selected from their countries of origin. Immigrant educational selectivity refers to the tendency of those who immigrate to the United States to be more highly educated than their counterparts who stay behind. Although most immigrant groups are highly selected compared to nonmigrants, there is substantial variation in the degree of educational selectivity depending on the country of origin and the timing of migration from a particular country.[20] What makes contemporary Asian immigration unique is that Asian immigrants are, on average, not only highly selected but also more highly educated than the average American, despite the tremendous heterogeneity in their countries of origin. We refer to this dual positive selectivity as "hyper-selectivity."

Second, hyper-selectivity has two notable consequences. First, Asian immigrants selectively import *class-specific* cultural institutions, frames, and mind-sets from their countries of origin and re-create those that are most useful for immigrant adaptation and second-generation mobility in their host society. One of the most notable cultural frames that they import is a strict definition of achievement and success—what we refer to as the "success frame." The frame entails earning straight A's, graduating as the high school valedictorian, earning a degree from an elite university, attaining an advanced degree, and working in one of four high-status professional fields: medicine, law, engineering, or science. So strict is the success frame that our interviewees consistently described grades on an "Asian scale" in which an A-minus is an "Asian F."

A second consequence of hyper-selectivity—and our third main point—is that it increases an ethnic group's capacity to generate "ethnic capital," which supports the cultural institutions and practices necessary to reinforce the success frame.[21] Asian immigrant parents understand that it is not enough to adopt a particular success frame; for any cultural frame to be effective, it needs to be buttressed by reinforcement mechanisms. In the absence of supporting mechanisms, the frame can change or evolve into diverse, competing frames.[22]

Reinforcement mechanisms include public resources, including those available in public schools, such as Advanced Placement (AP) and honors classes. They also include ethnic resources, which, in both their tangible and intangible forms, provide working-class coethnics with the relevant knowledge to navigate the U.S. educational system. Because knowledge is shared among coethnics through cross-class learning, working-class coethnics benefit from the resources generated by their middle-class counterparts.[23] However, this is only part of the story.

Fourth, an ethnic group's cultural frame also requires the recognition, validation, and reinforcement of "gateway institutions" such as schools.[24] Teachers and guidance counselors presume that Asian American students are smart, disciplined, high-achieving, and hardworking and treat them accordingly. As a result, they provide Asian American students with extra help with their coursework and college applications and are more likely to place them in competitive programs like gifted and talented education (GATE) and on academic tracks like AP and honors classes than they do with non-Asian students. When the higher expectations of teachers and guidance counselors are coupled with the institutional advantages accorded to Asian American students, the result is better grades and higher academic attainment.

Fifth, the high academic outcomes of Asian American students give rise to and reinforce ethnoracial stereotypes. Stereotypes are oversimplified, generalized beliefs about the characteristics or predominant cultural view of a particular group, and they have social psychological consequences.[25] One well-documented and empirically tested consequence is "stereotype threat," the fear of performing in such a way that confirms a negative group stereotype, which in turn depresses the performance of members of the negatively stereotyped group. Stereotype threat weakens the performance of high-achieving African American students, even in elite universities.[26] On the other hand, Asian Americans benefit from "stereotype promise," the promise of being viewed through the lens of a positive stereotype, which can enhance the performance of members of a positively stereotyped group.[27] Stereotype promise can enhance the performance of even the most mediocre Asian American students, leading them to work harder to excel in order to confirm the stereotype of Asian American exceptionalism.

Sixth, Asian immigrants have been raised in countries where the prevalent belief is that effort, rather than ability, is the most critical ingredient for achievement. Born and raised abroad, Asian immigrant parents transfer this belief as they raise their children in the United States. By contrast, native-born American parents believe that their children's outcomes are more heavily influenced by innate ability. The different weights that Asian immigrant and U.S.-born parents give to effort versus ability reflect a difference in mind-sets.[28] Differences in mind-sets, we argue, influence the willingness on the part of parents and families to invest in additional material and nonmaterial resources to improve their children's academic outcomes, resulting in differences in "achievement mind-sets" among their children.

Before proceeding, we add a note of clarification and caution: we do not propose that cultural frames, stereotypes, and mind-sets determine behavior; rather, we argue that they are linked in a way that makes certain "strategies of action" more likely, thereby making some group outcomes more likely than others.[29]

Seventh, Asian American achievement comes at a cost. Those who do not fit the narrowly tailored success frame feel like failures, underachievers, and ethnoracial outliers who distance themselves from coethnic peers and communities. Some choose to opt out of their ethnic identities because their outcomes, by not matching the success frame that they perceive as the norm for coethnics and for Asian Americans generally, make them feel inauthentically ethnic or Asian. Another facet of the "achievement paradox" is that even those Asian Americans whose outcomes match the success frame do not feel as successful as they would like because they measure their accomplishments against those of higher-achieving coethnics. Striving for success at all costs comes at a high price.

These seven points support our key argument: the Asian American achievement paradox cannot be explained by superior traits intrinsic to Asian culture or by the greater value that Asians place on education or success. Culture and ethnoracial status matter, but not in the essentialist way often touted by pundits and neoconservatives. We argue that the hyper-selectivity of Asian immigration leads Asian immigrant parents and their second-generation children to create and adopt a specific cultural frame about achievement and success that is supported by public and ethnic resources, reinforced in institutional contexts, and buttressed by social psychological processes. Together, these factors explain the Asian American achievement paradox, or the so-called exceptional academic outcomes of Asian Americans.

The Analytical Model

A sketch of our analytical model appears in figure 1.1. First, hyper-selectivity enables an immigrant group to generate ethnic capital and develop institutions, often through the ethnic community, where ethnic resources are generated and mobilized. Hyper-selectivity also helps group members tap into the host society's publicly available institutional resources, such as those offered in U.S. public schools. By contrast, hypo-selected immigrant groups are less able to generate the ethnic capital and to access ethnic and public resources. "Hypo-selectivity" refers to a dual negative selectivity in which an immigrant group is less educated than their nonmigrant counterparts and also less educated than the host society average.

The hyper-selectivity of Asian immigrants, coupled with their access to ethnic and public institutional resources, enables immigrants to construct and reinforce a success frame that fits squarely into the U.S. culture of mobility—which touts educational attainment as the surest route to success. In turn, the success frame, bolstered by stereotype promise and an achievement mind-set, perpetuates positive stereotypes of Asian Americans.

Reinforced by institutional resources, these cultural and social psychological processes can enhance the academic and work performance of Asian Americans, thereby giving them an advantage over their non-Asian peers.

Figure 1.1   *Cultural Frames: An Analytical Model*

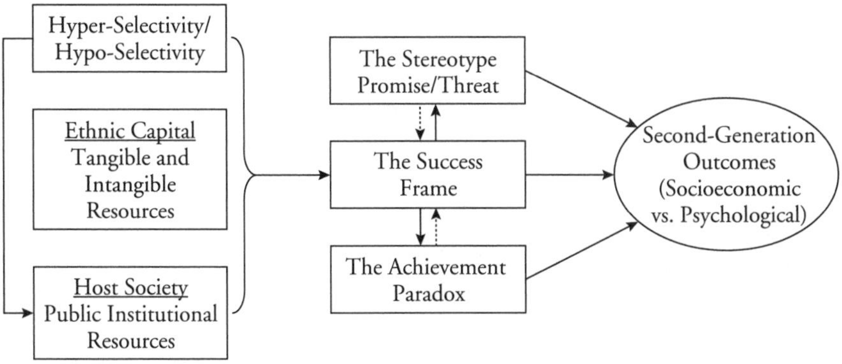

Source: Authors' conceptualization.

These advantages are especially salient because they occur in gateway institutions that distribute rewards and penalties, such as schools, workplaces, and the criminal justice system. By detailing how cultural frames emerge from historical, legal, institutional, and social psychological processes, we identify the mechanisms that produce convergent outcomes among second-generation Asian Americans, despite the unequal starting points of their immigrant parents. In doing so, we dispel the myths about the model minority stereotype and the exceptionality of cultural traits inherent among certain immigrant and ethnoracial groups. Furthermore, by dissecting the components of the Asian American achievement paradox, we illustrate how inequalities are reproduced at the high end of the educational distribution—which is just as critical as inequalities at the low end, yet far less studied. If our goal as researchers is to understand how ethnoracial inequality persists in spite of legislation to eradicate it, it is imperative to study both ends of the educational distribution.

Culture: Popular Discourse, Reflections, and Reemergence

Although popularly used to explain the variation in group outcomes, "culture" remains a slippery term because its conceptual exhaustiveness has limited its explanatory power.

The Popular Discourse on Culture and Achievement

In popular discourse, Asians and non-Asians alike often claim that Asian Americans exhibit exceptionally strong educational outcomes because Asian culture values and prioritizes education. For example, Chin Ho Liao of the

San Gabriel City Council has bluntly claimed, "Other ethnic groups don't put their kids' education as number one priority."[30] In his statement, council member Liao presumed that Asian Americans' educational outcomes are the result of the greater value their parents put on their children's education compared to other groups. His statement is in line with the arguments made by pundits and neoconservative culturalist scholars, who reduce culture to the innate traits and essentialist values of a particular group. In essence, because Asian Americans possess the "right" cultural values, they outperform their non-Asian peers, including native-born white Americans, with respect to educational attainment and median household incomes. Cultural values have also been employed to explain why Asian Americans have the lowest rates of incarceration, delinquency, and teenage births. This argument is so popular in American discourse that Asian Americans' values and traits have been brought to bear on the virgin territory of professional sports: this view attributes Jeremy Lin's success in the National Basketball Association to his playing and living "the right way."[31]

But beyond essentialist cultural arguments, where does culture fit into the debate about immigrant and second-generation socioeconomic outcomes? Before moving forward, we take a step back and briefly outline the intellectual history of the thorny and contested relationship between culture and achievement.

Reflecting Back: The Culture of Poverty Thesis and the Model Minority Antithesis

For decades, sociologists retreated from discussing the relationship between culture and achievement in large part because of the backlash and stigma of two cultural models that emerged in tandem in the 1960s: the "culture of poverty" thesis and the model minority antithesis.

Seeking to understand the persistent poverty among African Americans, Daniel Patrick Moynihan pointed to the "tangle of pathology" that was "capable of perpetuating itself" owing to the weak, dysfunctional black family structure.[32] The conclusions in his 1965 report "The Negro Family"—popularly dubbed "the Moynihan Report"—were based on the research of anthropologist Oscar Lewis, who sought to understand the intergenerational persistence of poverty in Third World countries. In his 1959 study of poverty among Mexican families, Lewis argued that while poverty is systemic in cause, it has intergenerational consequences: children who grow up poor are socialized to adopt particular values, aspirations, and behaviors that make them incapable of escaping their class position.[33] Once in place, the "culture of poverty" becomes autonomous, self-perpetuating, transmitted across generations, and immune to change.

Transferring Lewis's culture of poverty model to poor African Americans in the United States, Moynihan argued that eradicating poverty necessitated changing the cultural values, aspirations, and behaviors of the African American poor. Moynihan's conclusions proved to be attractive to U.S. politicians, policymakers, and the American public because they pointed to individual, familial, and cultural differences and deficiencies among poor African Americans rather than the gross structural inequalities that produced them.[34]

During the same period, scholars and journalists began to tout Asian Americans as the model minority who represented the antithesis to poor African Americans. The model minority antithesis emerged after the publication of two articles in 1966. The *New York Times Magazine* published "Success Story, Japanese-American Style" by sociologist William Petersen, and *U.S. News & World Report* published "Success of One Minority Group in U.S." by a staff writer. In both pieces, the authors extolled the "quiet" rise of Japanese and Chinese Americans, who persisted and overcame extreme hardship and racial discrimination to achieve extraordinary success, surpassing even U.S.-born whites. Most remarkable, the authors noted, was that Japanese and Chinese Americans attained success with no aid from anyone else. Since then, Asians have been publicly hailed and embraced as America's model minority.[35]

Social scientists, however, reacted differently to the culture of poverty thesis and the model minority antithesis. Rather than proactively engaging in a debate about the relationship between culture and poverty, many sociologists abandoned culture and turned their attention to the macro-structural causes of poverty and inequality.[36] They pointed to the change from a manufacturing to a service-based economy, the outsourcing of jobs from central cities to U.S. suburbs as well as to developing countries, the skills and spatial mismatch between jobs and residents in inner cities, residential segregation, and de facto school segregation.[37]

While social scientists expended a great deal of effort to deconstruct and debunk the culture of poverty thesis, they paid virtually no attention to the model minority antithesis. Sociologists were unconcerned about or uninterested in studying the high socioeconomic outcomes of Asian Americans, even those who hailed from poor and working-class immigrant backgrounds. Thus, they left the task of dispelling the model minority construct to historians and scholars in the humanities and Asian American studies, who leveled three main critiques.

First, the model minority thesis overlooks the heterogeneity among Asian immigrant ethnic groups and, subsequently, the variegated socioeconomic outcomes among those groups. For example, Cambodians, Laotians, and Hmong have higher poverty levels and higher high school dropout rates than the national average and even compared to African Americans and Latinos. Hence, not all Asian ethnic groups have model outcomes.

Second, these critics argue that the model minority construct has been strategically deployed to dismiss the significance of race and racial discrimination in determining the life chances of ethnoracial minorities. The logic is that if Asian Americans can make it in spite of their nonwhite ethnoracial status, then race does not matter. This line of reasoning has also been used in attempts to dismantle race-conscious policies like affirmative action. And third, the model minority trope is divisive: it pits Asian Americans against other ethnoracial minority groups, especially African Americans and, more recently, Latino Americans.[38]

While each point is valid, these scholars have stopped with these three points. Consequently, these critics have flippantly rejected the model minority thesis and rendered it moot, thereby leaving the discussion about culture and achievement at an intellectual stalemate.

For these reasons, evoking culture to explain either poor or exceptional outcomes has become tantamount to endorsing a neoconservative policy paradigm, and therefore, largely for political reasons, cultural analysis has yielded to structural analysis. For decades culture was reduced to a "last resort" residual explanation—one that social scientists turned to after controlling for all possible structural variables—to account for persistent ethnoracial gaps in education, earnings, and occupational status.[39]

The Reemergence of Culture

Culture has reemerged with a new generation of social scientists who have placed it at the forefront of the poverty and inequality research agendas.[40] This cadre of scholars has advanced the field in two fundamental ways. First, they reject the essentialist definition of culture as a core set of unchanging values, behaviors, practices, and norms that are immune to structural changes. Instead, they maintain that culture is dynamic and susceptible to change because it is supported by reinforcement mechanisms and changes in the absence of these mechanisms.

Second, the new generation of social scientists does not define culture as an all-encompassing category that includes a group's values, norms, aspirations, and behaviors. Rather, they conceive of culture more narrowly through analytical concepts such as frames, repertoires, toolkits, narratives, schemas, cultural capital, and boundaries. By defining culture through a more narrowly defined lens, scholars have been able to empirically measure and test its influence on a diversity of outcomes, including educational aspirations, employment, community involvement, political participation, welfare receipt, and teenage pregnancy.[41]

Although the study of culture has advanced tremendously since the culture of poverty thesis, there remain five glaring shortcomings. First, still largely absent from the newly emergent scholarship in culture is a focus on culture and immigration and, more specifically, on the role of culture in explaining the variation in immigrant and second-generation outcomes. Second, when culture has been evoked as an explanation, some immigration scholars have focused on the fitness and resilience of "cultural values," claiming that these values explain the academic achievement of immigrant children.[42]

Third, little attention has been paid to delineating how immigrant selectivity affects *which* cultural institutions, frames, and mind-sets immigrants import from their countries of origin and re-create in the host society. The more highly selected an immigrant group, the more likely it is that the highly selected elements from that group's country of origin will be imported to the host society. This is especially the case for many contemporary Asian immigrant groups in the United States, who are hyper-selected—that is, both more highly educated than their compatriots in their countries of origin and more highly educated than the native-born in their host society. Once here, immigrants re-create highly selected, class-specific institutions, frames, and mind-sets and readjust them to best fit the U.S. context. In addition, by re-creating cultural institutions in their ethnic communities, resources become available to ethnic group members across class lines, thereby expanding opportunity horizons and structures for working-class coethnics in ways that defy the status attainment model.

Fourth, also missing is an explanation of *how* success frames pass from immigrant parents to their U.S.-born and -raised children to produce desired outcomes. For example, the transmission of the success frame and the achievement mind-set, because it occurs in the face of daunting resettlement challenges for immigrant parents, should not be taken for granted. Born abroad, Asian immigrant parents must overcome a language barrier and cultural differences, which can generate intense intergenerational conflict with their U.S.-born children.[43] Yet in spite of the challenges, Asian immigrant parents transmit the success frame and achievement mind-set to their 1.5- and second-generation children.

Fifth, despite decades of criticism of essentialist arguments about culture, this view has endured in popular media and continues to resonate with the American public, as evidenced by the model minority stereotype and by the pundits and scholars who reinvoke it. In our view, if social scientists are to change the public rhetoric about essentialist cultural explanations, we must engage in the debate by providing a clearer, more compelling, jargon-free explanation, supported by empirical evidence. This task could not be more timely given the new ethnoracial diversity of the United States as a result of contemporary immigration, the growing inequality in socioeconomic outcomes among U.S. groups, and the misleading, facile rhetoric about the role of culture.

Immigration, Assimilation, and Moving Beyond the Black-White Binary

The timing of the debates about the culture of poverty thesis and the model minority antithesis was critical because these debates emerged during a defining moment in U.S. immigration history. In 1965 the United States passed the Immigration and Nationality Act, which abolished the national-origins quota system and replaced it with a skills-based and family reunification preference system. In ushering in a new stream of immigrants from Latin America, Asia, Africa, and the Caribbean, this change in the law transformed the landscape of the United States from a largely black-white society to one composed of multiple ethnoracial groups of diverse socioeconomic origins.[44] The arrival of non-European, nonwhite newcomers would broaden and reframe discussions about assimilation, culture, and group outcomes for decades thereafter.

In 1970 Latinos and Asians made up only 5 percent and 1 percent of the nation's population, respectively; in 2010 they accounted for close to 17 percent and 6 percent. Latinos now outnumber African Americans, and Asians are the fastest-growing group in the country. Although Asians and Latinos have altered the ethnoracial profile of the United States, research in immigration and culture has lagged behind America's new demographic realities.[45] In part, this is because the debate about culture and achievement was at an intellectual stalemate when America's newest immigrants began to arrive in 1965, but it is also because the debate had traditionally been framed within a black-white binary, giving relatively scant attention to Asians and Latinos.

Convergence to the Mean Versus Intergenerational Mobility

Contemporary immigration has also challenged the classic theory of assimilation. Although conceptions of assimilation have changed over time, classic and revisionist theories predicted a unidirectional and irreversible path leading to the eventual incorporation of *all* immigrants into an undifferentiated, unified, and white middle-class mainstream, based on the experience of European immigrants.[46] Today's new immigrants, however, are largely non-European, nonwhite, and diverse in socioeconomic backgrounds. The diversity of national origins, ethnoracial status, languages, and skill levels has ignited fears among nativists that today's immigrants and refugees are unable, or refuse, to assimilate as their European predecessors did in the past and thus pose a threat to America's national identity and culture.[47]

The concern about the unassimilability of contemporary immigrants is rooted in the question of whether immigrants are converging to the mean—and more specifically, to the white, middle-class mean. But it is not just nativists who presume that assimilation means convergence. The American public and academics often take it as a given that assimilation has normative connotations, the suggestion being that immigrants *should* converge and become more like native-born, middle-class, white Americans. In fact, scholars have often measured a group's success by the degree to which immigrants and their children become more like non-Hispanic whites, who make up the majority of the American middle class and therefore serve as the principal reference group against whom social scientists measure newcomers' progress. Some of the most influential second-generation studies—including the Children of Immigrants Longitudinal Study and the New York Second Generation

Study—have defined and measured incorporation as the convergence (or lack thereof) between the second generation and native-born Americans on socioeconomic measures, including education, earnings, residential integration, and homeownership.[48]

Relying on outcomes and convergence to the mean as the sole measure of successful assimilation, however, yields an incomplete portrait of immigrant and second-generation progress. We argue that a more sociologically complete assessment requires a consideration of "starting points" and the extent to which groups demonstrate intergenerational progress—that is, how much progress the children of immigrants make beyond their immigrant parents.[49] Incorporating starting points into the analysis is critical because we reach dramatically different conclusions about the degree to which an immigrant group is successfully assimilating into the U.S. social and economic structure depending on which measure we adopt.

We provide a baseball analogy to underscore the difference between outcomes (convergence to the mean) and mobility (how far the second generation progressed from the first). Most Americans would be more impressed by a batter who hits a double (someone who makes it to "second base" after her parents started from "home plate") than they would be by a pinch runner who comes in at third and fails to advance (someone who ends up on "third base" and whose parents started on "third base"). Because we tend to focus strictly on outcomes when we measure success, we praise the third-base runner but fail to acknowledge that she did not run far at all. However, if we were to consider starting points, we would shift our praise to the batter who hit a double, even if she only made it to second base.[50]

Segmented Assimilation

In 1993 Alejandro Portes and Min Zhou introduced "segmented assimilation" as a new theoretical framework to understand the intergroup variation in assimilation outcomes among today's new second generation.[51] What was novel about this theory was Portes and Zhou's consideration of both the diversity of contemporary immigrants and the diversity of America's mainstream. Rather than conceiving a single U.S. mainstream, they conceived of the American mainstream as stratified systems into which different second-generation groups assimilated. Segmented assimilation theory was pivotal for researchers who theorized that immigrants and their children do not follow a single assimilation pathway but rather multiple paths, and also that they assimilate into their host society at varying speeds.[52]

Segmented assimilation theory also addresses the ways in which the context of exit from immigrant groups' country of origin and the context of their reception in their host society affect their and their children's adaptation and outcomes.[53] The context of exit varies by a number of factors, including immigrants' social class and status in their homeland, the premigration material and nonmaterial resources that they import with them (such as money, human capital, and job skills), their means of migration, and their motivation, aspirations, and practices. The context of reception includes an immigrant group's position in the system of ethnoracial stratification, government policies that facilitate or hinder assimilation, public attitudes toward specific immigrant and ethnoracial groups, and the viability and strength of an ethnic community.

Portes and Zhou identified three paths of assimilation: assimilation into the white middle-class mainstream, downward assimilation into a socially marginalized status, and assimilation into the white middle class via selective acculturation and the use of ethnic resources. The first two paths are straight-forward and predictable because they are based on the status attainment model. By illustration, if an immigrant group is hyper-selected and has a large portion of middle-class members, the second generation is likely to reproduce their parents' middle-class status. On the other hand, if an immigrant group is highly selected vis-à-vis those left behind but has a large portion of poor and working-class members, the second generation will lack the supplemental external resources that help propel their mobility beyond that which would be expected from the status attainment model.

What propels immigrant group members from humble origins to move ahead is their access to "supplemental external resources." Supplemental external resources are those that are external to the family (including ethnic resources that are generated from the ethnic community) as well as publicly available resources (including those from the state and civil society). Because immigrant selectivity affects how much ethnic capital a group can generate, groups do not have the same capacity to generate resources conducive to second-generation achievement and mobility. The resulting differential access to externally available resources gives some second-generation members a competitive advantage over others, in spite of similar levels of poor parental human capital.[54] Thus, when we consider culture in our analyses, we under-score the role of cultural institutions and the resources they generate that facilitate socioeconomic attainment and mobility.

The Subject-Centered Approach and Minority Cultures of Mobility

In our work, we extend the theoretical research about assimilation in three ways. First, we measure assimilation and success as both outcomes and inter-generational mobility, and we illustrate how adopting different measures yields different conclusions about which second-generation group is the most successful.

Second, we consider the meaning that achievement and success may hold for second-generation groups by adopting what we describe as a "subject-centered approach." As social scientists we tend to adopt normative defini-tions of success, such as a college education, a high-status occupation, and homeownership, but how reasonable is it to assume that everyone holds the same markers of success? We take meaning seriously by placing the subjects' experiences and perceptions of success at the center of our analysis. In doing so, we open ourselves to the possibility that achievement and success may mean different things to different people, net of values.[55] So rather than a priori adopting normative assumptions about "success," we asked our interviewees to define success, to explain why they chose a particular pathway to achieve it, to detail the obstacles they encountered in their pathway, and to tell us which reference group they used when measuring their success.

Adopting the subject-centered approach proved illuminating, which brings us to the third way in which we extend the theoretical dialogue about assimilation. Contrary to the underlying assumption behind the classic and segmented assimilation models, which focus on convergence to the middle-class white mean, second-generation Chinese and Vietnamese do not turn to native-born, middle-class whites as their mobility prototypes when charting their paths to achieve success. Nor do they turn to native-born whites as the reference group when they measure their success. Rather, they turn to coethnics as their role models, mobility prototypes, and reference group for success and employ a distinctively minority culture of mobility to get ahead.[56] Hence, rather than striving to assimilate into the white, middle-class mainstream (the marker of successful assimilation in both classic and segmented assimilation theories), today's 1.5 and second generation are drawing on their toolkit of resources (in line with segmented assimilation), but assimilating beyond the white, middle-class norm.

A Preview of the Book

In the chapters ahead, we elaborate on our central argument based on our analytical model, outlined in figure 1.1, and support it with empirical data.

In chapter 2, we offer a historical review of Chinese and Vietnamese immigration to the United States and provide a profile of the main socioeconomic characteristics of these two distinct Asian ethnic groups in the United States and in Los Angeles. We detail the differences in their migration histories to the United States and also show how the hyper-selectivity of Chinese immigration and the high-selectivity of Vietnamese migration affect settlement patterns. Finally, we illustrate the pattern of second-generation convergence whereby the educational outcomes of the 1.5- and second-generation Chinese and Vietnamese converge, despite the dissimilar profiles of their immigrant parents.

In chapter 3, we illustrate how the hyper-selectivity and high-selectivity of Chinese and Vietnamese immigration have led to class-specific cultural frames about the meaning of achievement and success among their children—what we refer to as the success frame. As noted earlier, the success frame is exacting (one must earn straight A's, graduate as high school valedictorian, earn a degree from an elite university, go to graduate school, and work in one of four coveted, high-status, high-paying professional fields), but most remarkable is the consistency of the success frame, regardless of ethnicity, class, nativity, or gender. So prevalent is the success frame and so notable is Asian American academic achievement that doing well in school has been racially recoded as "an Asian thing" among Asians and non-Asians alike. The racial recoding has even recalibrated grades such that, on an "Asian scale," an A-minus is an "Asian F."

In chapter 4, we identify the strategies and resources—both tangible and intangible—that Chinese and Vietnamese immigrant parents use to reinforce the success frame. We argue that resources and strategies, rather than strict "Tiger Mother" parenting practices, are key to attaining the success frame. Tangible ethnic resources include after-school ethnic academies—classes, tutoring, college preparation, and enrichment programs—that supplement the education that 1.5- and second-generation Chinese and Vietnamese receive in their public schools. Intangible ethnic resources include cross-class networking and learning, which provide working-class coethnics with the relevant knowledge about high school rankings, AP classes, and the college admissions process. Together these resources arm the 1.5 and second generation with the necessary toolkit and roadmap to a top university and a high-status profession.

Moreover, supporting the success frame entails collective familial strategies that Chinese and Vietnamese immigrant families employ. Collective strategies do not, however, result in all children benefiting equally. When resources are thin, parents make calculated decisions to privilege one child over others based on gender and birth order. As a result, some siblings are disadvantaged because they make sacrifices by truncating their educational pursuits in order to better poise others to move ahead.

In chapter 5, we compare the success frame of the 1.5- and second-generation Chinese and Vietnamese with those of 1.5- and second-generation Mexicans and third-plus-generation whites and blacks. We highlight the distinctiveness of the Chinese and Vietnamese success frame by contrasting it with the diversity of the success frames adopted by the other groups. Although parents and their children uniformly value education, the frame through which they define "a good education" and "a good job" differs across ethnoracial groups. Furthermore, depending on the success frame an individual adopts, 1.5- and second-generation groups feel differently about how much success they had attained. The intergroup comparisons about the meaning and measurement of success underscore the significance of the "subject-centered approach"—placing the subjects' definition of success at the center of analysis—for better understanding the outcomes of the second generation and the pathways they pursue to achieve them.

In chapter 6, we engage with the literature on stereotypes in social psychology to analyze how the racialization of Asians serves as a form of "symbolic capital" in the context of American schools.[57] Teachers and guidance counselors make positive assumptions about the academic ability and work ethic of

Asian American students, regardless of class, nativity, gender, and ethnicity. As a result, Asian American students benefit from "stereotype promise," which can enhance their performance and create the self-fulfilling prophecy of Asian American exceptionalism.

Stereotype promise is not limited to schools; it also affects Asian Americans at the workplace and in the criminal justice system. All stereotypes have power, however, and we note that positive stereotypes that give Asian Americans a boost in school can negatively affect them later in their careers. As the second generation matures and seeks management and leadership positions, they may find themselves bumping up against and trying to break through a "bamboo ceiling."

In chapter 7, we delve more deeply into the meaning of success from the perspective of the Chinese and Vietnamese interviewees, highlighting the role of mind-sets. We find that Asian American students receive contradictory messages about the role of effort versus ability at home and in school. At home their immigrant parents believe that continued effort will result in improved outcomes, whereas in school teachers and peers assume that Asian American students possess natural abilities that result in exceptional outcomes. In both domains, Asian American students are expected to achieve, and this expectation is continuously reinforced by their parents, teachers, and peers. When they do not or cannot adhere to the success frame (which they perceive as the norm), Asian American students become vulnerable to low self-esteem and efficacy.

Moreover, regardless of how much success the 1.5- and second-generation Chinese and Vietnamese interviewees had attained, many did not feel successful because they measured their achievements against a selectively high reference group that included higher-achieving coethnics. However, in a surprising turn of logic, some of the lowest-achieving Chinese and Vietnamese interviewees felt the most successful because they measured their achievements against ethnoracially heterogeneous peers, whose educational and occupational outcomes were similar to or worse than theirs. These findings point to the multifaceted dimensions of the Asian American achievement paradox.

In chapter 8, we highlight the cost of focusing so narrowly on the success frame and the social consequences of exclusively measuring success by performance goals. Success at all costs comes at a high price, especially for those who fall short of attaining the success frame. Those who do not fit it feel like ethnoracial outliers who distance themselves from coethnics and reject their ethnic identities, both of which they believe are inextricably tied to exceptional achievement. Moreover, the exclusive focus on those who have attained the success frame explains why positive stereotypes of Asian Americans endure, even in spite of the bevy of disconfirming evidence. By extension, the circulation of exclusively confirming narratives about those who have attained exceptional outcomes by parents, their children, and the media reinforce the fallacious belief that the success frame is normative for Asian Americans.

We wrap up in chapter 9 by returning to the main theme of the book: the Asian American achievement paradox. We underscore that there is nothing essential about Asian culture or values that explains the academic achievement of Asian Americans. Rather, culture operates through institutions, frames, and mind-sets that are formed and re-formed through immigrant selectivity (and especially hyper-selectivity) and host-society adaptation. Through these linked processes, 1.5- and second-generation Chinese and Vietnamese converge in their educational outcomes and those from working-class backgrounds are able to override their poor parental human capital and defy the status attainment model. Nevertheless, academic achievement has been racialized as an Asian thing and "acting Asian" by Asians and non-Asians alike; decoupling ethnoracial status from achievement, we explain in this chapter, will benefit all groups, including Asian Americans.

We discuss the theoretical implications of our findings for debates about culture, success, and assimilation and point to the practical and policy lessons that we can draw from our research. We raise the question of how long the success frame will last given the heterogeneity of the Asian ethnoracial category, the birth of the third generation, the rising intermarriage rates among Asian Americans, and the growing Asian multiracial population. Finally, we point to fruitful directions for future research in light of the rapidly evolving nature of the Asian American category.

Both sociologists and social psychologists have been interested in questions about culture, success, and assimilation, but disciplinary boundaries have caused research in these fields to emerge independently rather than in tandem.[58] This book is an attempt to traverse those boundaries to provide a more complete understanding of the ways in which cultural institutions, frames, and mind-sets affect 1.5- and second-generation Asian American outcomes. In examining how immigrant educational selectivity, ethnic capital, and ethnic and public institutions influence the construction and operationalization of frames, stereotypes, and mind-sets among the 1.5 and second-generation Chinese and Vietnamese, we debunk the popularly held myths about cultural traits, the Asian American achievement paradox, and the model minority trope. By joining research in sociology and social psychology, we aim to provide a book that is far more than the sum of its disciplinary parts.

~ Chapter 2 ~

Immigration, Hyper-Selectivity, and Second-Generation Convergence

The Chinese and Vietnamese are the largest and fourth-largest Asian-origin groups in the United States, respectively.[1] Although they may both be racialized as "Asian" in the U.S. context, the two national-origin groups differ in migration histories, conditions of emigration, socioeconomic backgrounds, and resettlement patterns. In this chapter, we provide a brief historical account of Chinese and Vietnamese migration to the United States and show how these two groups vary with respect to hyper-selectivity and host-society reception—both of which affect their patterns of incorporation. Most remarkable, however, is that despite the enormous interethnic differences between the first generation, the second generation converges in their educational outcomes—the pattern we describe as "second-generation convergence."

We divide this chapter into five parts. First, we offer a historical overview of Chinese and Vietnamese immigration to the United States and underscore the diverse circumstances of the different waves of migration. Second, we introduce and define the concept of "hyper-selectivity." Third, we show the link between hyper-selectivity and "ethnic capital." Fourth, we highlight the ways in which ethnic capital, in a uniquely Asian American way, can help reduce the intraethnic class differences that drive social mobility, reflecting a minority culture of mobility among the 1.5- and second-generation Chinese and Vietnamese.[2]

In the fifth and final part of the chapter, we focus on the 1.5- and second-generation Chinese and Vietnamese in Los Angeles based on data from the Immigration and Intergenerational Mobility in Metropolitan Los Angeles (IIMMLA) survey. We compare the outcomes of the two Asian ethnic groups to Mexicans, whites, and blacks in Los Angeles. We also provide a profile of the interviewees who participated in our in-depth interview study of L.A.'s new second generation.

Divergent Origins

China and Vietnam are neighboring countries with a long history of both peaceful coexistence and intense conflict. China conquered and ruled over Vietnam for more than one thousand years from 111 BC to AD 939. Although Vietnam has undergone various regime changes and cultural transformations, some of its traditions and cultural ways trace to Chinese roots.[3] And as East Asians, Chinese and Vietnamese share a Confucian philosophical worldview.[4]

Cross-border movements of the Chinese and Vietnamese have been common and frequent through their long history, but the migration of the two groups across the Pacific to the United States took place under vastly different circumstances. The Chinese, whose history in the United States dates back to the late 1840s, are the oldest and largest Asian-origin group in the United States. By contrast, the Vietnamese, who emerged as an American ethnic group only at the end of the Vietnam War in 1975, are one of the newest Asian-origin groups. As of 2010, there were more than 4 million people of Chinese ancestry (including more than half a million multiracial Chinese) and 1.74 million people of Vietnamese ancestry in the United States.[5]

The rapid growth of both Asian-origin populations has been fueled by contemporary immigration, as reflected in the percentage of foreign-born in both groups. The Chinese population increased fifteenfold between 1960 and 2010, and the Vietnamese grew from insignificant numbers in 1960 to now outnumber Koreans (another fast-growing Asian-origin group) and the Japanese (the second-oldest Asian-origin group in the United States). The majority of both Chinese and Vietnamese are foreign-born. In 2010, 61 percent of the U.S. Chinese population were foreign-born, and among adults age eighteen and older the figure reached 76 percent. The percentage of foreign-born among the Vietnamese is even higher: two-thirds of Vietnamese in the United States were born abroad, and among those eighteen and older the figure soars to 84 percent.[6]

Since 1980, China has consistently been among the top five countries sending immigrants to the United States. According to the U.S. Bureau of Citizenship and Immigration Service, more than 2.3 million immigrants were admitted to the United States from China, Hong Kong, and Taiwan as permanent residents between 1970 and 2012. While not nearly as numerous, the number of Vietnamese who arrived in the United States during the same period totaled nearly 1 million. Unlike their Chinese counterparts, almost three-quarters of Vietnamese newcomers entered the country as refugees. Between 1975 and 1996, 20,000 to 30,000 Vietnamese migrated annually to the United States.[7] After 1996, the refugee influx slowed to a trickle, partly because of normalized relations between Vietnam and the United States, and also because earlier refugees began to sponsor relatives in Vietnam through the family reunification provision of the Immigration and Nationality Act of 1965, also known as the Hart-Celler Act.

Originating from the same region in Asia, the Chinese and Vietnamese in the United States may appear alike to non-Asian Americans, but their migration histories, premigration socioeconomic circumstances, contexts of reception, and patterns of settlement in the United States differ starkly.

Pre-1965 Chinese Immigration to the United States

Prior to the massive Asian influx, which has accelerated since the late 1960s, Asians in the United States were primarily Chinese and Japanese. There were much smaller numbers of Filipinos, even smaller numbers of Koreans and Asian Indians, and virtually no Vietnamese. The first group of Asians to arrive in the United States were the Chinese, who migrated half a century before the Japanese (the second-oldest Asian-origin group).

During the peak of the Gold Rush in the late 1840s, Chinese immigrants were the only visible Asian-origin group. Although the earliest Chinese immigrants were low-skilled, uneducated, illiterate men from the rural Canton region of South China, they hailed from areas that were more developed and less impoverished than other non-migrant-sending regions in China. As contract laborers, they emigrated in groups, often with men from the same villages, and financed their trans-Pacific journey through family savings and a tightly organized credit-ticket system. Their intent was not to settle in the United States but to sojourn—that is, to work and earn money with the goal of returning home in the near future.[8]

Upon arrival, the Chinese laborers initially worked in gold fields in the Sierra Nevada foothills; later they worked on the construction of the transcontinental railroad. When the railroad was complete, some Chinese laborers continued to work on it and helped stretch the railroad lines to the northern and southern ends of California. Others moved into agriculture, and still others moved to San Francisco and other cities where they found jobs in the cigar- and shoe-making industries or in domestic services.[9]

As low-wage, low-skilled, and nonwhite laborers, the Chinese were a visible out-group whose precarious status came to the fore when the U.S. economy took a sharp downturn in the mid-1870s. Well-organized native-white workers targeted the Chinese and accused them of building "a filthy nest of iniquity and rottenness" in the midst of American society and of driving away white labor by their "stealthy" competition. They referred to the Chinese as the "yellow peril," as the "indispensable enemy," and as "marginal members of the human race."[10] Rallying under the slogan "The Chinese Must Go!" the Workmen's Party in California successfully launched an anti-Chinese campaign in the early 1880s.[11] The U.S. Congress passed the Chinese Exclusion Act in 1882, renewed it in 1892, then extended it indefinitely; the act would not be repealed until World War II. With the passage of the Asiatic Barred Zone Act of 1917, U.S. immigration legislation excluded immigrants from Asia altogether.

Augmented by virulent anti-Chinese violence, legal exclusion drove Chinese laborers out of the mines, farms, woolen mills, and factories of the West Coast, and many of them returned permanently to China. Others stayed, however, and continued to work to support their families back home, hoping to accumulate enough wealth for a glorious homecoming in the near future.[12] Facing legal exclusion and societal hostility, the Chinese immigrants who remained gravitated toward San Francisco's Chinatown for protection, while others fled eastward. Chinatowns in the Northeast (particularly in New York) and in the Midwest grew and absorbed those who fled the extreme persecution in California.[13]

Pre–World War II Chinatowns were bachelors' societies with very few women. In 1890 the severely unbalanced sex ratio of the Chinese in the United States stood at 2,679 males for every 100 females.[14] The shortage of women combined with the "paper son" phenomenon and the illegal entry of male laborers during the exclusion era stifled the development of the Chinese American family and delayed the succession of generations of Chinese Americans.[15] Consequently, only 9 percent of the Chinese American population in 1900 was U.S.-born and a mere 3 percent were school-age children age fourteen or younger. Even today—one and a half centuries later— Chinese Americans remain predominantly first and second generation, unlike Japanese Americans, whose population includes a fourth generation despite their much later arrival in the United States.[16]

Although the Chinese Exclusion Act was repealed in 1943, the Chinese American population grew very slowly owing to the restrictive U.S. immigration quota system, which capped annual immigrant visas at 105 for Chinese. Even after World War II, when more women were admitted to the United States as war brides, the limited quota on Chinese immigrants did little to correct the severely imbalanced sex ratio. In the 1950s, the United States admitted a few thousand Chinese political refugees and their families, most of whom had already fled to Hong Kong and Taiwan before the Communist takeover and the founding of the People's Republic of China in 1949.[17] It was not until the 1965 passage of the Hart-Celler Act—which promoted both family reunification and high-skilled immigration—that Chinese immigration began to soar.

Post-1965 Chinese Immigration

The passage of the Immigration and Nationality Act in 1965 was a watershed moment in Chinese immigration. Between 1960 and 2010, the number of Chinese Americans grew from 237,000 to over 4 million. The importance of the growth in the Chinese American population goes well beyond numbers; it helped to balance the sex ratio and generated tremendous intragroup diversity among the U.S. Chinese population.

Unlike the earlier immigrants, who were low-skilled and originated from rural areas of the southern region of Guangdong Province, contemporary Chinese immigrants hail from diverse origins and socioeconomic backgrounds. Although the three main sources of Chinese immigration are mainland China, Hong Kong, and Taiwan, in recent years Chinese immigrants from Southeast Asia and the Americas have been added to the mix. Between 1980 and 2012, nearly two-thirds of Chinese immigrants came from mainland China, about 15 percent from Hong Kong, and close to 18 percent from Taiwan.[18] The diversity in countries of origin is emblematic of the diversity of Chinese immigration more generally, which is reflected in four primary ways.

First, while all ethnic Chinese share a single ancestral written language (which varies only in traditional and simplified versions of the characters), they boast a bevy of regional dialects, including Cantonese, Mandarin, Hakka, Minnan (Taiwanese), Fuzhounese, Chaozhounese, Shanghainese, Wenzhounese, and others.

Second, contemporary Chinese immigrants are a socioeconomically diverse lot. Those who arrive with few job skills, minimal education, and no English-language ability gravitate to poor urban ethnic enclaves and to low-wage work in the ethnic economy. Others arrive with extraordinarily high human capital and ample financial resources; they come armed with family savings, graduate school education, and labor market skills that far exceed those of the native-born average. Also noteworthy is the visible subgroup of student migrants among contemporary Chinese immigrants, who come to the United States on non-immigrant student visas with the intent to pursue advanced academic or professional degrees and then return home. Upon completing their graduate studies, however, many Chinese students find not only U.S. jobs that match their credentials and skill levels but employers willing to sponsor them. For political, economic, and family reasons, many decide to stay in the United States and apply for permanent residency under the sponsorship of their employers.

A third form of diversity among contemporary Chinese immigrants is their settlement patterns upon arrival. Traditional ethnic enclaves—such as Chinatowns in San Francisco, New York, Los Angeles, Chicago, and Boston—continue to flourish and receive new immigrants, but they no longer serve as the primary centers of initial settlement for all newcomers. As of 2010, less than 10 percent of Chinese in Los Angeles and New York lived in inner-city Chinatowns. The affluent and highly skilled bypass urban ethnic enclaves altogether and move into affluent suburbs or into new suburban ethnic enclaves known as "ethnoburbs."[19]

Most striking is the emergence of socioeconomically versatile ethnoburbs. Chinese ethnoburbs in southern California (such as Monterey Park and satellite cities in the San Gabriel Valley) are home to middle- and upper-middle-class Chinese whose incomes and levels of education surpass those of non-Chinese local residents.[20] With their resources, Chinese immigrants have revitalized declining local economies and created a thriving ethnic economy whose businesses, organizations, and institutions affect far more than neighboring residents; the wide range of services and resources in Chinese ethnoburbs attracts coethnics near and far, and across class lines, to meet the needs of a socioeconomically diverse population.[21]

Fourth, Chinese immigrants are more geographically dispersed than in the past. California remains home to the largest concentration of Chinese, accounting for 37 percent of the Chinese American population, followed by New York, which accounts for another 17 percent. Among U.S. cities, New York leads with the largest number of Chinese Americans (486,463), followed by San Francisco (171,974) and Los Angeles (66,509). However, even though the U.S. Chinese population remains concentrated in the West and in urban areas—nearly half live in California and New York—Chinese have begun to scatter across the country, with many penetrating new destination states where few coethnic predecessors have ever set foot, including Texas, New Jersey, Massachusetts, Illinois, Washington, Pennsylvania, Florida, and Maryland.[22]

In sum, the diversity of contemporary Chinese immigrants is reflected in these four primary ways: regional dialects, heterogeneous socioeconomic profiles, patterns of settlement, and geographic dispersion.

Vietnamese Refugee Flight and Subsequent Immigration

Unlike the long history of Chinese immigration to the United States, Vietnamese immigration is of much more recent vintage. Since the end of the Vietnam War with the fall of Saigon in 1975, the Vietnamese population in the United States has grown exponentially, from a near-negligible size in the early 1970s to 615,000 in 1990. Between 1990 and 2010, the Vietnamese population nearly tripled, to 1.74 million.[23] But even this figure understates the size of the Vietnamese-origin population, since it excludes no fewer than 200,000 Sino-Vietnamese (ethnic Chinese) who fled Vietnam and arrived in the United States as part of the larger refugee outflow from Southeast Asia.[24]

The most distinctive feature of Vietnamese immigrants in the United States is how they arrived: as refugees fleeing a war-torn country, they left their home country under horrendous conditions, without preparation, and without control over their final destination. With the exception of a small elite group, most Vietnamese refugees hailed from disadvantaged socioeconomic backgrounds; the majority of Vietnamese refugees had minimal formal education, few marketable job skills, little English-language proficiency, and scant knowledge of the ways of an advanced Western society. Compounding their class disadvantages was the severe trauma of their precarious flight, an experience fraught with emotional distress and anxiety that was exacerbated by their often uncertain, lengthy stays in refugee camps.[25] Lacking a preexisting ethnic community that could assist their acculturation into their new host society, the Vietnamese relied exclusively on the U.S. government and individual or institutional sponsors who determined where they would settle and what resources they would be given.[26]

Due to the bitterness of the war in Vietnam, the suddenness of South Vietnam's defeat in the spring of 1975, and the rumors that the Hanoi government intended to execute all former South Vietnamese civil servants, policemen, and officials and anyone who had served the Americans in any capacity, many Vietnamese fled the country by any means possible. The refugees arrived in three distinct waves. The initial wave comprised the elite and the middle class, who either were airlifted by the U.S. military immediately before and after the fall of Saigon or had means to pay their way out sometime in the following two years. Before 1977, a total of 130,000 refugees had fled Vietnam.[27]

The second mass exodus of Vietnamese were the "boat people," who escaped Vietnam on small, overcrowded fishing boats or overland to Hong Kong, Thailand, Malaysia, Indonesia, Singapore, and Australia. This wave began in 1978, peaked in 1979, and subsided by 1982. At that point, an estimated 400,000 refugees (about half of whom were Sino-Vietnamese) had resettled in the United States after spending varied periods of time in refugee camps in Asia.[28]

Disproportionately Sino-Vietnamese, the boat people were victims of anti-Chinese sentiment fueled by the China-Vietnam border conflict in 1979, and they became prime targets of the nationalization of private businesses.[29] Although they had low levels of education, lacked English-language ability, and arrived in the United States penniless, the Sino-Vietnamese came from an urban entrepreneurial class in South Vietnam. Upon arrival, many clustered in urban Chinatowns or in Chinese ethnoburbs and opened small businesses after their initial period of adjustment. Today, about two-thirds of the small businesses in Chinatown in Los Angeles are owned or operated by Sino-Vietnamese.

The third wave arrived in a more orderly fashion after the U.S. Congress passed the Refugee Act of 1980, which provided a systematic procedure for refugee admission as part of an ongoing process of resettlement. In the late 1980s, arrangements between the U.S. and Vietnamese governments provided those who wished to leave Vietnam with a legal means to do so. Admitted under programs such as the Orderly Departure Program and the Humanitarian Operation Program, former political prisoners and their families were able to leave their home country and settle anew. The third wave of refugees began in 1982 and continued through the mid-1990s.

After the normalization of U.S.-Vietnam diplomatic relations in 1995, immigration from Vietnam began to assume a different form. Though a substantial proportion of Vietnamese continue to be admitted as refugees, an increasing number have been admitted as immigrants. As more Vietnamese refugees have permanently settled in the United States and naturalized, they began to sponsor relatives from Vietnam and from other countries under the provisions of U.S. immigration legislation.[30]

Not only do Vietnamese refugees differ from Chinese immigrants with respect to the political contexts under which they exited their homelands, but they also differ in their initial pattern of settlement in the United States. Unlike the Chinese, Vietnamese had no ethnic communities and family networks in place to receive them. Moreover, because the United States admitted Vietnamese refugees as a response to a special emergency (rather than as part of an ongoing process of resettlement), the government's official resettlement policy aimed to disperse Vietnamese refugees across the country. The rationale was twofold: the government wanted to minimize the refugees' impact on local receiving communities, and officials believed that dispersion would more quickly incorporate refugees into America's economy and society.[31]

As U.S. government policy dispersed the Vietnamese refugees across the country, Vietnamese populations arose in nontraditional immigrant-receiving states, some in the Midwest and mountain regions. Over time, however, the Vietnamese began to gravitate to the metropolitan areas that were most popular for many recent immigrants of diverse nationalities; Vietnamese thus became concentrated in urban locales as a result of secondary migration and family networks. Nationwide, nearly two-thirds of the Vietnamese population reside in just two states today, California and Texas. California alone accounts for 38 percent (582,000) of the Vietnamese population in 2010, and Texas for 14 percent (211,000). Within California, three-quarters (76 percent) of the state's Vietnamese population reside in just three metropolitan areas: Los Angeles–Long Beach–Santa Ana (271,000), San Jose–Sunnyvale–Santa Clara (126,000), and San Diego–Carlsbad–San Marcos (44,000).[32] Sino-Vietnamese largely cluster in southern California's suburbs, including Garden Grove, Westminster, and Santa Ana (known as Little Saigon) in Orange County and El Monte, Rosemead, and San Gabriel in the midst of the most visible Chinese ethnoburbs in Los Angeles County.

Despite the severe conditions under which the Vietnamese fled their home country and in spite of their low levels of human and financial capital, Vietnamese refugees are assimilating remarkably well less than four decades after their arrival. For example, their average English proficiency rate increased from 27 percent in 1980 to 52 percent in 2010—a figure that exceeds the English proficiency rates for the overall foreign-born population in the United States. In addition, the proportion of college graduates among Vietnamese adults age twenty-five and older grew from 13 percent in 1980 to 25 percent in 2010, nearing the national average of 28 percent.

As their human capital steadily improved, so did their median household income: by 2010, the median household income of the Vietnamese was $56,300, which was significantly lower than that of Chinese ($80,600), but close to the U.S. average ($61,000). The poverty rate among Vietnamese also decreased to 14 percent in 2010, from 28 percent in 1980, compared to 10 percent of Chinese families and 11 percent of all U.S. families living in poverty. Although they lag far behind the Chinese on socioeconomic indicators, and behind Americans more generally, the Vietnamese have demonstrated remarkable socioeconomic progress since 1980.

Converging Patterns of Immigrant Adaptation

Immigrants are a self-selected lot. They differ from nonmigrants with respect to behavioral characteristics, such as motivation and ambition, and also with respect to demographic, socioeconomic, and health variables, including age, gender, skills, health, and education. We begin this discussion of converging patterns of immigrant adaptation by looking first at educational selectivity.

Educational Selectivity Versus Hyper-Selectivity

"Educational selectivity" refers to immigrants' average number of years of educational attainment vis-à-vis the average for non-immigrants in their country of origin. Researchers have consistently shown that most immigrant and refugee groups in the United States are positively selected. Their positive selectivity, in turn, has resulted in better immigrant outcomes compared to their coethnic natives.[33]

However, the degree of positive educational selectivity varies considerably across national-origin groups. Sociologist Cynthia Feliciano has shown a range of net difference indexes for immigrant and refugee groups in the United States, with a high of 0.667 for the Chinese, a moderate high of 0.589 for the Vietnamese, and a low of 0.200 for the Mexicans.[34] She argues that varied degrees of positive selectivity among immigrant groups drive the general American perception about the groups' educational profiles. For example, the low degree of selectivity of Mexican immigrants leads Americans to perceive all Mexicans as poorly educated. This perception endures even though the overall educational level of Mexicans in Mexico is relatively high: close to one-third have had formal schooling. On the other hand, the high degree of positive selectivity of Indian immigrants creates the perception that all Indians are highly educated, despite the fact that the vast majority of Indians in India lack formal schooling.[35]

Building on these insights from existing research on educational selectivity, we propose a new concept: "hyper-selectivity." Hyper-selectivity is a relative concept that includes two comparative dimensions of *above-average* educational attainment: the overall percentage of college graduates in an immigrant group compared with the overall percentage of college graduates among non-immigrants in the country of origin; and the overall percentage of college graduates in an immigrant group compared with the percentage in the host country. We advance the concept of educational selectivity in two ways. First, rather than comparing only immigrants and nonmigrants, we argue that it is critical to compare immigrants to their host society. Second, rather than using average years of education to measure educational selectivity, we compare the percentage of an immigrant group with a BA degree or higher because a college education has become the minimum educational requirement for entry into professional, middle-tier jobs in the labor market. This dual positive selectivity—hyper-selectivity—is germane given the changing skill requirements in a knowledge-intensive economy such as the United States and other advanced economies.

Hyper-selectivity is consequential for immigrant and second-generation incorporation because it determines the amount of ethnic capital (or group-level human capital) and the type of ethnic resources that an immigrant group can generate and access upon arrival in the host country. Hyper-selected immigrant groups are better poised to form strong ethnic communities and ethnic institutions, which generate supplemental resources conducive to mobility. Because the resources are offered in ethnic communities, they give poor and working-class coethnics an advantage over their counterparts who are not members of hyper-selected groups. Hence, hyper-selectivity can mitigate the disadvantage of poor socioeconomic status and reduce class differences within an ethnic group.

Later in the chapter, we provide an illustrative example of hyper-selectivity and its consequences by profiling Chinese immigrants in the United States. We also discuss how Vietnamese refugees differ from Chinese immigrants; the former are highly selected but not hyper-selected. In the chapters ahead, we flesh out how hyper- and high-selectivity affect opportunity horizons and structures for 1.5- and second-generation children.

The Hyper-Selectivity and Selectivity of Chinese and Vietnamese Immigrants

Figure 2.1 offers a glimpse into the hyper-selectivity and selectivity of Chinese and Vietnamese immigrants, respectively. Half of Chinese immigrant adults age twenty-five or older has at least a bachelor's degree, compared to only 4 percent of adults in China; this means that Chinese immigrants in the United States are more than twelve times as likely to have a college degree as those who did not immigrate.[36] We should also note that nearly half of the college-educated Chinese immigrants have attained advanced degrees (a master's degree or a doctorate), mostly from U.S. universities. Vietnamese immigrants are also highly selected: nearly one-quarter (23 percent) of Vietnamese immigrant adults have at least a bachelor's degree, compared to 5 percent of adults in Vietnam; thus, Vietnamese immigrants are nearly five times as likely to have graduated from college as nonmigrants. Moreover, a sizable proportion of college-educated Vietnamese immigrants completed their bachelor's degree or attained an advanced degree in the United States after fleeing the war. On this dimension of educational selectivity, both groups are highly selected.

Figure 2.1   *Immigrant Selectivity: Chinese, Vietnamese, and Mexican Immigrants Age Twenty-Five and Older with a Bachelor's Degree or Higher*

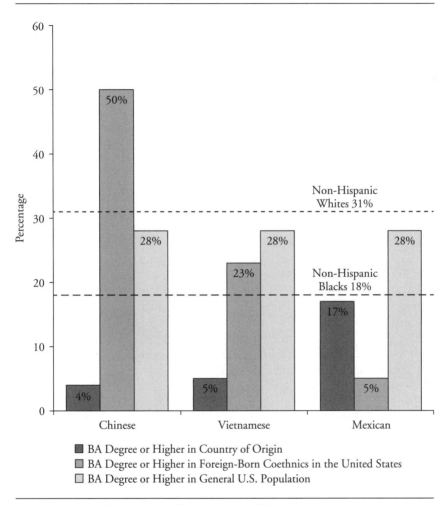

BA Degree or Higher in Country of Origin
BA Degree or Higher in Foreign-Born Coethnics in the United States
BA Degree or Higher in General U.S. Population

Source: Authors' compilation based on U.S. Census Bureau (2010a).

Relative to the general population in the receiving country, Chinese immigrants are also hyper-selected. With a college graduation rate of 50 percent, they are much more highly educated than the general U.S. population (28 percent), the U.S. foreign-born population (27 percent), non-Hispanic whites (31 percent), and non-Hispanic blacks (18 percent). The hyper-selectivity of Chinese immigrants translates into high median household incomes, which for Chinese American families was $81,000 in 2009—higher than the median income for all American families ($61,000). It was also higher than the median household income for non-Hispanic white families ($68,200) and non-Hispanic black families ($39,800).[37]

In contrast to Chinese immigrants, the Vietnamese in the United States showed a lower college graduation rate compared to the general U.S. population (23 percent versus 28 percent). However, their rate of college graduation was significantly higher than that of other ethnoracial minority groups. We see the same pattern with respect to annual household income: while the $56,300 annual income of Vietnamese households in 2009 was lower than that of average American and non-Hispanic white households, it was significantly higher than the annual income of non-Hispanic black households. Although Vietnamese immigrants are not hyper-selected as are Chinese immigrants, they benefit from the hyper-selectivity of the Chinese because they are racialized as Asian American; the hyper-selectivity of Chinese immigrants (the largest Asian immigrant population in the United States) drives the general American perception that all Chinese immigrants and all Asian immigrants more generally are highly educated. Also critical to note is that Vietnamese immigrants are a bifurcated group: while a significant portion are poorly educated and have not graduated from high school, another significant portion are highly educated and have attained at least a college degree. For example, based on the IIMMLA survey data, we find that Vietnamese immigrant fathers and mothers are less likely than native-born blacks and whites to have graduated from high school: 15.6 percent of Vietnamese fathers and 30.5 percent of Vietnamese mothers have not graduated from high school. At the other end of the educational spectrum, however, nearly one-third of Vietnamese immigrant fathers (31.9 percent) and 16.1 percent of Vietnamese immigrant mothers have attained a BA degree or more.

Hence, while Vietnamese immigrants exhibit lower levels of education on average than the general U.S. population, close to one-third of Vietnamese immigrant fathers have a college degree. These are the elite and middle-class refugees who fled Vietnam before the fall of Saigon. This point deserves mention because the positive educational selectivity of both the Chinese and Vietnamese immigrant populations in the United States determines which cultural institutions, frames, and mind-sets will be transferred and re-created in the new host-society context.

The pattern of educational selectivity differs starkly for Mexican immigrants in the United States. While Mexican immigrants are positively selected based on their average years of education compared to nonmigrants, they are negatively selected based on our measure of selectivity—the percentage of college graduates.[38] In Mexico, nearly one-fifth (17 percent) of the adult population have at least a BA or equivalent degree compared to only 5 percent of Mexican immigrants in the United States. A greater portion of the Mexican population has a BA degree or higher than both the Vietnamese population

(5 percent) and the Chinese population (4 percent). In addition, not only are Mexican immigrants negatively selected with respect to the percentage who are college educated, but they are also more poorly educated compared to the U.S. national average and compared to other ethnoracial minorities, like non-Hispanic blacks. We refer to this dual negative educational selectivity as "hypo-selectivity." The hypo-selectivity of Mexican immigration drives the general American perception that all Mexicans are poorly educated and over-shadows intergenerational progress.

U.S. Government Assistance to Vietnamese Refugees

In addition to their positive educational selectivity, Vietnamese refugees have another distinct advantage over other U.S. immigrants: they received govern-mental and institutional assistance as they settled into their new host society. As refugees, the Vietnamese relied on the U.S. government and government-sponsored resettlement agencies known as VOLAGs (voluntary agencies).[39] From the U.S. government's perspective, integrating Vietnamese refugees was a matter of developing a comprehensive program of support that would result in their eventual economic independence.

Unlike other immigrant groups (including Mexicans), almost all Vietnamese refugees began their lives in the United States on welfare. The three cash assistance programs that were most commonly utilized by Vietnamese refu-gees were Aid to Families with Dependent Children (AFDC), Supplemental Security Income (SSI), and Refugee Cash Assistance (RCA). AFDC (super-seded in 1996 by Temporary Assistance for Needy Families, TANF) and SSI were forms of public assistance (or welfare) available to U.S. citizens. AFDC provided assistance to low-income families with children, and SSI to the elderly and the disabled poor. Refugees who were ineligible for these forms of assistance generally received RCA during their first six to eighteen months. Given the precarious circumstances of their flight from Vietnam, U.S. govern-ment assistance was critical to the initial settlement of the Vietnamese refugees and their economic incorporation. As they established a foothold in their new homeland, the Vietnamese developed their own ethnic communities from which ethnic resources were generated and utilized to aid group mobility.[40]

Hyper-Selectivity, Ethnic Capital, and Ethnic Community Development

Ethnic Capital   Hyper-selectivity is structurally advantageous for an immi-grant group because it gives group members access to supplemental resources that are developed within the ethnic community through ethnic institutions. Drawing on the economist George Borjas's concept of "ethnic capital" as a theoretical launching point, we explain the link between hyper-selectivity, ethnic capital, ethnic community development, and ethnic resources.

Borjas argues that the development of children's skills depends not only on their parents' skills but also on the quality of the ethnic environment in which their parents make their human capital investments.[41] In applying his concept of "ethnic capital" to capture differences in group-level capital—which he measures as the average levels of skills and earnings of an ethnic group—Borjas finds that parental human capital yields greater earnings returns in children in environments with higher-quality ethnic capital. In essence, Borjas argues, ethnic capital has an independent effect on children's outcomes and their intergenerational mobility. Borjas's theoretical model of ethnic capital is illuminating, but it falls short in explaining precisely *how* ethnic capital benefits in-group members. For example, the model cannot account for how ethnic resources can help group members tap into publicly available institutional resources beyond the ethnic community. Furthermore, the model cannot explain why ethnic capital has different effects on the intergenerational outcomes of different ethnoracial groups.

We extend Borjas's thesis by providing the analytical link between hyperselectivity, ethnic capital, ethnic community building, and ethnic resources. Hyper-selected immigrants are poised to create ethnic capital given their high human and economic capital. Ethnic capital is consequential because it facilitates ethnic community development through the creation of institutions, businesses, and organizations. Those institutions, businesses, and organizations, in turn, provide the supplemental ethnic resources that aid first-generation adaptation as well as second-generation educational attainment. Ethnic institutions serve another critical function: they help coethnics access publicly available resources that aid mobility, especially for those in the second generation who come from working-class backgrounds. In the following section, we provide examples of the development of the Chinese and Vietnamese ethnic communities in Los Angeles.

Ethnic Community Development in Los Angeles   The greater Los Angeles metropolitan region—which includes Los Angeles, Orange, San Bernardino, Riverside, and Ventura Counties—is home to the largest number of Chinese and Vietnamese Americans in the United States. About 15 percent of all Chinese and 20 percent of all Vietnamese in the United States lived in the region as of 2010, and most reside in California's suburbs, as figures 2.2 and 2.3 indicate.

Although the old Chinatown in Los Angeles continues to receive newcomers, the vast majority of Chinese now live in newly established Chinese ethnoburbs in the San Gabriel Valley (situated east of Los Angeles, north of Puente Hills, south of the San Gabriel Mountains, and west of the Inland Empire). The San Gabriel Valley encompasses thirty-one municipalities and fourteen unincorporated communities of Los Angeles County. Chinese Americans are concentrated in eight of these, with Monterey Park being the first suburban Chinatown.[42] Since the 1990s, the Chinese have also resettled farther east

Figure 2.2   *Geographic Distribution of the Chinese Population in the Los Angeles Metropolitan Region, 2010*

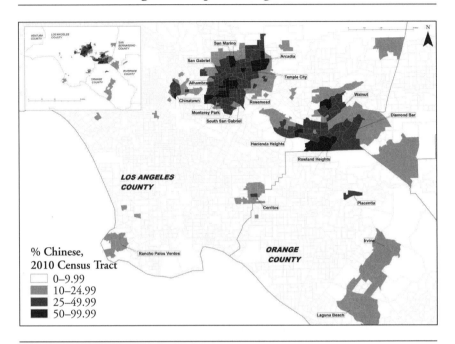

Source: Authors' compilation based on U.S. Census Bureau (2010b).

into wealthier suburbs, such as Hacienda Heights, Rowland Heights, Walnut, and Diamond Bar, as well as south and west into Rancho Palos Verdes, Irvine, and Laguna Beach. Although the Chinese were only 4 percent of California's population in 2010, they made up more than 20 percent of the population of twenty-one U.S. cities. Twenty of these were suburban cities, and fifteen were in Los Angeles.

By comparison, the Vietnamese are a much smaller group than the Chinese and make up less than 2 percent of California's population. They are also less dispersed than the Chinese in the region, mainly clustering in two areas, Orange County and the San Gabriel Valley. The three suburban cities in Orange County (Garden Grove, Westminster, and Santa Ana) represent the core of Little Saigon—home to the largest Vietnamese population of any metropolis outside of Vietnam, Little Saigon accounted for 107,000 Vietnamese in 2010. Over 40 percent of Westminster's population, 28 percent of Garden Grove's, and 7 percent of Santa Ana's were Vietnamese. Those who reside in Chinese ethnoburbs, including Rosemead, San Gabriel, South San Gabriel, and El Monte, are predominantly Sino-Vietnamese.

Figure 2.3   *Geographic Distribution of the Vietnamese Population in the Los Angeles Metropolitan Region, 2010*

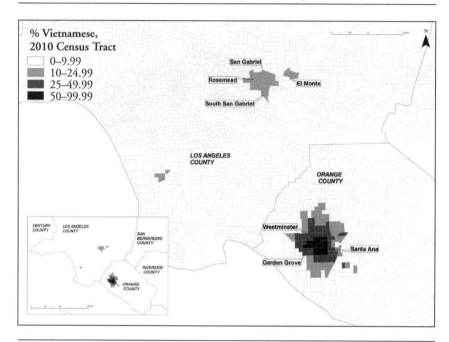

Source: Authors' compilation based on U.S. Census Bureau (2010b).

Both the Chinese and Vietnamese communities have seen rapid growth in their respective ethnic economies, as measured by the increase in ethnic-owned businesses and the revenues generated by these businesses. Chinese-owned firms increased more than seventeenfold in a thirty-year span between 1977 and 2007, from 23,270 to 423,609 firms (27 percent of all Asian-owned firms), with receipts of $142.8 billion (28 percent of all receipts from Asian-owned firms). Los Angeles County had the largest number of Chinese-owned firms in 2007 at 61,758 (15 percent of all Chinese-owned firms in the United States).

The size of the annually updated English-Chinese bilingual telephone directory, the Southern California Chinese Consumer Yellow Pages, provides an observable indicator of the number of Chinese-owned businesses in the region—it is four inches thick. Chinese-owned firms span a diversity of sectors, including significant numbers in the professional, scientific, and technical services sector, the accommodations and food services sector, and the repair, maintenance, personal, and laundry services sector. As of 2007, there was one Chinese-owned firm for every nine Chinese Americans. By comparison, the comparable ratio was one African American–owned firm for every twenty African Americans, and one Mexican-owned firm for every thirty-one Mexicans.[43]

Vietnamese-owned firms grew from near-zero in 1977 to 229,149 firms (15 percent of all Asian firms) in 2007, with receipts of $28.8 billion (6 percent of all receipts from Asian-owned firms). Los Angeles County had the largest number of Vietnamese-owned firms in 2007 at 17,695 (8 percent of all Vietnamese-owned firms). Unlike Chinese-owned firms, which offer a diversity of services, Vietnamese-owned firms are more clustered: more than two-thirds of the Vietnamese-owned firms are concentrated in service sectors such as repair, maintenance, personal, and laundry, as well as in the retail trade sector. Vietnamese-owned U.S. firms accounted for 3 percent of all U.S. businesses in these sectors.

The growth in Vietnamese-owned businesses is impressive. In absolute numbers, the number of Vietnamese-owned firms has surpassed the number owned by Filipinos (the second-largest Asian-origin group) and even surpasses those owned by Koreans (the most entrepreneurial Asian-origin group).[44] As of 2007, there was one Vietnamese-owned firm for every eight Vietnamese Americans. Even though most Vietnamese-owned firms are small mom-and-pop shops, they provide a strong foundation for community building as well as a path to social mobility for newcomers.

The benefits of ethnic entrepreneurship extend far beyond the dollars generated by these firms; ethnic-owned firms create employment opportunities for coethnics, while also generating a host of ethnic resources that can be utilized by the first and second generations.[45] For example, Chinese immigrant entrepreneurs use their ethnic and transnational networks along with their bilingual skills to open new business ventures, including a sophisticated ethnic system of supplementary education. Chinese ethnic communities and ethnic newspapers are dotted with signs for Chinese language schools, after-school tutoring, academic enrichment programs, and cultural enrichment programs (such as music, dance, and sports) that arm the children of Chinese immigrants with supplemental skills that help them excel academically.[46]

The development of an ethnic community is also consequential for the formation of the cultural institutions, frames, and mind-sets that affect second-generation educational outcomes, as we detail more fully in the chapters ahead. Cultural institutions provide both tangible and intangible ethnic resources. Tangible resources include supplemental educational programs within the ethnic community, and intangible resources include knowledge about how to access the most coveted publicly available resources.[47] Hyper-selectivity plays a critical role here. An ethnic group composed of hyper-selected immigrants has a greater capacity to create cultural institutions and to support a strict success frame and an achievement mind-set—each of which is critical to attaining mobility in the host-society context.

Through formal and informal reinforcement mechanisms, ethnic institutions promote collective strategies of mobility in which educational achievement is paramount. For example, by lauding as heroes those who attain the success frame and by sanctioning those who adopt trajectories that diverge from it, these institutions buttress a specific path to mobility and provide the resources to achieve it.[48] Cultural institutions, frames, and mind-sets, combined with publicly available institutional resources, are especially useful for poor and working-class coethnics in helping to mitigate their class disadvantage, as we reveal in the chapters ahead.

The Coming of Age of the Second Generation in Los Angeles: A Profile from IIMMLA

The Immigration and Intergenerational Mobility in Metropolitan Los Angeles survey is a multistage, multi-method survey of a randomly drawn, representative sample of young adult children (age twenty to thirty-nine) of foreign-born parents in metropolitan Los Angeles conducted in 2004. For the Mexican-origin population, the survey also included a third-plus-generation sample (children of native-born parentage).[49] Table 2.1 provides selective demographic and family characteristics of 1.5- and second-generation Chinese and Vietnamese in the sample (along with the characteristics of 1.5- and second-generation Mexicans, third-plus-generation Mexicans, non-Hispanic blacks, and non-Hispanic whites for reference).

Given the relative recency of Vietnamese migration to the United States, the Vietnamese in the IIMMLA survey are more likely than their Chinese counterparts to be in the 1.5 generation (meaning that they were born abroad but arrived before the age of thirteen). Given their refugee status, they also have a greater propensity to become naturalized U.S. citizens. There are notable differences between the two Asian groups in family characteristics as well, and between them and the comparison groups, as shown in table 2.1. Educational attainment is a measure of family socioeconomic status (SES), and on this measure the Chinese come out ahead. The 1.5- and second-generation Chinese are more likely to have highly educated parents than all other groups, including native-born whites: 61 percent of the Chinese have a college-educated father and 42 percent have a college-educated mother, whereas the comparable figures for native-born whites are 47 percent and 36 percent, respectively.

The high level of parental human capital reflects the hyper-selectivity of Chinese immigration to Los Angeles; Chinese immigrants in Los Angeles are both more highly educated (as measured by the percentage who have attained a bachelor's degree or higher) than those who did not immigrate and also more highly educated than the general U.S. population. Chinese immigrants in Los Angeles also exhibit another form of hyper-selectivity: they are more highly educated than their coethnics in other metropolitan areas in the United States, such as New York and Honolulu.[50]

Table 2.1   Selected Characteristics of the New Second Generation in Los Angeles

	1.5- and Second-Generation			Third-Plus-Generation		
Characteristics	Chinese	Vietnamese	Mexican	Mexican	Black	White
Demographic characteristics						
Female	43.5%	49.9%	49.7%	52.0%	53.7%	50.6%
1.5 generation	54.7	70.6	34.4	—	—	—
Second generation	45.3	29.4	65.6	—	—	—
Parental characteristics						
Father with no English proficiency	7.0	7.9	15.2	—	—	—
Mother with no English proficiency	7.8	12.0	19.1	—	—	—
Father with no high school diploma	7.5	15.6	54.5	17.2	10.9	3.5
Mother with no high school diploma	12.2	30.5	58.0	22.4	9.0	4.4
Neither parent with a high school diploma	6.0	12.0	30.3	9.3	1.7	0.7
Father with a bachelor's degree or higher	61.3	31.9	7.3	14.7	35.0	46.5
Mother with a bachelor's degree or higher	42.3	16.1	5.3	11.3	28.0	36.3
Parent ever been undocumented	1.0	0.6	10.4	—	—	—
Parent ever remitting money to home country	45.8	72.1	61.7	—	—	—

(Table continues on p. 40.)

Table 2.1 (Continued)

Characteristics	1.5- and Second-Generation			Third-Plus-Generation		
	Chinese	Vietnamese	Mexican	Mexican	Black	White
Family situation						
Parents own a home	86.5	58.8	62.8	73.1	67.5	89.2
Both parents married	85.5	83.6	72.0	53.8	43.3	51.9
Grew up living with both parents	85.6	83.1	72.2	62.2	45.4	64.8
Have college-educated siblings	76.4	69.9	30.0	35.6	41.4	52.9
Neighborhood environment						
Grew up where drugs are a big problem	3.0	7.0	22.9	14.0	22.7	6.4
Grew up where gang activity is a big problem	5.0	11.5	31.0	18.2	23.5	5.4
Grew up where crime is a big problem	4.0	8.0	22.5	16.2	21.5	6.6
Total in sample	400	401	844	400	401	402

Source: Rumbaut et al. (2004).

On the other end of the educational attainment spectrum are Mexican immigrant parents, the majority of whom have not graduated from high school—a measure of low family SES. Close to 60 percent of 1.5- and second-generation Mexicans have a father *or* a mother with less than a high school education, and for 30 percent *both* parents lacked a high school diploma (compared to only 6 percent of the Chinese and 12 percent of the Vietnamese). Mexican immigration reflects not only a low degree of immigrant selectivity but also hypo-selectivity—that is, on average, those who migrate are less likely to be college educated than their counterparts in Mexico and they are less educated than the U.S. population (see figure 2.1).

Vietnamese immigrant parents—who migrated to the United States as refugees—fall in between the Chinese and Mexican parents. Like Mexican immigrant parents, they exhibit lower levels of educational attainment than native-born white and black parents, but they differ from their Mexican immigrant counterparts in three ways. First, close to one-third of Vietnamese immigrant fathers have a college degree—attesting to the educational bifurcation among Vietnamese immigrant adults. Second, their educational and socioeconomic disadvantages are tempered by their favorable host-society reception, including generous in-kind resettlement assistance from the U.S. government. Third, as an Asian-origin group, the Vietnamese are perceived by non-Asian Americans as similar to Chinese immigrants and thus as highly educated.

Profiles of the 1.5 and Second Generation from the IIMMLA

Turning to the educational profiles of the children of immigrants, we find that the 1.5- and second-generation Chinese exhibit the highest levels of education, reflecting the intergenerational transmission of advantage of high parental human capital: nearly two-thirds of the 1.5- and second-generation Chinese (63 percent) graduated from college, and of this group 22 percent also attained a graduate degree. Notably, none of the 1.5- and second-generation Chinese students in the IIMMLA survey had dropped out of high school. Although the educational attainment of the 1.5- and second-generation Chinese may appear exceptional, the patterns are consistent with the classic status attainment theory, in which children's educational outcomes reflect the advantages they accrue from their highly educated parents.[51]

Of the second-generation groups, the Mexicans exhibit the lowest educational outcomes, which is also consistent with the status attainment theory and reflects severe parental socioeconomic disadvantages. However, what gets lost in presenting cross-sectional, intergroup comparisons is the enormous *intergenerational* mobility that Mexicans have achieved, within just one generation. For example, though more than 55 percent of Mexican immigrant parents did not graduate from high school (see table 2.2), this figure dropped to 14 percent within one generation. In essence, the 1.5 and second

Table 2.2   Mobility Outcomes of the New Second Generation in Los Angeles

	1.5- and Second-Generation			Third-Plus-Generation		
Outcomes	Chinese	Vietnamese	Mexican	Mexican	Black	White
Median age	27.0%	25.0%	28.0%	29.0%	31.0%	30.0%
Positive outcomes						
Educational attainment						
No high school diploma	0.0	1.0	13.8	9.5	6.7	3.7
High school diploma	4.5	6.7	32.7	30.3	24.2	17.7
Some college	32.4	44.1	35.9	41.4	45.1	32.5
Bachelor's degree	41.5	37.7	12.6	14.5	18.8	31.8
Graduate degree(s)	21.6	10.5	5.0	4.3	5.2	14.3
Current school enrollment						
Currently enrolled in school	37.0	48.1	28.7	23.4	31.6	24.9
Vocational school	4.1	7.8	22.3	20.2	14.1	10.8
Community college	18.9	25.9	40.9	40.4	43.8	26.5
Four-year college	47.3	47.2	19.4	22.3	28.1	27.5
Graduate school	29.7	19.2	16.1	17.0	14.1	34.3
Negative outcomes						
Having children as a teen	0.0	2.2	12.5	12.8	12.0	2.9
Incarceration	1.8	3.2	9.8	15.0	19.3	10.6
Total in sample	400	401	844	400	401	402

Source: Rumbaut et al. (2004).

generation nearly doubled the high school graduation rates of their parents. Moreover, the college graduation rate of 1.5- and second-generation Mexicans (18 percent) is far lower than the rate for the Chinese (63 percent), but it is more than double that of their Mexican immigrant fathers (7 percent) and triple that of their immigrant mothers (5 percent). Thus, when we measure attainment intergenerationally rather than cross-sectionally, the children of Mexican immigrants exhibit the greatest educational gains of the three second-generation groups.[52] In this respect, the children of Mexican immigrants are successfully assimilating and doing so rapidly.[53]

It is also critical to note that undocumented parental status matters for the children of Mexican immigrants. On average, children whose parents are undocumented attained two fewer years of education compared to those whose parents had migrated legally or those who had entered the country as undocumented migrants but legalized their status, and this difference holds even after controlling for all other parental socioeconomic factors.[54] Moreover, this two-year difference of eleven versus thirteen years of education is critical because it separates the high school graduates from the high school dropouts.

While the second generation made impressive gains, the intergenerational progress did not continue at the same pace into the third generation. Third-plus-generation Mexicans continue to lag behind other groups by a significantly large margin, revealing the extremely disadvantaged parental SES from which Mexican immigrants came when they arrived in the United States, including their undocumented status.[55] Moreover, as sociologists Edward Telles and Vilma Ortiz have argued, third-generation disadvantage may also stem from the negative stereotyping to which Mexican immigrants and Mexican Americans are subjected.[56]

Of the three second-generation groups, perhaps the most intriguing is the Vietnamese, of whom nearly half (48 percent) had attained a college degree or higher and only 1 percent had failed to complete high school. What makes their pattern of educational attainment intriguing is that their immigrant parents (especially their mothers) exhibit lower levels of education than both native-born blacks and whites, but within one generation the 1.5- and second-generation children surpass both native-born groups and move closer to the Chinese—a pattern that points to "second-generation convergence" among the two Asian ethnic groups. That the children of Vietnamese refugees, especially those of low family SES, converge toward the Chinese rather than toward either native-born blacks or native-born whites highlights the shortcomings of the status attainment model in explaining second-generation outcomes.

Moreover, the status attainment model cannot explain how even the children of poorly educated Chinese immigrants attain high educational outcomes. The IIMMLA data show that low parental education does not impede the educational attainment of second-generation Chinese, as it does for other groups. In fact, in the IIMMLA sample, second-generation Chinese whose parents did not graduate from high school are even *more* likely to have

Figure 2.4   *Holders of a Bachelor's Degree or Higher Among 1.5- and Second-Generation Chinese, Vietnamese, and Mexicans, as Well as Third-Plus-Generation Mexicans, Blacks, and Whites with Fathers and Mothers Who Do Not Have a High School Diploma*

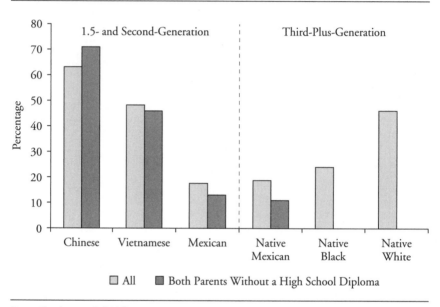

Source: Rumbaut et al. (2004).

earned a BA compared to all second-generation Chinese (71 percent versus 63 percent), as figure 2.4 shows.

Two more vexing patterns are revealed by figure 2.4, which shows educational attainment among those whose parents had not graduated from high school. First, regardless of parental education, the percentage of 1.5- and second-generation Chinese and Vietnamese who attained a BA degree or higher surpasses, or is equal to, the percentage for native-born whites.[57] Among those whose parents did not graduate from high school, close to three-quarters of the Chinese (71 percent) and nearly half of the Vietnamese (46 percent) attained a BA or higher. Second, parental education is more significant for the Mexicans than it was for both Asian groups. That low family SES does not impede the educational attainment for nearly half the Vietnamese and three quarters of the Chinese suggests that ethnoracial status and culture affect second-generation outcomes in ways that researchers have not fully examined.[58] Moreover, that low parental SES is more consequential for

Mexicans than for the two Asian ethnic groups suggests that hyper-, high-, and hypo-selectivity and their resultant consequences also matter.

Finally, we point out that, at twenty-five, the median age of the 1.5- and second-generation Vietnamese is relatively young. Their median age is younger than that of the 1.5- and second-generation Chinese (twenty-seven years) and Mexicans (twenty-eight years) and younger than native-born whites (thirty years) and blacks (thirty-one years) as well. This is relevant because some of the 1.5- and second-generation Vietnamese had not completed their education at the time of the survey, nor even at the time of our follow-up interview; it is reasonable to assume that in a few years the educational attainment of the Vietnamese will be even higher and that they will continue to converge with their Chinese counterparts.

A Glimpse at the Interviewees from the L.A. Qualitative Study

The chapters that follow focus on the experiences of the 1.5- and second-generation Chinese and Vietnamese based on face-to-face, in-depth, life-history interviews in a qualitative study that we conducted between 2006 and 2009. In our study, titled "Becoming 'Ethnic,' Becoming 'Angeleno,' and/or Becoming 'American': The Multifaceted Experiences of Immigrant Children and the Children of Immigrants in Los Angeles,"[59] we sought to examine how members of today's 1.5 and second generation define "success." We also aimed to understand how national origin, class, and ethnoracial status influence how much "success" they attain, which reference group they choose when measuring their success, and how stereotypes affect their performance. By placing the subjects' experiences at the center of our analyses, we adopted what we refer to as "a subject-centered approach"—that is, we allowed the subjects to define the meaning of success rather than making assumptions a priori, as we often do as social scientists.

We selected forty-one Chinese and forty-one Vietnamese, with an even gender and generation balance, from those who indicated in the IIMMLA survey that they would be willing to participate in a follow-up study.[60] Because our sample was drawn from the pool of those who were willing to participate in a follow-up study, it is not a random sample of all IIMMLA survey respondents, but rather a random sample of those who were willing to participate. Figure 2.5 provides the geographic distribution of our interviewees across the L.A. region; the triangular dots denote the Chinese interviewees, and the round dots the Vietnamese interviewees.

Table 2.3 offers a profile of our interviewees selected from the IIMMLA for in-depth, face-to-face interviews. Of our Vietnamese interviewees, four are Sino-Vietnamese, and one is multiethnic Korean-Vietnamese. Among the Vietnamese and Chinese interviewees, only one is multiracial, a Chinese-white male.

Figure 2.5   *Geographic Distribution of the Chinese and Vietnamese Interviewees in the L.A. Qualitative Study in the Los Angeles Metropolitan Region*

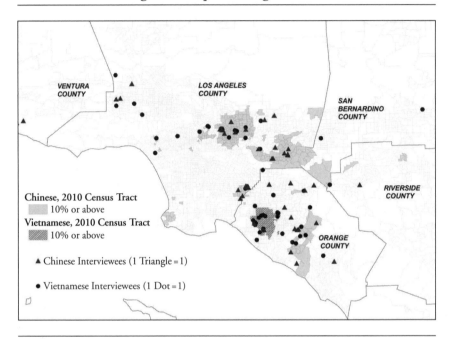

Source: Lee and Zhou (2009). For more details of the study, see note 17, chapter 1.

The overall trend in 1.5- and second-generation educational attainment among our Chinese and Vietnamese interviewees is similar to that in the IIMMLA survey, which shows a pattern of second-generation convergence between these two Asian ethnic groups. However, compared to the IIMMLA survey data, our Chinese and Vietnamese interviewees come from families in which the fathers and mothers had much lower levels of English-language proficiency; in addition, Chinese fathers and Vietnamese mothers are more likely to have dropped out of high school. The characteristics of the Mexican interviewees are similar to those in the IIMMLA data. However, our black and white interviewees are selected from a middle-class subset of the IIMMLA data and exhibit higher parental SES and educational attainment than the black and white IIMMLA survey respondents. In the chapters ahead, we turn to the in-depth interviews to unveil the patterns and mechanisms that produce second-generation convergence among the children of Chinese and Vietnamese immigrants.

Table 2.3   A Profile of Interviewees from the L.A. Qualitative Study

	1.5- and Second-Generation Chinese	1.5- and Second-Generation Vietnamese	1.5- and Second-Generation Mexican[a]	Native-Born Black[b]	Native-Born White[b]
Male (number)	21	21	28	6	6
Mean age (year)	30.8	27.9	33.5	38	38
Generation (number)					
1.5 generation	20	21	26	—	—
Second generation	21	20	28	—	—
Education (self)					
No high school diploma	0.0%	0.0%	3.6%	0.0%	0.0%
High school graduate or some college	39.0	48.8	78.2	72.7	33.3
Bachelor's degree	41.5	41.5	9.1	27.3	16.7
Graduate degree(s)	19.5	9.8	9.1	0.0	50.0
College attendance (self)					
Attended junior college	27.5	35.9	70.6	75.0	27.3
Attended four-year college	52.5	53.8	14.7	25.0	18.2
Attended graduate school	20.0	10.3	14.7	0.0	54.5

(Table continues on p. 48.)

Table 2.3   (Continued)

	1.5- and Second-Generation Chinese	1.5- and Second-Generation Vietnamese	1.5- and Second-Generation Mexican[a]	Native-Born Black[b]	Native-Born White[b]
Education (parents)					
Father with no English	33.3	33.3	44.9	0.0	0.0
Mother with no English	34.1	47.5	64.7	0.0	0.0
Father with no high school diploma	12.2	17.9	52.7	0.0	0.0
Father with college degree or higher	60.1	36.6	1.8	54.5	75.0
Mother with no high school diploma	12.2	22.5	58.2	9.1	0.0
Mother with college degree or higher	53.7	24.4	1.8	36.4	41.7
Parents own home	92.5	57.5	71.2	90.9	100.0
Total number of cases	41	41	55	11	12

Source: Lee and Zhou (2009), and see chapter 1, note 17.
a. One Mexican case and one black case have no respondent ID.
b. Native-born whites and blacks are of middle-class family background.

Summary

In this chapter, we traced the historical and contemporary origins of Chinese and Vietnamese immigration to the United States. Although contemporary Chinese immigrants and Vietnamese refugees arrived in the United States under different political and socioeconomic circumstances, their children—the 1.5 and second generation—exhibit similar educational outcomes, a pattern that we define as "second-generation convergence." Second-generation convergence defies the expectations of the classic status attainment model, which privileges parental human and cultural capital.

Second-generation convergence, however, is not happenstance. Rather, it is a product of the historic changes in U.S. immigration law in 1965 to give preference to applicants with high levels of education and high skills. The legal changes in immigration also extended privileges to refugees like the Vietnamese, who received U.S. government assistance to aid their transition into their new host society.

The change in U.S. immigration law has resulted in the hyper-selectivity of Chinese immigration—that is, Chinese immigrants in the post-1965 wave are positively selected on two counts. First, they are more likely to be college educated than their counterparts who did not immigrate, and they are also more likely to be college educated than members of the host society. Vietnamese refugees are not hyper-selected but rather highly selected. Moreover, they are an educationally bifurcated group: about one-third of Vietnamese immigrant fathers in Los Angeles have graduated from college. By contrast, Mexican immigrants are hypo-selected: they are less likely to have graduated from college compared to Mexican nonmigrants, and they are also less likely to have graduated from college compared to the general American population.

Hyper-selectivity and high immigrant selectivity determine the class-specific cultural institutions, frames, and mind-sets that immigrants transport from their countries of origin and re-create in the United States. Hyper-selected and highly selected groups can generate more ethnic capital, which gives coethnics access to supplemental resources through ethnic institutions. These advantages cross class lines and extend to those from poor and working-class origins who lack human capital, skills, and cultural capital—points upon which we elaborate more fully in the chapters ahead. In that analysis, we further debunk the argument that second-generation convergence is a product of essentialist cultural traits or values. We show that educational outcomes are driven by access to cultural institutions, frames, and mind-sets, coupled with the group position of Asians in the U.S. ethnoracial hierarchy, in a way that defies the status attainment model. In short, we show why class matters less for the 1.5- and second-generation Chinese and Vietnamese than for other ethnoracial groups, thereby helping to explain the Asian American achievement paradox.

~ Chapter 3 ~

The Success Frame and the Asian F

As early as 1967, the sociologists Peter Blau and Otis Dudley Duncan noted that the strongest predictor of a son's occupational attainment is his father's occupation—a key finding that they published in their pioneering study *The American Occupational Structure.*[1] Blau and Duncan's study shows that life chances are unequal out of the starting gate because advantages and disadvantages are transmitted intergenerationally. If a son is fortunate to be born with a father who is highly educated and holds a high-status job, he is likely to reproduce those advantages in adulthood.

Since Blau and Duncan's pioneering study, sociologists have followed their lead and advanced the classic status attainment model, which emphasizes the role of family socioeconomic status (SES) and cultural capital in determining a child's educational and occupational outcomes.[2] Not only does the classic status attainment model account for differences in educational outcomes among the children of U.S.-born white parents, but it also explains the comparatively low educational attainment among ethnoracial minority children like African Americans and Latinos.[3]

The status attainment model also sheds light on the educational lag among the children of Mexican immigrants, especially among those whose parents arrived without the protection of legal status. Researchers have shown that Mexican immigrants who arrived as undocumented immigrants and are unable to legalize their status transmit their disadvantage intergenerationally, as evidenced by the poorer educational outcomes of their children, even after controlling for all socioeconomic and demographic factors. The disadvantage of undocumented status is so extreme that it negatively affects the educational outcomes of the third generation.[4]

While the status attainment model explains the reproduction of advantage and disadvantage for some groups, it cannot explain the high educational outcomes for the children of poor and working-class Chinese and

Vietnamese immigrants. For example, U.S. census data show that even Chinese and Vietnamese children from poor families routinely surpass their non-Hispanic white middle-class peers in educational attainment.[5] That class does not hamper educational attainment for 1.5- and second-generation Chinese and Vietnamese as it does for Mexicans and other ethnoracial minority groups points to the vexing Asian American achievement paradox.

The patterns of educational achievement among the 1.5- and second-generation Vietnamese and Chinese in Los Angeles provide further evidence of the achievement paradox. The majority of Vietnamese immigrants in Los Angeles arrived after the mid-1970s as poorly educated refugees who did not graduate from high school, but their U.S.-born children graduate from high school and college at much higher rates than their parents, and they also surpass the educational attainment of native-born whites and blacks. Furthermore, the children of Chinese immigrants whose parents did not graduate from high school are actually *more* likely to earn a college degree than their coethnic peers whose parents have college degrees (see table 2.2 and figure 2.4).

Unable to explain the Asian American achievement paradox, some pundits and neoconservatives point to culture and, more specifically, cultural traits and values as the facile, go-to explanation. Although we agree that culture matters, the question remains: How does it matter? Put differently, what is cultural about Asian Americans' educational outcomes? In this chapter, we draw on our rich, in-depth interview data to address two main questions: How do Chinese and Vietnamese immigrant parents and 1.5- and second-generation children frame achievement and success? And why do they construct such a narrow conception of success? We approach these questions by making four points.

First, we explain how Chinese and Vietnamese immigrants and their children frame achievement and success—what we refer to as "the success frame." Second, we explain why immigrant parents insist that their U.S.-born and U.S.-raised children adopt the success frame. Third, we show how the success frame becomes group-specific, how academic success has become racially recoded as "an Asian thing," and how Asian Americans have become the reference group for academic success. Fourth, we reveal that cultural frames—including the success frame—emerged from a specific legal and historical context after the passage of the Civil Rights Act of 1964 and the Immigration and Nationality Act of 1965. We underscore that failing to embed the success frame within the legal and historical context from which it emerged can easily lead to fallacious and incomplete explanations about the role of culture in explaining the achievement paradox and Asian Americans' outcomes more generally.

Cultural Frames and
the Subject-Centered Approach

In the vast literature on culture, we find the concept of "frames" useful in understanding 1.5- and second-generation educational outcomes. Following in the footsteps of sociologist Erving Goffman, we define a frame as an analytical tool by which people observe, interpret, and make sense of their social life.[6] Most plainly, frames are ways of understanding how the world works; by understanding the frames people adopt in their decision-making process, we may begin to understand variation in behavior.

Our in-depth, life-history interviews with 1.5- and second-generation Chinese and Vietnamese, as well as our interviews with 1.5- and second-generation Mexicans and native-born whites and blacks, provided a wealth of data bout their experiences and trajectories. Based on themes that emerged from the interviews, we identified different cultural frames cited by group members for "a good education" and "success." For example, some groups frame a good education as graduating from high school, attending a local community college, and earning an occupational certificate that allows them to work as electricians, mechanics, or nursing or dental assistants. Others adopt a much narrower frame that involves getting straight A's and graduating as the high school valedictorian, gaining admission to an elite university, and earning a graduate degree in medicine, law, science, or engineering. Hence, groups may value education equally, but they may construct remarkably different frames of what a "good" education is and what success means depending on the frame that is accessible to them and that they eventually adopt.

This is a point that we as social scientists often overlook when we study outcomes because we take for granted the middle-class, normative frame for success, which involves graduating from a reputable university, possibly earning an advanced degree, and securing a high-status professional job. But how reasonable is it to assume that everyone subscribes to the same success frame, or that everyone chooses to follow a singular route to achieve it? In our analyses, we follow John Skrentny's call to "go deeper" to examine the *meaning* of success from the perspectives of the 1.5 and second generation in Los Angeles.[7] We consider the possibility that success may mean different things to different people—net of their values—and jettison the assumption that all immigrants and their children frame success through a singular, normative lens. We also jettison the assumption that the new second generation uses native-born whites as their reference group when measuring their success, which is the underlying assumption in classic assimilation and segmented assimilation models. Instead, we adopt a "subject-centered approach" that places the subjects' definition of success at the center of our analysis and allows for the possibility that the second generation has adopted alternative measures of success, as well as alternative reference groups.

Culture is critical to the subject-centered approach because the success frame that members of the 1.5 and second generation adopt is influenced not only by family SES but also by the ethnic capital and ethnic resources generated by their community. A hyper-selected immigrant group is equipped with higher-than-average ethnic capital or group-level resources, including the presence of a sizable middle class.[8] A prominent and visible middle-class presence within an ethnic group benefits less-advantaged coethnics because members of the middle class create the success frame and also provide the institutional resources to support it. Because ethnic resources are preferentially available to ethnic group members, middle-class resources become ethnic resources that cut across class lines to benefit poor and working-class coethnics—a point that we develop further in the following chapter.[9] In this way, 1.5- and second-generation Chinese and Vietnamese from poor and working-class backgrounds are able to take advantage of middle-class resources and employ a middle-class culture of mobility to help override their class disadvantage in their quest for intergenerational mobility.[10]

Constructing the Success Frame as a Good Education

One of the most striking findings from the interviews is that nearly all of the 1.5- and second-generation Chinese and Vietnamese framed success in terms of a good education; moreover, nearly all used the same markers to frame a good education: high school is mandatory; college is an expectation; and an advanced degree is essential to success. This definition of a good education is critical because it is only with this kind of good education that one can work in one of the four coveted, high-salaried, high-status professions that represent the pinnacle of success in this frame: doctor/pharmacist, lawyer, scientist, or engineer. (The Vietnamese interviewees added pharmacist as a high-status profession because the responsibilities of a pharmacist in Vietnam are more akin to those of a medical doctor in the United States.)

So essential is a good education for the success frame that the interviewees explained that their immigrant parents could not understand why graduating from high school was cause for celebration for Americans. Caroline, a thirty-five-year-old, second-generation Chinese woman, explained:

> The idea of graduating from high school for my mother was not a great, congratulatory day. I was happy, but you know what? My mother was very blunt, she said, "This is a good day, but it's not that special."
>
> She finds it absurd that graduating from high school is made into a big deal because you should graduate high school; everyone should. It's not necessarily a privilege; it's an obligation. You must go to high school, and you must finish. It's a further obligation that you go to college and get a

bachelor's degree. Thereafter, if you get a PhD or a master's, that's the big thing; that's the icing on the cake with a cherry on top, and that's what she values.

Furthermore, college was so critical to the success frame that the interviewees could not recall when they first learned that college was an expectation. They maintained that "they always knew" that they would go to college, but could not explain exactly how they knew. In fact, the idea of not going to college was tantamount to "blasphemy," as Daniel, a thirty-eight-year-old 1.5-generation Chinese male, described it: "Any Asian that doesn't go to college, that's like blasphemy. We're kind of brainwashed to the point that almost every single Asian kid thinks college is a necessity. Only after that can you start pursuing other options." Annie, a twenty-eight-year-old 1.5-generation Vietnamese female, echoed these sentiments and explained that her parents expected her not only to go to college but to go beyond college:

> INTERVIEWER: So what were your parents' educational expectations for you? High school? College? Beyond?
> ANNIE: Beyond.
> INTERVIEWER: Beyond college?
> ANNIE: Yes.

However, as Tony, a second-generation Chinese male, specified, the expectation was not simply to go to college but to go to an elite college. When we asked how his parents would have felt had he chosen not to go to college, Tony responded with amusement:

> I would have been disowned or something like that. [*laughs*] No, I would have been convinced to do otherwise. But honestly, by then it was very well ingrained value-wise that that was probably just going to happen. I mean, it was assumed or understood that [I would go to] college, and a really good college at that. Any college would have been a disappointment.

Like Tony, the vast majority of our Chinese and Vietnamese interviewees were well aware of the status differences among the colleges in California, and they distinguished among the "UCs" (the University of California schools, which are the most elite public universities), the "Cal States" (California state universities), community colleges, and elite private schools like Stanford and the Ivys. Furthermore, even within each of the college tiers the interviewees could detail the hierarchical rankings and reputational strengths among them.

The goal for most of the Chinese and Vietnamese interviewees was to gain admission to a UC because they are California's leading public institutions—and preferably UC Berkeley or UCLA because they are the most competitive and prestigious of the UC schools. In fact, the majority of our Chinese and Vietnamese interviewees reported that they had applied to more than one UC school, regardless of whether they intended to enroll. For example, Annie, the

1.5-generation Vietnamese interviewee quoted earlier, applied to three UC schools and one Cal State school (and was admitted by all except UCLA). Considering her family's limited financial resources, she chose to accept admission to the Cal State school for her undergraduate education, but her decision factored in her plans to attend a UC for graduate school. Moreover, her admission to the UC schools (despite her decision not to attend) allowed her parents to brag about this feat.

Not only was a specific educational track critical to the success frame from the perspective of immigrant parents, but parents also strongly disapproved of and admonished any deviation from it. For example, when Annie changed her college major from biochemistry to liberal arts and abandoned her plans to attend medical school and become a doctor, her parents could not understand her decision and were upset and disappointed in her. As Annie explained, "With Asian parents, they just want you to be a doctor or a lawyer or a pharmacist. It brings you more fame. Like a higher status."

The "Asian F"

So exacting is the success frame that our Chinese and Vietnamese interviewees explained that their immigrant parents expected them to earn straight A's in high school because a 4.0 GPA (a straight-A grade point average) or higher was the route to a top UC school.[11] So prevalent is the straight-A expectation that several of the interviewees described grades on an "Asian scale" as "A is for average, and B is an Asian fail." However, most had an even stricter definition of an Asian F, clarifying that "an A minus is an Asian fail"—a sentiment reflected in an episode of the popular television series *Glee* aptly titled "Asian F." So widespread is the Asian F metaphor that the popular comedian and television host Jon Stewart jokingly referred to National Basketball Association player Jeremy Lin's 3.1 GPA at Harvard as an "Asian F."

Philip, a thirty-four-year-old second-generation Chinese male, underscored just how narrowly his parents defined "doing well in school." A's and A-pluses were the expectation, he explained: "You got an A-minus and my parents would ask, 'Why couldn't you get an A?' You got an A. 'Why couldn't you get an A-plus?' So, yeah, we were expected to be very high-achievers." Similarly, Tony, a second-generation Chinese male, explained that as far back as he could remember, beginning in grade school, his parents had expected him to earn straight A's. He just "understood" this message, he said:

> As far as I can remember, I've always felt like working hard, and being smart, and doing the best you could, and having high expectations, like straight A's in high school, or grade school for that matter. It was always just something that was understood.

Most remarkable is that regardless of class background, the Chinese and Vietnamese recounted the same success frame: getting straight A's in high school, attending a top UC school, earning an advanced degree, and working in one of the top four professions.

Figure 3.1   *Self-Reports of Receiving Mostly A's in High School Among Male and Female 1.5-, Second-, and Third-Plus-Generation Immigrant Children, by Ethnic Group*

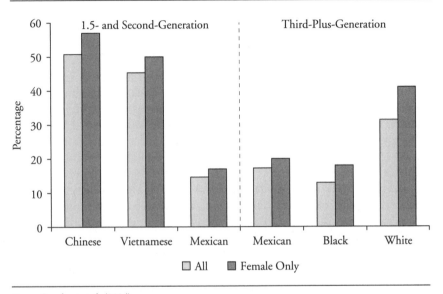

Source: Rumbaut et al. (2004).

Why Parents Push the Success Frame

The premium that Asian immigrant parents and Asian American students place on grades stems from a specific narrative about how to attain success in the United States. To secure "a good job" one needs a good education, and to get into a university that promises a good education one needs to work hard to get good grades in high school. The strict success frame for educational achievement that the Chinese and Vietnamese immigrant parents adopt and pass on to their 1.5- and second-generation children reflects their belief that it is *only* through a good education and good grades that one is able to secure a good job—that is they delineate a singular success frame and a singular path to achieve it. The positive association between a good education and a good job is one that Asian American adolescents adhere to more strongly than non-Asian adolescents.[12]

Most Asian Americans do not get straight A's, but the Immigration and Intergenerational Mobility in Metropolitan Los Angeles (IIMMLA) data reveal that they are more likely to get mostly A's compared to other groups. Figure 3.1 shows the percentages of IIMMLA respondents who reported getting mostly A's in high school by ethnic group and gender. The 1.5- and second-generation Chinese and Vietnamese respondents were much more likely than other groups to report having earned mostly A's. Although females received better grades than males across all ethnoracial groups, the intergroup pattern remained the same.

There is another reason why Chinese and Vietnamese immigrant parents adopt a strict success frame that includes only a narrow set of professions that require high educational credentials and convey high earnings that go beyond status attainment. Asian immigrant parents recognize that despite their children's native-born status, as nonwhite Americans they are still vulnerable to racial discrimination and bias in the labor market. Believing that upward social mobility is possible in the United States—as a result of the civil rights movement—but fearing that their children will face racial discrimination because of their nonwhite status and immigrant origins, Asian immigrant parents shepherd their children onto the path that they believe is most likely to lead to a successful professional outcome.

Fields such as medicine, law, science, and engineering require exceptional educational achievement, credentials, and "hard" skills that may obviate or lessen potential discrimination and bias. Consequently, Asian immigrant parents direct their children into elite colleges, specific majors, and particular occupations so that they will be better protected from subjective evaluation.[13] From the Asian immigrant parents' point of view, entering a technical field that requires an advanced degree is a conservative approach to a high-status, successful outcome and one that leaves the least wiggle room for non-Asian employers, customers, clients, and peers to subjectively evaluate and discriminate against their children.[14]

Hence, aside from status attainment, their desire to protect their children from potential bias and discrimination is another critical reason why Chinese and Vietnamese immigrant parents set definite parameters around the success frame and discourage their second-generation children from deviating from it. Creative fields such as writing, filmmaking, acting, art, design, and politics leave their children more open to subjective evaluation by employers, customers, and clients, and consequently more open to potential critique and bias. As a 1.5-generation Chinese female recounted her mother's words of advice about pursuing math and medicine as opposed to interior design, "in math there's always a right answer; one plus one always equals two. It's not that way in the arts." From Asian immigrant parents' point of view, taking the most conservative approach is also the most surefire path to success, which is why they frame success so narrowly defined for their children.

The Consistency of the Success Frame

Most remarkable was the consistency of the success frame, regardless of parents' level of education, occupational status, migration history, class background, or residential segregation. For example, when we asked Maryann, a twenty-four-year-old, second-generation Vietnamese woman who grew up in the housing projects in downtown L.A., how she defined success, she said, "Getting into one of the top schools" (which by her account included UCLA, Berkeley, Yale, Harvard, Princeton, and Stanford) and then working in one of the "top professions" such as "doctor or lawyer." When we asked Maryann how she knew about the top schools and top professions, she said, "[From] other parents who have kids. We know a few families who have kids who've gone to Yale, and they're doctors now, and they're doing really well for themselves."

What is noteworthy about Maryann's account of the success frame is that her Vietnamese parents arrived as refugees in the United States with only a sixth-grade education. They do not speak English, they work in Chinatown's garment factories, and they live in L.A.'s housing projects surrounded by poor Mexican immigrant neighbors. In spite of Maryann's low familial SES and residential segregation from more privileged coethnics, she recounted a success frame that mirrored that of her middle-class peers. However, as Maryann noted, she learned about the frame from her parents' coethnic network of friends and adopted it because she and her parents knew of other second-generation Vietnamese who had attained it. Because immigrant parents circulate the success frame within their coethnic networks and relay confirming narratives about those who attain it to their second-generation children, information cuts across class and generational lines.[15] This is how the success frame—which middle-class coethnics construct—reaches less-privileged, residentially segregated, working-class coethnics.

Although Maryann had not graduated from one of the "top schools" that she listed, she did graduate from a Cal State school and was working toward a master's degree in education at the time of the interview. Despite the extraordinary intergenerational mobility that she had already attained, she felt that she had departed from the success frame because her GPA was "only a 3.5," and also because she had attended a Cal State rather than a UC school. Furthermore, she added, her parents, along with other Vietnamese immigrant parents, did not regard teaching as a high-status profession because, in their view, "anyone can become a teacher." Maryann also felt that she paled in comparison to her twin sister, who had graduated as the high school valedictorian, had been admitted to and graduated from Berkeley (the most elite UC school), and was attending medical school.

Measuring her accomplishments against those of her twin sister and other high-achieving coethnics who were marching in step with the success frame, Maryann felt "average" and did not feel successful, despite the extraordinary intergenerational mobility that she had attained. Maryann was not unique among other Chinese and Vietnamese interviewees who described themselves as "average" or "not really successful." Those who graduated with GPAs of 3.5 or 3.6 consistently pointed to coethnic peers whose GPAs were 4.0, and even those who earned GPAs of 4.0 pointed to others whose GPAs were even higher. Hannah, for example, was a twenty-five-year-old, second-generation Vietnamese woman who had graduated third in her high school class with a GPA of 4.21, was voted "most likely to succeed" by her senior class, and had earned admission to UCLA and Berkeley. When we asked whether her parents were proud of her academic achievements in high school, Hannah shrugged her shoulders and casually replied, "It would have been better if I was first or second."

Across the board, the Chinese and Vietnamese interviewees looked not to native-born whites but to high-achieving coethnic peers or siblings as their reference group when measuring their success. Those who did not meet the success frame when comparing themselves against those who did consequently felt unsuccessful, inadequate, or average. Some even admitted that they felt like ethnic outliers or failures. For example, Carolyn, a thirty-five-year-old second-generation Chinese, described herself as her family's "black sheep" because she had only a 3.3 GPA in high school, went to a Cal State school, and worked as a filmmaker rather than a doctor or lawyer like her cousins.

Likewise, Maggie, a thirty-five-year-old 1.5-generation Chinese, described herself as her family's black sheep because she deviated from the success frame, unlike her two sisters who attained it. Maggie's sisters were straight-A students, high school valedictorians, graduates of elite private universities, and graduates of a top medical school and top business school. By stark contrast, Maggie ditched classes in high school and decided to forgo college to follow her passion to open her own martial arts studio. She told us that her mother, disgusted with her decision, kicked Maggie out of the house and branded her the "shame" of the family, predicting that she would forever be a "failure."

Our interviewees who departed from the constricting success frame, rather than rejecting or challenging it, were more likely to reject their ethnoracial identities, claiming that they did not feel Chinese, Vietnamese, or Asian. Moreover, they distanced themselves from their "successful" coethnic peers and coethnic communities because their educational and professional outcomes had departed from what they perceived as the norm for Asian Americans, a point upon which we elaborate in forthcoming chapters.

The Ethnoracial Coding
of the Success Frame

So closely tied is the success frame with ethnoracial status that Vicky, a second-generation Chinese woman who graduated from a top UC school and is now working toward her master's degree in public administration, felt the urge to clarify her status: "Just because I'm not a doctor or lawyer doesn't mean that I'm not Chinese." Not only did Vicky recognize that she did not fit the success frame because she was pursuing an alternative career path, but she also felt the need to proclaim her Chinese ethnicity because she was neither a doctor nor a lawyer—professions that she perceived as the norm for second-generation Chinese. Although Vicky may have acquired the success frame from her family and coethnic peers, as her statement reveals, the frame has become ethnicized and racialized.

Regardless of whether our Chinese and Vietnamese interviewees agreed with the constricting success frame, each was keenly aware of it, and most attributed it to their ethnoracial culture or to their Asian, Chinese, or Vietnamese upbringing. Throughout the interviews, the 1.5- and second-generation Chinese and Vietnamese noted that doing well in school not only is the expectation or obligation but also has become racialized as "acting Asian" and the Asian thing. Here the interviewees conflated not only ethnicity and race but also ethnic culture and Asian culture, often using racial and ethnic categories and descriptors interchangeably. Moreover, they reduced ethnic and Asian culture to high educational expectations and achievement. (As noted in chapter 1, note 8, we use the term "ethnoracial" to reflect the fluidity with which the interviewees moved from ethnic to racial categories, but distinguish between racial and ethnic categories when it is salient.)

Although the racial coding of academic achievement as acting Asian and the Asian thing is new, the racial coding of academic achievement is not. Conflated with race for decades, academic achievement was formerly the province of whites, as Signithia Fordham and John Ogbu assert in their oft-cited article "Black Students' School Success: Coping with the Burden of 'Acting White.'"[16] Fordham and Ogbu proposed the "acting white" hypothesis to explain the black-white achievement gap: they argue that black students consciously disengage from academic learning and reject schooling because they consider doing well in school a "white thing."[17] Other researchers have strongly critiqued the "acting white" thesis by showing that poor black and Latino students do not hold an anti-achievement ideology, but rather lack the dominant cultural capital required to enable their mobility.[18] In addition, Prudence Carter found that acting white reflects dress styles, speech patterns, and cultural codes among black and Latino youth rather than an anti-achievement ideology.[19]

In light of these findings, we asked our interviewees whether they believed that to do well in school is to act white. None of the 1.5- and second-generation Chinese and Vietnamese interviewees had heard of this; moreover, none associated academic achievement with white students. However, rather than dissociating race from achievement entirely, the interviewees described doing well in school as the Asian thing. For example, Debra, a 1.5-generation Chinese woman, explained:

> Doing well in school is the Asian thing. You just see a lot more Asians being valedictorians, being top ten, never getting in trouble with the teachers, and entering into the good UC's and the Ivy League schools. And I even heard jokes from my best friend, this Caucasian girl, she liked hanging around with Asians because she knew that Asians were good students. The ones I that I hung around with ended up at Harvard, Stanford, Cal [Berkeley].

Rebecca, a twenty-six-year-old second-generation Vietnamese who had just graduated from law school, echoed Debra's sentiments. Doing well in school was not framed as acting white at her high school; on the contrary, the white students were known as the jocks, cheerleaders, and partiers who were not concerned about their grades:

> The white people were associated with being the jocks, the cheerleaders; they didn't care about academics. The Asians—we weren't the pretty blondes, we didn't do the cheerleading. We focused more on our classes. For example, if you looked at all the AP students, they were predominantly Asian, and the whites were considered the partiers and the ones that went out and did the whole jock thing.

Furthermore, when we asked Rebecca whether doing well in school was considered "uncool," she flatly answered, "No, I didn't feel that way. If anything, it was a thing to have on your side." Hence, not only was doing well in school racially coded as the Asian thing for our interviewees, but it had no association whatsoever with whiteness, antiblackness, or the "cool" factor.[20]

The Chinese and Vietnamese interviewees were not the only ones who racialized academic achievement as the Asian thing; the Mexican interviewees also described academic achievement as the province of Asians. During our interviews with the 1.5- and second-generation Mexicans, they described Asians as "educated," "smart," "dedicated," and "hardworking." For example, when we asked Claudia, a second-generation Mexican mother of three children, how she would describe the Chinese and Vietnamese in Los Angeles, she answered without hesitation, "Very smart." When we asked her why she believed this, she explained that the majority of her daughter's peers in the GATE (gifted and talented education) program were Asian. Claudia added that, because her daughter was also "very smart," she had decided to adopt the Asian success frame herself:

> She [my daughter] is very smart. I try to give her support. I was told the Asian people—and I am not sure if this is true, but I was told this—that they are told when they are small that they *have* to go to school and *have* to be a doctor or *have* to be something. So when they are told when they are small, and you keep on telling them they will be something, they are like, "I have to be this when I grow up, and I have to do it, and my parents are pushing for school." That is what I am doing with my daughter, so we will see.

Having learned that Asian parents reinforce a narrow success frame, Claudia was doing the same with her daughter, in the hopes that her daughter would model herself after her Asian American peers.

Like Claudia, Nancy, a second-generation Mexican woman, had also noticed a difference in the way her parents and her Chinese friend's parents reinforced the success frame. Nancy explained that, while her parents wanted her to do well in high school and go to college, they never specified what that meant or how they expected her to achieve those goals. Comparing her parents to her Chinese friend's parents, Nancy noticed a clear difference in the way both sets of parents conveyed their educational expectations of their children; unlike her parents, her friend's Chinese parents relayed strict and concrete expectations about academic achievement. When we pressed Nancy to elaborate, she explained:

> I don't know if that has something to do with the culture, but I had a friend who is Chinese, and she had strict parents. You had to get an A; it's kind of hard to explain. My mom never said to me to "get an A." She said, "Do your best"—you know? Sometimes my dad, once in a while, he would say, "Finish school, go to college," but he wouldn't get into much detail.

Nancy noted that both her parents and her friend's Chinese parents held high aspirations for their children and expected them to do well in school and go to college. However, her friend's parents specified the route to attaining this goal, making it tangible in a way that her parents did not or were not able to do. Unable to explain the different types of advice that she and her Chinese friend received, Nancy speculated that the differences must have been cultural.

In ethnoracially diverse urban contexts like Los Angeles, the frame for academic achievement has moved beyond the black-white binary to reflect the country's new ethnoracial diversity. Because of the hyper- and high-selectivity of East Asian immigration, academic achievement has become racially recoded as the Asian thing, especially in cities that have witnessed a stream of high-skilled Asian immigrants. The reshuffling of the ethnoracial order in the domain of education has consequently changed the reference group to whom the second-generation Chinese and Vietnamese turn as their model for success: rather than modeling themselves after native-born whites, they measure their success against high-achieving coethnics and panethnics.

The movement away from native-born whites as the reference group for success is also evident in studies of second-generation Mexicans who turn to middle-class coethnics or other high-achieving ethnoracial groups as their mobility prototypes. For example, Jody Vallejo finds that second-generation Mexicans look to successful coethnics, rather than whites, as their role models.[21] Moreover, Robert Smith shows that in New York City second-generation Mexicans do not look to native-born whites as their models of success, nor do they turn to coethnics; instead, the children of Mexican immigrants turn to another ethnoracial minority group—native-born blacks.[22] They selectively seek out, emulate, and associate with academically successful black peers in their high schools because adopting a black racial identity signals American nativity, popularity, and academic prowess.

By contrast, a Mexican identity holds little social status, especially since the Mexican immigrant population is relatively new and the Mexican-origin population relatively small compared to other immigrant populations in New York City. Given their relative recency, small size, and low status, Mexican students conflate Mexican ethnicity with powerlessness, poor and working-class origins, and foreign-born, undocumented status. In addition, because second-generation Mexicans in Smith's study attend schools primarily with blacks (but not with whites or Asians), they model themselves after the high-achievers in their schools, who happen to be black rather than white or Asian, with whom, in any event, they had little contact.[23]

The shift from native-born whites as the reference group for success is also evident in Tomás Jiménez and Adam Horowitz's study of Silicon Valley, California, an area that has witnessed an influx of highly skilled immigrants from East and South Asia.[24] No longer perceived as exceptional, native-born white students have been reduced to "just all right," while Asians have become synonymous with academic excellence. While just all right may be just fine for whites, just all right does not make the cut for Asian Americans. The success frame is so narrowly constructed that it is the standard by which all Asian Americans are measured and judged, by themselves as well as by others. As a result, Asian Americans whose achievements are just all right feel that they are below average, that they are failures, and that they are the black sheep in their families and ethnic outliers against the perceived norm of Asian American exceptionalism.

The Historical and Legal Context of the Success Frame

Unable to explain Asian Americans' academic outcomes, most of our interviewees, Mexicans included, pointed to cultural differences and, in particular, to their belief that "Asians value education" more than other ethnoracial groups. This essentialist cultural argument has several flaws. First, it does not take into account the effects of immigrant educational selectivity and hyper-selectivity. As we showed in chapter 2, educational selectivity and hyper-selectivity result in a sizable ethnic middle class that is highly educated, highly skilled, and economically resourceful. The middle class generates the ethnic capital, creates ethnic institutions, and constructs the success frame. Members of the ethnic middle class also selectively import cultural institutions and practices from their countries of origin and re-create them in the United States to ensure the realization of the success frame—a point upon which we elaborate in chapter 4.

Second, the essentialist cultural argument also fails to account for the historical specificity of the success frame. It is worth remembering that Asian immigrants to the United States have not always been highly educated and highly selected, much less hyper-selected.[25] Less than a century ago, Asian immigrants were low-skilled, low-wage manual laborers who lived in crowded ethnic enclaves, segregated from other Americans. Described as illiterate, "undesirable immigrants" and "marginal members of the human race" full of "filth and disease," they were denied citizenship, denied the right to intermarry, residentially segregated, and, in the case of Japanese Americans, forced into internment camps.[26]

Yet despite decades of institutional discrimination and racial prejudice, the status of Asians has changed dramatically over the course of several decades. Today, some pundits and scholars hail Asian Americans as exceptional and as the nation's most successful minority group.[27] Based on socioeconomic indicators alone, there appears to be merit to this designation. Despite the heterogeneity in the population, Asian Americans are the most highly educated group in the country and have the highest median household incomes, the highest rates of intermarriage, and the lowest rates of residential segregation.[28]

How has the status of Asian Americans changed from unassimilable to exceptional in a relatively short period of time? The answer lies in the changing political landscape of the United States, combined with the change in U.S. immigration laws. In the 1960s, the civil rights movement, spearheaded by African Americans, led to the passage of the Civil Rights Act of 1964, which outlawed segregation in public places and prohibited discrimination in employment based on race, gender, or national origin. Their fight for equality also resulted in the passage of the Voting Rights Act of 1965, which secured for African Americans equal access to and opportunities to enjoy the basic privileges and rights of U.S. citizenship. These sweeping legal changes led Americans to believe that race would decline in significance and no longer obstruct the opportunity structure for black Americans, as well as for other nonwhite Americans.

These radical legal changes coincided with the passage of the 1965 Hart-Celler Act, which altered the demographic landscape of the United States by opening the door to immigrants from Latin America, Asia, Africa, and the Caribbean. The Hart-Celler Act not only ushered in immigrants from different parts of the globe but also gave rise to a new socioeconomic profile of immigrants. Among Asian immigrants, for example, those who came to the United States after 1965 were more highly educated than those who had migrated in the nineteenth and early twentieth centuries. Not only are contemporary Asian immigrants more highly educated than their predecessors, but they are also more highly educated than the U.S. average. As the 2012 Pew Report shows, more than three-fifths (61 percent) of adults between the ages of twenty-five and sixty-four who immigrated from Asia in recent years had at least a bachelor's degree—more than double the national average for the U.S. population (28 percent). In addition, contemporary Asian immigrants are more highly educated than nonmigrants in their countries of origin—reflecting the hyper-selectivity of Asian immigration (as shown in figure 2.1).

How Hyper-Selectivity Affects the Perception of Asian Americans

The general perception that all Asian Americans are highly educated and high-achieving is driven by not only the hyper-selectivity and high-selectivity of most Asian immigrant groups but also the tendency of Americans to make assumptions about all Asians based on a select group of contemporary Asian immigrants in the United States. In other words, Americans tend to make assumptions about Asians based on a select group of contemporary Asian immigrants in the United States. As we illustrated in chapter 2, however, Asian immigrants in the United States like the Chinese and Vietnamese are only a thin slice—and a highly selected thin slice—of the general populations in China and Vietnam, about 95 percent of whom have not graduated from college. Hence, to make racial, ethnic, or cultural generalizations about Asian immigrants based on such a hyper-selected group is fallacious reasoning—a third flaw of the cultural essentialist argument. This logic is akin to making generalizations about Americans based only on those who graduated from Ivy League universities.

Many of our interviewees did the same; they credited Asian Americans' exceptional outcomes to Asian cultural values. Most of the 1.5- and second-generation Chinese and Vietnamese we interviewed did not recognize the role of hyper- and high-selectivity in the construction and perpetuation of stereotypes about Asians as academic high-achievers. Kevin, a twenty-seven-year-old second-generation Chinese, and Jesse, a thirty-three-year-old 1.5-generation Chinese, were among the few who did. Kevin, who graduated from a UC school and worked as an account manager, explained that, for example, because of the high cost and difficulty of emigrating from China to the United States, only the most educated and affluent are able to do so. He also astutely added that if travel from Asia were less costly and immigration laws less restrictive, Americans would see more class heterogeneity among Chinese immigrants:

> The people that do cross the ocean can afford to. If you go to Asia, there are just as many poor Chinese cleaning toilets, and those people don't have those means to get across. I think if it's the right sample size, you'll see similarities between all races. If it was cheaper to cross the Pacific Ocean and get a working visa, things are going to start changing, but it's not going to happen in our generation.

Jesse, who also graduated from a UC school and now worked for a professor doing research, echoed Kevin's point, adding that because of the hyper-selectivity of Asian immigration (which he metaphorically described as a "filter"), Americans tend to meet only highly educated Asian immigrants:

> In order for the Asians to get here, they had to go through a process. I'm sure there are other Asians in other cities elsewhere in the world who don't value education or who aren't able to get an education, but of course in the U.S. we never see them face to face because they never make it here.

I mean, you can find the poor anywhere in the world, except that we only see the top [Asians] because immigration filters out the people who can't make it here. Whereas if you are from Mexico, it is very easy to walk across the border; the filter is not there.

We are only seeing the top from these Asian countries coming in. I think a lot of the perception is that people tend to ignore that filter. When we see these people come from Asian countries, they only seem to value education because we are only getting the people who value education coming in.

As both Kevin and Jesse insightfully articulated, not all Asians are highly educated, and by extension, not all embrace or can attain the success frame. However, Chinese and Vietnamese immigrants in the United States are more likely to do so because of their hyper-selectivity and high educational selectivity, respectively.

The success frame emerged from the historical context of liberalized immigration laws and the belief in a more open opportunity structure for non-white Americans, including immigrants. Moreover, the hyper-selectivity and high educational selectivity of Asian immigration provide the material bases for Asian immigrants like the Chinese and Vietnamese to import the success frame, re-create it in their new host society, and support it with middle-class resources. As we detail in the following chapters, hyper-selectivity and high educational selectivity play a critical role in Asian immigrant parents' ability to support and reinforce the success frame—in the absence of which that frame would change or become more heterogeneous.

Summary

Family socioeconomic status is one of the strongest predictors of attainment, but as we show in this chapter, it does not affect all groups equally. Low SES among some Asian groups, such as Chinese and Vietnamese immigrants, does not hamper the educational outcomes of their 1.5- and second-generation children as it does for the children of Mexican immigrants, native-born whites, and native-born blacks. Unable to explain this Asian American achievement paradox, pundits and neoconservatives have turned to essentialist explanations of culture: there must be something unique about Asian culture and values that leads to these exceptional educational outcomes. Culture does play a role, but not in the way that pundits often claim.

We maintain that to understand the role of culture in immigrant and second-generation outcomes, we must factor in the role of hyper-selectivity and high educational selectivity among immigrant groups. The hyper-selectivity and high selectivity affect the formation of the success frame for Chinese and Vietnamese immigrants and their children. The success frame involves getting straight A's, earning admission to a top university, going to graduate school, and working in one of four high-status professions: medicine, law, science, or engineering. Most remarkable is the consistency of the success frame among our Chinese and Vietnamese interviewees, regardless of their parents' education, occupational status, migration history, or class background.

The strict success frame for educational achievement among Chinese and Vietnamese immigrant parents and their 1.5- and second-generation children reflects the parental belief that it is *only* through getting a good education and earning excellent grades that one is able to secure a good job—a belief that delineates a singular success frame and a singular pathway to achieve it. But there is another reason why Chinese and Vietnamese immigrant parents adopt a success frame that encompasses a narrow set of professions. Believing that upward social mobility is possible in the United States—as a result of the civil rights movement—but fearing that their nonwhite and immigrant-origin children will face racial bias and discrimination because of their ethnoracial status, Asian immigrant parents shepherd their children onto the path that will most likely lead to a successful professional outcome.

Asian immigrant parents direct their children into elite colleges, specific majors, and particular occupations in which they feel their children will be better protected from subjective evaluation, bias, and potential discrimination. From the Asian immigrant parents' point of view, entering a technical field that requires an advanced degree is the surest protector against bias from non-Asian employers, customers, and clients. This is also why Asian immigrant parents discourage their second-generation children from entering more creative fields such as writing, filmmaking, acting, art, design, and politics, which would leave their children more open to subjective evaluation and bias.

In light of the achievement paradox, the narrow success frame, and Asian Americans' educational outcomes, academic achievement has become racially recoded as acting Asian and the Asian thing by Asian and non-Asian students alike in Los Angeles. The new racialization of achievement has also recalibrated grades along an Asian scale, such than an A-minus is now an Asian F. This new racial recoding is evident not only in Los Angeles but also in other metropolitan areas that have experienced large-scale, highly skilled Asian immigration, such as Silicon Valley, California.[29]

As academic achievement has moved beyond the black-white binary, so too has the reference group for success. The nonwhite, nonblack children of contemporary immigrants are not turning to native-born whites as their reference group; rather, the children of Chinese and Vietnamese immigrants turn to high-achieving coethnics as their barometer for success, and they employ a minority culture of mobility to attain it.[30] In the following chapter, we focus on the resources that Chinese and Vietnamese immigrant parents use to support the success frame. Although some of these resources are preferentially available to coethnics, many are not exclusive to Asians.

~ Chapter 4 ~

Reinforcing the Success Frame

In the previous chapter, we explained how Chinese and Vietnamese immigrant parents construct a strict success frame for their children, expecting them to get straight A's in high school, attend a prestigious university, earn an advanced degree, and secure a high-status, well-paying job in one of the four coveted professions: doctor, lawyer, scientist, or engineer. However, simply adopting a success frame does not ensure the desired outcome. For a frame to be effective, it needs to be supported by reinforcement mechanisms, in the absence of which the frame can change and diversify.

Chinese and Vietnamese immigrant parents recognize that in order for their children to attain the success frame, they need to buttress it with reinforcement mechanisms in the form of resources and strategies. These resources and strategies—rather than strict "Tiger Mother" parenting practices—are key to achieving the success frame.[1] In addition, the reinforcement mechanisms must be strong enough not only to support the success frame but also to counteract the appeal and pressure to assimilate into white or black middle-class youth culture.[2] Furthermore, the reinforcement mechanisms must be durable enough to withstand the intense bicultural and intergenerational conflict that can erupt between Asian immigrant parents and their U.S.-born children.[3] Given the pressure that both immigrant parents and their U.S.-born children face in the United States combined with the potential for intergenerational conflict, how have Chinese and Vietnamese immigrant parents managed to ensure that their children adopt the success frame?

In this chapter, we answer this question, first, by identifying the strategies that Chinese and Vietnamese immigrant parents employ to take advantage of publicly available resources to guarantee that their U.S.-born and U.S.-raised children are placed in the most competitive and rigorous academic environments in their public schools. Second, we describe the *tangible* ethnic resources that Chinese and Vietnamese immigrant parents draw upon to reinforce the success frame, such as the elaborate system of supplementary education available in their ethnic communities. Third, we identify the *intangible* ethnic resources and strategies that both immigrant parents and their 1.5- and second-generation children depend on to realize the success frame: the parents' belief in a mind-set that privileges effort over ability; collective strategies that maximize family mobility; and the cross-class learning that occurs within ethnoracially homophilous peer networks.

Here we paint a broader picture by adopting a global, comparative perspective to illustrate that ethnic resources like the supplementary education systems in ethnic communities and ethnic strategies such as the collective familial strategy for mobility are not solely U.S.-born institutions and strategies but rather are imported from immigrants' countries of origin, readjusted, and then re-created to best fit the U.S. context. That Chinese and Vietnamese immigrants are hyper-selected and highly selected, respectively, means that the institutions, frames, and mind-sets that they import are not simply ethnic resources and strategies but *class-specific* ethnic resources and strategies. As such, these resources and strategies arm the 1.5 and second generation with a toolkit that aids educational achievement, even in spite of low parental human capital.

Taking a broader view offers another insight: it helps us understand that Chinese and Vietnamese immigrant parents and their children adopt a dual frame of reference to gauge the rigor of supplementary education programs in the United States and in Asia. That those in the United States are less rigorous, demanding, and time-consuming makes them more palatable for U.S.-born children, who compare them to the arduous supplemental system in their parents' countries of origin.

Combined, these strategies and ethnic resources explain the pattern of "second-generation convergence" as well as the ability of children of working-class Chinese and Vietnamese parents to override their class disadvantage and achieve academic outcomes that defy the status attainment model. However, we caution that not all children of Chinese and Vietnamese immigrants benefit equally from ethnic resources and strategies, especially in households where economic resources are thin. Gender and birth order determine which children in working-class households are most likely to benefit—and thus which are better poised to attain the success frame.

Familial Strategies to Support the Success Frame

Based on our in-depth, life-history interviews with 1.5- and second-generation Chinese and Vietnamese, we learned that the success frame is reinforced by four strategies. First, Chinese and Vietnamese immigrant parents deliberately buy or rent homes in neighborhoods based on the reputation and quality of the local public schools, especially the high schools. Second, parents, in the belief that the most rigorous learning environment will position their children for admission to an elite college, demand that their children be placed in honors and Advanced Placement (AP) classes in high school. Third, parents point to the highest-achieving siblings and coethnic peers as the reference group for success. Those who have attained the success frame become the mobility prototypes and role models for their fellow ethnics, and they also serve as proof that the success frame is within reach.[4]

These three strategies are not unique to Chinese, Vietnamese, or Asian immigrant parents and families, but the fourth strategy is. Chinese and Vietnamese immigrant parents rely on ethnic resources and strategies, including ethnic channels and ethnic networks, to acquire and distribute pertinent information about neighborhood quality, school rankings, and supplemental educational programs that will help to keep their children a step ahead of their peers. Some of the ethnic resources are tangible, such as the elaborate system of supplementary education available in ethnic communities. Other ethnic resources and strategies are intangible, including the belief in effort over innate ability to improve academic achievement, a collective strategy for mobility, and cross-class learning among coethnic peers.

These strategies and resources build "ethnic capital"—that is, the institutional investments that parents make in their ethnic communities to support success frames and achievement mind-sets.[5] As a result of middle-class parental investments, tangible and intangible ethnic resources become available to ethnic group members, regardless of class. In turn, access to ethnic capital allows poor and working-class coethnics to mitigate their familial SES and expand their opportunity horizon, that is, what they perceive is possible to achieve based on class resources alone.[6]

Selectively Buying or Renting a Home Based on the School District

One of the primary strategies that immigrant parents rely upon to reinforce the success frame is to provide their children with an environment that is conducive to learning by buying a home or renting an apartment based foremost on the quality of the neighborhood's school district. Homeownership, house size, and house quality are therefore less important for Chinese and Vietnamese immigrant parents than living in a neighborhood with a strong public school district. Moreover, these immigrant parents will go to great lengths to move so that their children can attend the most competitive public schools.[7] Although choosing to move to a neighborhood based on the strength of the school district is not a uniquely Chinese, Vietnamese, or Asian cultural practice, what is unique is the ease and frequency with which poor and working-class Asian immigrants draw on their familial and coethnic networks to place their children in more competitive public schools in middle-class neighborhoods.

Here, hyper-selectivity and high-selectivity matter: for immigrant groups that are hyper-selected and highly selected, working-class members benefit from the disproportionate number of coethnics who can afford to move into middle-class neighborhoods with strong school districts. Although low-SES parents may be unable to move into the same neighborhoods, middle-class coethnics can sponsor their children and take legal guardianship of them so that they may attend more resource-rich schools, as Christopher's case attests.

Christopher—Transferring Guardianship Christopher is a twenty-seven-year-old second-generation Vietnamese whose refugee parents have only a fourth-grade education, yet despite their poor human capital, Christopher graduated from the University of Texas with a degree in computer science. He now works as a financial analyst for a management consulting firm and earns an annual salary of $70,000, which is more than his parents' combined earnings. Despite his family's low socioeconomic status, Christopher benefited from having high-achieving cousins who served as his academic role models and as mobility prototypes whose paths he emulated. In addition, at the advice of their friends, Christopher's parents (who live in a low-income, predominantly Vietnamese immigrant community in Westminster) transferred legal guardianship of their son to one of their coethnic friends so that he could attend a more competitive public high school in an affluent neighborhood in Orange County. Not only did the transfer of guardianship provide Christopher with a more resource-rich high school education, but it also shielded him from potential involvement in the Vietnamese gangs that were a serious concern in his parents' poor neighborhood.

Hence, Christopher's parents tapped into their class-diverse ethnic networks to learn how they could provide their son with a better education in spite of their socioeconomic disadvantage. They placed Christopher in the most competitive school they could find, and that learning environment armed him with the requisite toolkit to support the success frame and put him on an equal footing with his middle-class coethnic peers. Although Christopher's case may appear extreme, it reveals the popular practice of transferring guardianship of children among Chinese and Vietnamese immigrant parents to relatives and coethnic friends when the parents cannot afford to move to neighborhoods with highly ranked, resource-rich public schools.[8]

Honors and Advanced Placement Classes

A second strategy that Chinese and Vietnamese immigrant parents utilize is placing their children in honors and AP classes so that their academic milieu is as rigorous as possible. Here, employing a global comparative framework is fruitful. The educational systems in many East Asian countries focus on grades and high-stakes testing, which require hours of study that extend well beyond the school day. Educated immigrant parents from East Asia who have successfully made it through the intense educational system in their home country perceive the American educational system as less rigorous and less competitive by comparison. They also believe that students are assigned relatively little homework and are easily able to pass classes because American academic standards are lax. However, Asian immigrant parents are also aware that the American educational system is heterogeneous: the quality of education differs both among schools and within them. Recognizing that heterogeneity, they strive to place their children in the most competitive schools and also insist that they be placed in the most competitive academic tracks, classes, and programs.

Asian immigrant parents insist that their children enroll in honors and AP classes for four reasons. First, these parents believe that their children will receive the most rigorous education in these classes compared to general education classes. Second, they recognize that grades in honors and AP classes are weighted to reflect the rigor of these programs, so that a B in an AP or honors class is the grade-point equivalent of an A in a general education class. Hence, the payoff for taking more AP and honors classes is a boost to a student's grade point average (GPA), sometimes even beyond a 4.0 (which denotes straight A's). Third, parents insist that their children are placed in AP and honors classes because peers affect students' academic aspirations and performance; students with academically oriented and high-achieving peers are more likely to have higher educational expectations and higher academic outcomes than those with low-achieving peers.[9] And fourth, parents recognize that each of these factors enhances the probability that their children will gain admission to a top university.

Most of the Chinese and Vietnamese respondents mentioned that they were enrolled in AP or honors classes, and most expressed that being on this track was an expectation that came from several sources—their parents, their teachers, and both their coethnic and non-coethnic peers. So prevalent was that expectation that those who were not enrolled in AP or honors classes felt like ethnoracial outliers. For example, Patty, a twenty-seven-year-old 1.5-generation female, said that she was different from her Asian friends in high school because they were in AP classes and excelled in school and she did not:

> I have a lot of friends who do, like, really well in school. Actually, most of my friends did really well in high school. . . . When I was in high school, I just felt that those honor classes, or AP, were like so far, like, above me; it's not something I would [be] capable of. I think most Asians, or at least most of my friends that I know of, they all did really well, either, like, perfect or close to perfect.

Others mentioned that their parents insisted that they enroll in AP classes, even though they felt ill equipped to handle the workload at that level of instruction. For example, Sue, a 1.5-generation Chinese, said that her non-English-speaking mother insisted that she enroll in all honors classes during her freshman year in high school, even though both she and her teacher believed that she belonged in the general education English class. Sue admitted that she worked twice as hard in honors English and only managed to earn an above-average grade. Her mother "made me go after school simply to make sure that I had sufficient preview and review of each English class according to the course syllabus and did the required homework well. I ended up working more than twice as much for that class. She still felt I wasn't working hard enough when I had a B." While Sue put in double the effort to earn a B in the class, her mother insisted that she stay in the honors English class because she, like other Chinese and Vietnamese parents, believes that a B in an honors or AP class is better than an A in a general education class.

Chinese and Vietnamese immigrant parents learn that providing their children with the most effective public school education entails having them enroll in the most competitive high schools and having them enroll in the most competitive classes.

Supplementary Education: Tutoring, College Prep, and Summer School

A third strategy that parents rely on to support the success frame is providing their children with supplementary education that takes place outside of the normal school day—after-school tutoring, college prep courses, SAT prep classes, and summer school. Researchers describe supplementary education as the "hidden curriculum of high academic achievement" that middle-class American parents routinely provide for their children.[10] For example, Annette Lareau finds that both white and black-middle-class parents pack their children's schedules with a slew of after-school activities—for example, piano, violin, and tennis lessons, as well as tutoring and supplemental educational classes. She describes this middle-class strategy as "concerted cultivation"—the effort by parents to make their children as well rounded and competitive as possible.[11]

Affluent parents spend even more economic resources on supplementing their children's education; parents whose children attend New York's elite private high schools, for instance, spend several hundred dollars an hour on tutors for the SAT exam and for specific class subjects, which can add up to as much as $35,000 a year—nearly the equivalent of one year's tuition at an elite New York City private school.[12] So prevalent is the practice of concerted cultivation among middle-class and affluent parents that they now invest more of their resources (both money and time) in their children's education than ever before, resulting in an ever-widening class gap among American children.[13]

No class gap is evident, however, among the children of Chinese immigrants, and it is less evident among the children of Vietnamese immigrants. In other words, low SES does not hamper the educational attainment of Chinese and Vietnamese children. Access to supplementary education in the ethnic community is key here. For both 1.5- and second-generation Asian ethnic groups, class does not restrict access to middle-class resources as it does for their Mexican, white, and black peers because there are alternatives in addition to those offered in the mainstream economy. The hyper- and high-selectivity of Asian immigration enables Asian ethnic groups like Chinese and Vietnamese to build parallel systems of supplementary education in ethnic communities that make educational services available at a range of prices and therefore accessible to coethnic group members across class lines.[14] A majority of our Chinese and Vietnamese interviewees reported that they had enrolled in some type of after-school, weekend, or summer program to supplement the education they received in their public schools. So common was the practice that the interviewees believed the practice to be universal among Asians.

Tangible Ethnic Resources: What Makes Ethnic Supplementary Education Unique

Although the strategies that Chinese and Vietnamese immigrant parents employ to supplement their children's education are not unique to Asian ethnic groups, two aspects of this supplementary education are uniquely Asian American, meaning that they are born out of the U.S. Asian immigrant experience. To understand what is distinctively ethnic about these practices and how immigrants' countries of origin and the hyper-selectivity and high-selectivity of Asian immigration reinforce the success frame, it is useful to widen the lens once again and adopt a global, comparative approach.

A Global Comparative Approach to Supplementary Education

In both China and Vietnam, high school students prepare for years to take a nationwide, comprehensive, standardized exam that is the sole basis of university admission. Because one's career is closely tied to one's educational performance, the stakes and rewards of doing well on the college entrance exam are extremely high—and further heightened by the low odds of being accepted into a university, especially an elite one. In China, only three in five high school students who take the test make the cut. The odds of making it into a Vietnamese college are even lower: one in six. Given the high stakes and poor odds, Chinese and Vietnamese parents who can afford to do so enroll their children in supplemental educational programs as early as elementary school.

Supplementary education is not exclusive to China and Vietnam; it is also the norm in middle-class households in South Korea, Japan, Taiwan, and Singapore.[15] The impending national examinations and the consequences of their performance on the exam for their career trajectories strongly influence the educational practices of students, beginning in elementary school and going through middle school and into high school. Therefore, on top of their regular school day, students spend as many as seven hours in after-school academies—which begin at the end of the regular school day and end sometime between 10:00 PM and 1:00 AM.

The private after-school academies in mainland China, Hong Kong, Taiwan, and Singapore (called "buxiban" in these four countries) and in South Korea (where they are called "hagwon") are reputed to be the most rigorous in the world. The supplementary education industry in these countries is targeted not only at high school students but also at middle school and elementary students and even at preschool children. In South Korea, after-school academies are also geared to students who failed the nationwide exam and thus failed to gain admission to college on their first (or second) attempt. In Seoul, legions of students who do not earn admission to college immediately after high school spend the following year in a hagwon like the Daesung Institute (one of the country's most prestigious academies) to improve their scores on the nationwide university admissions exam. At the Daesung Institute, students spend fourteen-hour days intensively preparing for this exam—which pays off for the 70 percent of Daesung Institute graduates who earn admission to one of Seoul's top three universities.

So ubiquitous are hagwon and so pervasive is the practice of putting in such long hours that the South Korean government, concerned that students are spending too much time studying, has now implemented a curfew of 10:00 PM on hagwon.[16] But rather than changing their institutional practices to abide by the government's new curfew, hagwon have merely adapted to the government's restriction by putting more lessons online for students to study after-hours at home.[17]

Hyper-selected Asian immigrants have imported this particular practice of supplementary education to the United States, modified it, and re-created it to fit the U.S. context with the goal of shepherding their children into elite U.S. universities. The system of supplementary education is distinctively ethnic in three ways. First, the ethnic system of supplementary education is an integral part of the ethnic enclave economy anchored in the ethnic community.[18] It includes a range of private institutions—from small mom-and-pop operations to large learning and tutoring centers—and a range of price points so that not only middle-class but also working-class families can arrange supplementary education for their children.[19]

Second, these supplementary education systems emerge in parallel with and in addition to those offered by mainstream institutions and are priced differently. Some of our interviewees admitted to having taken supplementary education classes in the ethnic and mainstream economies. While the mainstream economy offers popular SAT prep courses from Kaplan and the Princeton Review, the ethnic economy offers SAT prep courses as well as extra help in class subjects such as math.[20] This ethnic system of supplementary education provides additional resources beyond those offered in the mainstream U.S. system of supplemental education to help second-generation Chinese and Vietnamese students excel on standardized tests like the SAT exam, as well as in their regular subject classes in elementary, junior high, and high school.

Third, ethnic supplementary education programs also include cultural enrichment programs specifically tailored to enhance students' chances of earning admission to an Ivy League school or prestigious university. Cultural enrichment programs include arts academies, classical music schools, ethnic language schools, sports programs, and programs to visit ancestral homelands so that U.S.-born and -raised children can "rediscover their roots."[21]

In these three ways, ethnic supplementary education is distinct from the supplemental education that middle-class white and black American parents provide for their children, and it enhances the academic outcomes and extra-curricular profiles of the children of Chinese and Vietnamese immigrants in uniquely ethnic ways.

Vanessa and Audrey: A Dual Frame of Reference   Taking the global comparative approach also helps in understanding the dual frame of reference that Chinese and Vietnamese immigrant parents and their children adopt to gauge a rigorous school day and study schedule. Supplementary education in East Asian countries is the norm, especially for middle-class children, and some of our 1.5-generation interviewees who came to the United States in their preteen years could vividly recall the long hours of studying that they put in each day, as well as the stress induced by this fiercely competitive educational system.

Vanessa, a twenty-five-year-old 1.5-generation Taiwanese-Chinese, told us that the main driver for her family's migration to the United States was to get away from the intense educational system in Taiwan. Witnessing the severe stress that Taiwan's educational system placed on Vanessa and her two younger sisters, her parents decided to leave the Taiwanese educational system shortly before Vanessa was about to take the high school entrance exam, which would have determined which high school she would attend. Recalling her grueling schedule in Taiwan, where each hour of her day was devoted to education, Vanessa described the toll on her physical and emotional health:

> VANESSA: I would wake up at like 6:00 every morning and then go to school until 6:00 at night. And then I would eat dinner, like, every day in the car because my dad would buy me something in the car to eat. And then after, like, an hour or so, I would go to another, like, school, like an after-school thing for whatever subject, like English, math, or physics, or whatever you can imagine. I didn't leave after-school until 11:00.
> INTERVIEWER: So from 6:00 in the morning until 11:00 at night?
> VANESSA: Every day. I was thirty pounds lighter than what I am [now]. I was like a bone-skinny person, just totally not healthy.
> INTERVIEWER: Did your friends do that too?
> VANESSA: Yeah, everybody did that, starting in middle school, so it was a nightmare.

Vanessa described the U.S. educational system as "relaxed" compared to the intensity and long hours in Taiwan, even though she attended supplemental educational classes after school, on weekends, and during the summers in the United States. Her account of her typical school day in Taiwan illustrates that when immigrants and their children compare supplementary education in their country of origin and in their host society, they use a dual frame of reference and judge the latter as far more laid-back.

Audrey, another 1.5-generation Taiwanese-Chinese, had Vanessa's experience. Now a high school math teacher, she acknowledged that she studied more than her white peers in high school, but also admitted that her extra hours of studying were far short of the hours that her cousins in Taiwan had invested in their schooling:

> It's nothing like Taiwan. In Taiwan, my relatives and cousins, they go to school in the morning, and then in the afternoon they go to more school until night. So they constantly have school. And they have Saturday school, and I think maybe half Sunday, so it's totally nothing compared to the Asian countries.

Not only do Chinese and Vietnamese immigrants adopt a dual frame of reference in their evaluation of supplementary education in the United States, but the 1.5 and second generation do too; they are aware of the rigorous supplementary education system in Asia and recognize that after-school and summer school supplementary classes in the United States pale by comparison. This dual frame of reference also helps the children of immigrants place the long hours of supplemental study imposed on them by their parents within a comparative context, which makes after-school and weekend programs more palatable for U.S.-born and -raised children.

But for the 1.5 and second generation, personal experience with the supplementary education system in East Asia is not a prerequisite for adopting a dual frame of reference. Such a frame is adopted when parents as well as instructors and tutors in the ethnic community regale the children of immigrants with stories about how easy they have it compared to their peers in Asia. In addition, the dual frame of reference is reinforced by summer vacations and trips to the parents' ancestral homelands during which U.S.-born children "get in touch with their roots" and learn firsthand about the intense study routines of their cousins who did not immigrate. The dual frame of reference explains how Asian immigrant parents make supplementary education a routine part of their children's normative schedules without generating severe backlash or intergenerational conflict.

Jason: How Supplementary Education Overrides Low SES   To highlight how family strategies and supplementary education improve students' academic performance and help them override low parental human capital and familial socioeconomic status, we profile Jason, a twenty-five-year-old second-generation Chinese who benefited from a variety of ethnic resources.

Jason grew up in a working-class neighborhood in Long Beach with parents who did not attend college. He attended elementary school in a neighborhood that he described as "the bad area" in Long Beach, but as soon as his parents could afford it, they moved to a modest home in Cerritos because they learned from the Southern California Chinese Consumer Yellow Pages—the four-inch-thick, 2,500-page directory that provides a list of the area's ethnic businesses as well as the rankings of the region's public high schools and the country's best universities—that Cerritos High School ranked "in the teens" for academics. Unable to speak English, Jason's Chinese parents turned to an ethnic resource that they could understand and trust when deciding on a neighborhood in which to buy a home, with the foremost criterion being the strength of the school district.

When Jason first moved from the working-class neighborhood in Long Beach to Cerritos in seventh grade, he was unprepared for the rigorous academic culture of Cerritos Middle School. When we asked what he meant, he explained that unlike his school in Long Beach, "Cerritos is a school that definitely prepares you for college." He had stood at the top of his class in his elementary school in Long Beach, but Jason was placed on the regular academic track in Cerritos after taking the entrance exams and posting average scores. As he explained, "I came out of elementary school in Long Beach, and I was below the expectation level of Cerritos. I couldn't get into the honors classes."

Dismayed by Jason's test results and his placement on the general academic track, his parents immediately enrolled him in an after-school Chinese academy, which he attended for three hours every day after school. When Jason took the exam for high school, his scores bumped him up into the AP program. Jason's supplementary education did not stop there: it also included an SAT preparatory course in ninth grade and then another in tenth grade so that he would be well prepared to take the SAT exam in eleventh grade. Not only did Jason's parents turn to the "Chinese Yellow Book" for information about neighborhoods and school districts, but they also turned to it for information about SAT prep courses and tutoring services.

Jason's parents' investment in supplementary education, along with his hard work, paid off. He graduated in the top 10 percent of his senior class with a GPA of 3.6, and later he graduated from a top University of California (UC) school. Jason is now in his third year of law school, and along with his JD, he is working toward his MBA and a master's in law, which he will receive in the following year. Recognizing the difficulty of landing a job in one of the top corporate law firms in Los Angeles, Jason decided to earn "extra degrees" so that he will stand out among his peers in that competitive job market. When asked about the salary he would like to earn, he nonchalantly replied that he expects to earn "a nice salary of 200K or so"—a figure that far exceeded his parents' combined earnings.

What is remarkable about Jason's educational mobility and occupational aspirations is that his parents did not graduate from high school, had little understanding of the American school system, did not speak English, and could not help their son with his schoolwork. Furthermore, they could not help him with his college or law school applications. However, they knew about supplementary education in Asia and were able to turn to both tangible and intangible ethnic resources and strategies within their reach to compensate for their lack of human and economic capital. The ethnic resources included the after-school Chinese academy and SAT prep courses in which they enrolled Jason and their strategy of buying a home in Cerritos because of its strong public school, both of which they learned about from the "Chinese Yellow Book." As non-English-speakers, Jason's parents tapped into their ethnic capital, which provided Jason with the appropriate toolkit to attain the success frame, in spite of his class disadvantage.

Hannah: Staying a Step Ahead   Supplementary education was such an integral part of the adolescence of our Chinese and Vietnamese interviewees that they hardly characterized it as "supplementary." Hannah, a twenty-five-year-old second-generation Vietnamese who graduated third in her class with a 4.2 GPA, explained that her summers were scheduled with summer school and tutoring:

> Summertime, besides going to summer school every single year, we also did tutoring classes to get ahead. Like in junior high and stuff, we were taking a class ahead, like math classes. If we were going to take geometry, then we were doing it in the summertime, or algebra in the summertime, the summer before. In the Asian community, I think everyone does tutoring.

By taking a class the summer before taking it during the academic year, students repeated the subject, thereby gaining an insurance policy that they would receive excellent grades and remain a step ahead of their peers.[22]

Supplementary Education: The Relationship Between Culture and Achievement

Before continuing, we reiterate four critical points about supplementary education that provide a more complete understanding of the relationship between culture and achievement among Asian Americans. First, supplemental education classes (or after-school academies) exist in ethnic communities across the United States in part because they are transported from sending countries.[23] Asian immigrants like the Chinese and Vietnamese transfer cultural institutions and practices from their countries of origin, modify them, and re-create those that are best suited for their new host society.

Second, because of the hyper-selectivity and high-selectivity of East Asian immigrants to the United States, those who migrate are much more highly educated than their coethnics who stay behind. Hence, the cultural institutions and frames that they transfer and re-create are not just *ethnic*-specific but also *class*-specific. With a more highly educated, middle-class stream of contemporary East Asian immigrants coming to the United States, the institutions and frames that they bring with them are largely middle-class institutions and frames. In addition, hyper-selected and highly selected East Asian immigrants have the human and economic capital to generate ethnic capital and to re-create these institutions and frames in their new host society.

Third, using a dual frame of reference, Chinese and Vietnamese immigrants realize that supplementary education in the United States is not nearly as demanding and rigorous as the supplemental educational practices in their countries of origin. Although many 1.5- and second-generation Chinese and Vietnamese children devote a few hours after school and part of their Saturday to supplementary classes or tutoring sessions, the time and effort they put in pale in comparison to the schedule that they would have to endure had their parents not migrated.

Fourth, East Asians such as Chinese and Vietnamese invest in supplementary education because they adhere to the belief that increased effort, rather than ability alone, pays off and is the major avenue to improvement and success.

Intangible Resources and Strategies: The Effort Mind-Set, Collective Strategies for Mobility, and Cross-Class Learning

The success frame is also supported by intangible ethnic resources and strategies, including Asian immigrant parents' belief in the "effort effect," their collective strategies of familial mobility, and the cross-class learning that occurs through ethnoracially homophilous peer networks.

The Effort Mind-Set

Scientists have long wrestled with the question of whether intelligence is fixed or can be improved through effort, and they have debated whether ability is more important than effort (or vice versa) in determining a child's academic outcomes. Social psychologists have also sought to explain cultural differences in beliefs about the roles of effort and ability—a perspective advanced by Harold Stevenson and Shin-ying Lee, who compared the academic performances of Chinese, Japanese, and American children and identified stark cultural differences between Chinese and Japanese mothers, on the one hand, and American mothers, on the other.[24]

Stevenson and Lee find that American mothers and their children give greater weight to ability as a determinant in their child's academic performance compared to Chinese and Japanese mothers, who place more weight on effort. They also find that, compared to American mothers, Chinese and

Japanese mothers expect their children to put more effort into their school-work in the belief that increased effort is the major avenue to improvement and that it would lead to continuous improvement in their children's grades, in relation to both their past performance and that of their peers. Stevenson and Lee conclude that the belief that effort leads to improvement is one of the central reasons why Chinese and Japanese students spend more time on their academic work than their American peers, and also why parents enroll their children in supplemental education classes.

They also find that Chinese and Japanese families devote a greater portion of their family resources to their children's academic activities—including house-hold space, funds, and parental time—compared to their American counter-parts. For example, Chinese and Japanese students are given more study space and educational resources (including computers) even after controlling for class differences—a finding replicated in later empirical research on Asian Americans' educational achievement.[25] However, a recent study released by the Bureau of Labor Statistics (BLS) contradicts the finding that Asian American families invest more of their resources in their children's education. The authors of the BLS study, Tian Luo and Richard Holden, find that, although Asian families spend more on their children's education than African American and Latino families, these racial differences in investment in children's education disappear after controlling for family income.[26]

While the debate about differences in parental investment in children's edu-cation continues, our research provides a fuller explanation of how Chinese and Vietnamese immigrant parents' belief in the effort effect—the mind-set that intelligence can be improved by increased effort—leads them to shepherd their children into supplementary classes to improve their grades and test scores. This belief is a critical *intangible* resource that, coupled with tangible resources like supplemental education programs, becomes an effective strategy to improve students' academic performance.

Immigrant parents pass their belief in the effort effect to their U.S.-born and -raised children, who also associate effort with improved performance and recognize that increased effort may set them apart from their non-Asian peers. Take Audrey, whom we quoted earlier: she highlighted the role of effort in achievement and staunchly rejected the claim that Asian American stu-dents are innately smarter than others. Drawing on her experience as a child of Chinese immigrants and as a high school teacher, Audrey explained that high-achieving Asian American students excel academically because they put more time and effort into their schoolwork and therefore outperform their peers: "A lot of people think that Chinese people are smarter. No, they are not smarter. It's that they are pushed more to do their homework, and they spend more time doing the assignments." Having taught both honors and general math classes, Audrey noticed the different levels of effort that students put into their homework assignments and during class: "I teach an honors class, and the reason [the Chinese students] do well is because, one, they're paying attention and, two, they do their homework. You look at the regular kids, and it's not that they're dumb; it's just that they don't put in as much effort." This difference in the amount of effort that her students invested in their work affected their academic performance.

Audrey also recalled that when she was a high school student herself she spent more time on her homework than her white peers because she considered herself "not smart," particularly in math. But she compensated for her weakness in math by investing more time and effort in her math homework, with the help of a math tutor. As a result, her math performance improved and she surpassed her white peers in the subject.

Asian Americans' belief in the effort effect is also reflected in findings from the Pew Research Report, which shows that Asian Americans, compared to the general American population, are more likely to believe that individuals can get ahead and make it if they are willing to work hard (69 percent versus 58 percent). Moreover, fewer Asian Americans believe that hard work and determination are no guarantee of success compared to the general American population (40 percent versus 27 percent)—underscoring that Asian Americans are more likely than Americans generally to believe in the primary role of effort in getting ahead.[27] Based on national representative data, sociologists Amy Hsin and Yu Xie reaffirm the role of effort. Based on their measurements of academic effort in terms of teachers' assessments of students' classroom behavior and attitude, Hsin and Xie find that the academic achievement gap between Asian and white students is explained by differences in effort rather than differences in cognitive ability or class.[28]

Immigrant parents' belief in the effort effect thus leads them to invest more of their resources in increasing the effort that their children devote to enhancing their educational outcomes.

A Collective Strategy for Mobility

The belief that increased effort improves performance pertains to not only the individual effort of children but also the collective effort of family members, including parents and siblings.[29] Stevenson and Lee point to the integral involvement of Chinese and Japanese mothers, fathers, and older siblings in children's academic activities, describing it as a collective familial strategy of mobility.[30] Our study also shows the pivotal role in the educational attainment of younger children played by their older siblings, some of whom help to financially support their younger brothers and sisters so that they can focus on their schoolwork.

Thy: A Rotating System of Sibling Support   We describe the collective effort of older siblings supporting younger siblings as a "rotating system of sibling support." Sibling support can be both material and nonmaterial. Nonmaterial support includes helping younger siblings with homework, advising them about enrolling in AP and honors classes, and helping with their college applications. Material support may take the form of contributions to household income so that younger siblings are shielded from having to work while in school. This is the form that the rotating system of sibling support took in Thy's family.

Thy, a twenty-five-year-old, second-generation Vietnamese woman, graduated from a UC school and now works as a credit analyst. She explained that her older siblings had contributed to the household income so that she did not have to take a part-time job in high school and college. Now that she has graduated from college and secured a full-time job, she contributes to the household income so that her younger siblings could also have a chance to concentrate on their schoolwork without having to work part-time:

> THY: Each of us were about two or three years apart, so when you get a job [after college], it is not really said, but it is kind of expected that when you get a job, you kind of help them [my parents] out later. That's what I am doing right now.
>
> INTERVIEWER: Explain that a little bit more.
>
> THY: By the time I got into college, my brother and my sister already had a job, so they helped my parents with the rent and with their insurance too.
>
> INTERVIEWER: So they helped you guys, but then when you get a job, you give back to them and help them out?
>
> THY: Uh-huh [yes]. Because there are eight of us, so the first two would do it, and then the next two, and then me and Teresa. The younger siblings, they were just going to high school and studying, as I was doing before.
>
> INTERVIEWER: So now you help your parents financially?
>
> THY: Uh-huh [yes]. I give them about $300 a month.

Although Thy graduated from college three years earlier, she continues to live with her parents and contributes $300 a month to the household income. By remaining in her parents' home, Tran is able to provide the supplemental income needed to continue the rotating system of sibling support, which allows her two younger siblings to focus exclusively on their schoolwork. With the financial help from their older siblings, the younger siblings are shielded from having to contribute to their personal and household expenses by working part-time while they are still in high school.

When we asked Thy whether she resents the obligation to forfeit part of her paycheck to her familial household to help support her younger siblings, she said that she does not because her older brother and sister had done the same for her. Now that she and her sister Teresa have graduated from college, they model themselves after their older siblings, without questions or resentments. Although giving back to the family household is an obligation, Thy does not perceive it that way.[31] When Thy's younger brother and sister graduate from college, they will be expected to follow suit, even though there will be no younger siblings behind them; they will contribute to the household in order to help support their aging parents. Hence, the strategy for mobility is not solely an individual strategy but rather a collective one that involves all family members, including older siblings who do their part to ensure that their younger brothers and sisters are poised to get ahead.

David and Mai: Prioritizing One Child over Another   Adopting a collective familial strategy for mobility does not always benefit each sibling, however, nor does it always benefit each sibling equally, as David's family's strategy illustrates. David is a twenty-five-year-old, 1.5-generation Vietnamese male who is beginning his second year of medical school. His parents migrated from Vietnam to the United States in 1990 when David was seven and his sister was fourteen. Like other highly educated professionals, David's parents experienced downward mobility upon arrival: his father, once a military officer, took a job in a manufacturing plant, and his mother, who had been a nurse, stayed at home to care for her two children. David's parents settled in a low-income neighborhood in south Los Angeles that was riddled with Asian and Latino gangs. Given the neighborhood environment, David's parents insisted that he come directly home after school, where his mother kept an eye on him and closely monitored his homework.

David was on the college preparatory track and took AP classes during high school. His strong academic record earned him admission into several UC schools, and he chose to attend the one that was closest to his parents' home so that he could save money by continuing to live there. David took out a school loan to pay his tuition, but his parents paid for all of his other expenses, including his books, personal expenses, and a car. Despite their meager household income, David's parents insisted that he not work during high school or college because they did not want him to become "distracted" from his studies. They had high hopes for David and expected him to go to medical school, or at the very least earn a master's degree.

In college, David majored in computer engineering, earned a 3.8 GPA, and graduated in four years. Upon graduation, David landed a job as a computer engineer, earning a salary of $65,000 a year. He worked at this job for one year while he studied for the MCAT exams, and he continued to live at home with his parents. Although David was earning a paycheck that far exceeded his father's earnings, his parents never asked him to contribute to the family household; instead, they insisted that he pay off his college loans and save the remainder for medical school. David's high MCAT score and stellar college record earned him a place in a competitive medical school.

David benefited from his parents' decision to keep him focused on school rather than on work, but his sister (seven years his senior) was not as fortunate. His sister graduated from the same college as David, but their parents asked her to contribute to the household income immediately after graduating from college so that they could purchase the home they now own.

Moreover, her contribution to the household income freed David of the obligation to do the same. The income contribution from David's sister not only helped their parents purchase their home but also helped defray the expenses of David's car and insurance. While her contribution to the family income helped propel the family into homeownership and allowed David to focus exclusively on schoolwork, it also truncated her own educational aspiration to pursue an advanced degree.

When we asked whether his parents held different educational expectations for the two siblings, David candidly answered, "Yeah, they did. They expected me to go get a higher education than my sister." We asked David to recount his sister's educational trajectory and describe how it differed from his own:

> DAVID: She's a chemist. She got her chemistry degree at a UC. She got a bachelor's degree, and she has been working since.
>
> INTERVIEWER: Did she want to get a higher degree?
>
> DAVID: She wanted to continue to get a master's or higher degree, but at the time my parents needed help financially, so my sister just started working after she graduated. After she started working, our family bought a house and she was a big help. So, yeah, that was part of why she didn't continue.
>
> INTERVIEWER: Did you ever have to help support your parents financially?
>
> DAVID: No, my parents didn't want me to get distracted from school. Even though I worked [after college], I didn't need to contribute financially.
>
> INTERVIEWER: Your sister helped so you didn't have to?
>
> DAVID: Yeah, that's true.

David's parents' decision to favor one child over another is not unique. Another interviewee, Mai, a 1.5-generation Vietnamese female, is also the privileged child among her siblings. Mai is the youngest of four daughters in her family, and her sisters are much older—thirteen, twelve, and eleven years her senior. Because her sisters were young adults when they migrated to the United States and Mai was only eight years old, they had vastly different immigrant incorporation experiences. Mai's oldest sister arrived in the United States at the age of twenty-one and dropped out of community college shortly after enrolling in order to contribute to the household income. The two middle sisters also had to help support the family, but as the youngest daughter in her family, Mai was shielded from this responsibility, which enabled her to focus exclusively on school and graduate from college. At the age of twenty-five, Mai is now a third-year medical student.

In another example, Lilly, a thirty-three-year-old, 1.5-generation Chinese woman whose family immigrated to the United States when she was only one year old, explained that her parents devoted more attention and resources to her brother's educational attainment than hers. Lilly's older and only brother had experienced more pressure to achieve the success frame than she did because, as the son, he will carry the family name:

> They put a lot of hope in my brother because of the Chinese tradition. The son is focused on, having a very important role, to be the one that is successful and do good in school and have a good career. For a daughter, it was, as long as you finish school, that was it. My brother, of course, he had to do well and set a good example and make a name for the family because he carries the family's name.

The gendered expectations of Lilly's parents had additional consequences: they circumscribed her choice of colleges. With her brother already enrolled in a private university when she was a senior in high school, Lilly's parents explained, she would have to limit her options to Cal States rather than private universities or UCs because they could not afford to pay two private school tuitions simultaneously. Despite having been admitted to a UC school, Lilly had to forfeit the acceptance because tuition was far lower at a Cal State school. In addition, the Cal State school where she enrolled offered the added incentive of a stronger financial aid package:

> LILLY: At first I wanted to go to [a private university in southern California], but there was the money problem, so I had to go to Cal State.
>
> INTERVIEWER: Did you get into the other schools?
>
> LILLY: Yes, I did. I got into a UC, but still, my parents didn't have more money, so I just went to Cal State. I felt that I was going to the cheapest school.
>
> INTERVIEWER: Was it your decision or your parents' decision?
>
> LILLY: It was both my parents' and myself. Both of us had talked about it. It was just, okay, you find a college that's not expensive because my brother at the time went to a private university, and it was very expensive. My parents were paying a lot of money, so I had to find a school that didn't cost that much, so that was the reason why I applied for Cal State. I got a good financial package.
>
> INTERVIEWER: Did your brother not get financial aid?
>
> LILLY: Oh, he did too, but still, it's a private university, so you still have to contribute some money, so my parents still had to put some money in and pay every-month installments for his education.

With economic resources that were too limited to provide both children with private college educations, Lilly's parents decided to invest the bulk of their resources in her older brother. But rather than resenting the decision, Lilly described it as a collective one—and also as one that was personally beneficial, because it relieved her of the pressure to strive for the success frame. As she explained, her parents were content with her "mediocre grades" of "A's and B's"; moreover, she did not feel that she had to pursue one of the "four professions." This lack of pressure gave Lilly the freedom to pursue a career as a school counselor—a career that would have been out of the question for her older brother.

In households where economic resources are limited, Chinese and Vietnamese immigrant parents make calculated decisions to invest their resources in one child, typically a son, because traditionally sons are financially responsible for caring for their aging parents once they grow too old to care for themselves. Furthermore, birth order matters, especially for the 1.5 generation: the youngest in the family is the one who is most likely to be most acculturated and therefore is most likely to succeed in school and in the labor market in the family's new host society. In this collective strategy for familial mobility, gender and birth order affect which child gains priority and which loses out.

Like the system of supplementary education, prioritizing one child is an age-old mobility strategy of poor families in East Asia and one that is imported from immigrants' countries of origin. A family pools its resources to support one son (typically the eldest), with the understanding that when the son succeeds he will support the entire family. When parents in economically disadvantaged households in East Asia place all of the family resources on one son—rather than thinly spreading them among several children—they are making a calculated choice to maximize the odds of family mobility. But unlike the traditional East Asian practice, which typically benefits the oldest son, the strategy as practiced with the 1.5 generation often makes younger children the beneficiaries of family resources, because parents believe that their arrival in the United States at a younger age strengthens their chances for success in school and the labor market. Older children—especially older daughters—typically lose out when family resources are too slim to be doled out equally among all siblings.

Homophily and Cross-Class Learning

Intangible resources—including friendship and peer networks that fall along ethnic and panethnic lines—also serve as reinforcement mechanisms that help the children of Chinese and Vietnamese immigrants attain the success frame. Because L.A.'s public high schools and the academic tracking within them are highly segregated, friendship networks are more ethnoracially homophilous than one might otherwise expect considering the diversity in Los Angeles. Based on our interviewees' experiences, most of the students in high school AP and honors classes were Asian, making friendships across racial lines less possible and less likely. However, coethnic and panethnic friendships that crossed class lines were not uncommon among 1.5- and second-generation Chinese and Vietnamese, and they served as a form of ethnic capital for those whose parents hailed from poor class backgrounds.

Cindy and Kenneth: Cross-Class Learning and Peer Effects   Cindy, a thirty-two-year-old 1.5-generation Chinese, is a prime example. Cindy came to the United States at the age of three with her parents, neither of whom graduated from high school. Her father completed the sixth grade in Hong Kong, and her mother went to school through eighth grade. In addition, their lack of English-language proficiency had relegated her parents to low-wage service work all of their lives; her father always worked in ethnic restaurants, and her mother was a cleaning lady. Although neither of her parents could give her advice about high school or college, Cindy said that she "always knew" that she would go to college.

We asked Cindy to explain how she always knew she would go to college. She modeled herself after her friends, she responded. She followed in their paths, and they pushed her to excel. Then we asked her about the ethnic backgrounds of her friends in high school: they were "all Asian," she said, and more specifically, "Chinese, Vietnamese, Taiwanese." How did these Asian friends affect her academic performance in school? "I think we just pushed each other to the same level," she replied. "You don't want to do poorly because your friend was doing better than you, so, you know, you just kept up." We asked her to elaborate on which friends she decided to follow and what she meant by "keeping up with her friends." "Well, in high school, they took up all the AP classes, they took zero period, and they went to all the UCs, and you just knew." In short, Cindy modeled her behavior after her high-achieving Asian peers.

Kenneth, a 1.5-generation Vietnamese, had a similar experience. Kenneth is from a low-SES family background; poor and uneducated, his parents had been relegated to service jobs in the ethnic economy their entire lives. When we asked him who had most influenced him in high school, Kenneth pointed to his "ABC" friends in his AP classes:

> In high school, you know, the classes I took were all AP, the students I hung around with—they were all smart kids, they were like ABC kids and, you know, . . . being around these kids gives me the motivation to always try to keep up with them and try and get the grade level that they do.

ABC is an acronym for American-Born Chinese, but like most of our interviewees, Kenneth used the term to refer to U.S.-born Asians regardless of ethnicity.

For Cindy and Kenneth, high-achieving coethnic and panethnic peers served as mobility prototypes and role models who were essential reinforcement mechanisms; not only did they learn that the success frame was possible by watching their friends, but they also learned how to achieve it by emulating their behavior. When their friends took tests to get into AP classes, they did the same, and when their friends enrolled in "zero period"—when students learn about the college admissions process—Cindy and Kenneth followed suit. Their high-achieving ABC friends also set the standard for academic achievement and became the reference group by which they measured their progress.

Peers and reference groups affect educational aspirations and outcomes and can be even more influential than teachers' and parents' encouragement.[32] In fact, the positive effect of peers can outweigh the "less than perfect" parenting of Asian parents.[33] By surrounding themselves with high-achieving coethnic and panethnic peers, 1.5- and second-generation Chinese and Vietnamese who come from disadvantaged family backgrounds, like Cindy and Kenneth, benefit from cross-class interactions and learning.[34]

Cindy's parents' limited economic resources circumscribed her college choices and constrained her from choosing a college that would have required leaving her parents' house, so she chose to attend a nearby Cal State school. Since Cal States are more affordable than UCs and she could live at home while attending the nearby Cal State school, Cindy calculated that this would be the most cost-effective college option. By making these choices, Cindy did not have to work during college; freed of the burden of balancing school and work, she was able to graduate in the normative time of four years. She now works as a claims adjuster for an insurance company, earning $65,000 annually—which far exceeds her parents' combined salaries.

Interactions that cross class lines help working-class immigrants and their children acquire the class-specific knowledge and strategies they need to achieve the success frame and navigate gateway institutions such as schools. The knowledge acquired through cross-class interactions is an invaluable intangible resource for those whose lack of cultural capital and exclusion from more affluent and middle-class networks would otherwise prevent them from being privy to such information.[35] Thus, cross-class learning does not happen exclusively in ethnic institutions; it also occurs in public institutions like schools, where students acquire knowledge from one another.

Sometimes cross-class learning occurs as an unintended consequence of membership in a public institution, even one as seemingly inconsequential as a day care center. Mario Small finds that poor and working-class mothers in New York City who enroll their children in day care centers expand the size and usefulness of their personal networks. Something as simple as a field trip for children outside of the city expands their opportunity horizon because it enables these mothers for the first time to envision a life beyond the poor, urban neighborhoods where they live. Furthermore, mothers who send their children to day care also engage in cross-class contact with people and institutions beyond those in their typical daily routine in their neighborhood.[36]

Similarly, Annette Lareau and Jessica McCrory Calarco show that working-class parents who live in socioeconomically diverse neighborhoods are more likely to have contact with middle-class parents through their children's activities and sports and through their jobs as day care providers. As a result, working-class parents pick up class-specific, socioemotional strategies that prove useful when they interact with school officials and their children's teachers. In these ways, middle-class parents serve as cultural mentors to their working-class counterparts who benefit from these cross-class interactions.[37]

Like the working-class parents in Lareau and Calarco's study, poor and working-class Chinese and Vietnamese students benefit from cross-class learning from and interactions with their middle-class peers. Through formal and informal means, middle-class peers disseminate information that working-class coethnics pick up and use, including knowledge about which classes to take in high school, the importance of enrolling in zero periods, the benefit of being in AP and honors classes, and the usefulness of SAT prep courses.

Poorly educated, working-class Chinese and Vietnamese immigrant parents want their children to gain admission into elite colleges, but they lack the knowledge, the financial resources, and the experience to map out a mobility strategy to make this happen. What they lack in human capital and class resources, however, they compensate for with ethnic capital: they and their children tap into readily available, tangible, and intangible ethnic resources that provide Asian immigrant children with a toolkit of resources and strategies that improve their educational outcomes and help them attain the success frame, even in spite of their humble origins.

Summary

Chinese and Vietnamese immigrant parents rely on a set of strategies and resources to reinforce a strict success frame. While some of the strategies are class-specific, others are ethnic-specific. High-SES families—regardless of ethnoracial status—rely on class resources to raise their children through "concerted cultivation," buying a home in a neighborhood with resource-rich public schools and paying for supplementary education and academic enrichment programs. In the absence of class resources in low-SES families, ethnic resources—both tangible and intangible—come into play. Ethnic resources differ from class resources in that they are not limited to middle-class and affluent families; they are preferentially available to members of an entire ethnic group irrespective of class.

What is unique in Chinese, Vietnamese, and other Asian ethnic communities is that they have developed an ethnic system of supplementary education in parallel to the existing supplementary education available in non-Asian, middle-class communities.[38] This elaborate ethnic system of supplementary education—which is absent in other ethnoracial minority communities and enclaves—offers a diversity of educational classes and tutoring in a wide price range; some of this supplementary education is freely available through ethnic churches and community centers and thus accessible to working-class coethnics.[39]

Cultural institutions like Asian immigrants' sophisticated system of supplementary education serve coethnics, but they are not intrinsic to an immigrant or ethnic group. By adopting a global, comparative perspective, we have shown that cultural institutions emerge as a result of the hyper-selectivity and high educational selectivity of East Asian immigration to the United States. Because those who immigrate tend to be much more highly educated than nonmigrants, the cultural institutions, frames, and mind-sets that immigrants transport and re-create in their host society are influenced by their educational selectivity. Therefore, these transported institutional arrangements are not merely ethnic-specific but also class-specific. Hyper-selectivity and high-selectivity within an immigrant group have other consequences as well: they offer poor and working-class coethnics the opportunity to engage in cross-class learning with their middle-class peers, who serve as mobility prototypes and whose educational pathways lower-SES coethnics can emulate.

Adopting a global, comparative approach yields other critical insights: Chinese and Vietnamese immigrants strongly support supplementary education because they firmly believe in the "effort effect" mind-set—that is, that there is a linear relationship between effort and outcomes. Asian immigrant parents believe that increased effort, rather than innate ability alone, will yield stronger academic outcomes among their children, and they have passed this belief on to their U.S.-born children. Belief in the effort effect mind-set explains why immigrant parents are convinced that supplementary education will improve their children's educational outcomes. Moreover, when U.S.-born and U.S.-raised children adopt a dual frame of reference by comparing the U.S. supplementary education system to the more demanding system in their parents' countries of origin, they realize that the extra classes and tutoring that they endure pale in rigor by comparison. Consequently, the children of immigrants are less likely to reject supplemental education, as might the children of U.S. native-born parents, who lack the dual frame.

Finally, the quest for mobility is not only an individual effort but a collective one in Chinese and Vietnamese immigrant households. Collective strategies for mobility, however, do not benefit all 1.5- and second-generation children equally: gender and birth order determine the child to whom the most resources will be devoted in his (typically) quest to attain the success frame. These mobility strategies and resources—both tangible and intangible—enable 1.5- and second-generation Chinese and Vietnamese to attain exceptional academic outcomes and help to explain the Asian American achievement paradox.

In the following chapter, we compare the success frames of native-born whites and blacks, as well as those of 1.5- and second-generation Mexicans. By comparing the success frames of these groups to that of the 1.5- and second-generation Chinese and Vietnamese, we unveil interethnic differences as well as some surprising interethnic similarities. The intergroup comparisons also highlight how uniquely narrow and specific the Asian American success frame is compared to that of other ethnoracial groups.

~ Chapter 5 ~

Comparing Success Frames

Chinese and Vietnamese immigrant parents and their children construct a strict success frame that includes a specific educational pathway to one of four elite professions, and they employ familial, institutional, and ethnic resources and strategies to reinforce this frame. In this chapter, we compare the success frame of 1.5- and second-generation Chinese and Vietnamese to the success frames of other groups, including 1.5- and second-generation Mexicans and third-plus-generation whites and blacks in Los Angeles. We address the central question: how unique is the success frame of the 1.5- and second-generation Chinese and Vietnamese? To compare success frames, we adopt a subject-centered approach that places the subjects' definition of success at the center of analysis. We focus on how members of these groups frame success, the reference group they turn to when they measure their success, and whether they feel successful.

The ethnoracial status of the Chinese and Vietnamese interviewees is critical to the "subject-centered approach" because the success frame that members of the 1.5 and second generation adopt is influenced not only by family socioeconomic status (SES) but also by ethnic capital. Hyper-selected and highly selected immigrant groups (like Chinese and Vietnamese, respectively) have a sizable middle class, which leads to higher-than-average ethnic capital, particularly for the Chinese.[1] A sizable middle-class presence within an ethnic group benefits working-class coethnics because the middle class constructs the success frame and also provides the resources and strategies to reinforce it. Moreover, for these groups, high-achieving coethnics are the reference group by which they measure their success.

For the Chinese and Vietnamese interviewees, there is a singular success frame, and a singular path to achieve it. By contrast, the success frames of Mexicans, whites, and blacks are more diverse and are influenced by class, nativity, ethnoracial status, and—in the case of Mexicans—their "hypo-selectivity."

Hypo-selectivity is a dual negative selectivity in which an immigrant group, on average, is less educated than their nonmigrant counterparts in their country of origin, and also less educated than the host country. We found that groups construct remarkably different frames of what a good education, a good job, and success mean depending on the frame that is accessible to them and that they eventually adopt. Although the success frames differ across groups, there are also some surprising intergroup similarities, which provided further evidence that the essentialist understanding of culture (that some groups value education more than others) does not hold. Finally, we note that members of today's 1.5 and second generations do not turn to native-born whites or blacks as their reference group for success, nor do they look to these groups as mobility prototypes. Our finding that they turn to coethnics instead yields additional, unanticipated findings about which group members feel most successful.

The Success Frame for Mexicans:
The Variegated Pathways to Success

A glance at the Immigration and Intergenerational Mobility in Metropolitan Los Angeles (IIMMLA) data shows that the college graduation rates for 1.5- and second-generation Mexicans are much lower compared to their Chinese and Vietnamese counterparts: 18 percent for Mexicans compared to 63 percent for Chinese and 48 percent for Vietnamese. The popular conclusion from such data has been that Asian ethnic groups are more successful than their Mexican counterparts. However, by focusing solely on group outcomes, we overlook "starting points" and, therefore, miss out on another measure of success: intergenerational mobility.

Starting Points: Measuring Success
Among Second-Generation Mexicans

Although only 18 percent of 1.5- and second-generation Mexicans have graduated from college, this figure is double the rate for their immigrant fathers, and triple the rate for their immigrant mothers. Moreover, 86 percent of 1.5- and second-generation Mexicans have graduated from high school, meaning that they have nearly doubled the high school graduation rate of their immigrant parents. In addition, more than one-third of Mexicans (36 percent) have attained some college education. Hence, when we consider starting points and define success as the progress from one generation to the next, the children of Mexican immigrants are the most successful.

However, because social scientists (and the American public more generally) tend to measure success as a static measure of educational attainment vis-à-vis other groups (and especially in relation to middle-class whites), we lose sight of the fact that group members begin their quest for mobility at different points on a starting line. By evaluating success as a dynamic measure of intergenerational mobility, we gain an alternative perspective about the success of second-generation groups. The children of Mexican immigrants, whose parents are "hypo-selected"—that is, they have lower college graduation rates than Mexican nonmigrants *and* lower college graduation rates compared to the U.S. mean—have much further to climb to reach parity with other second-generation groups like Chinese and Vietnamese. The hypo-selectivity of Mexican immigrants also puts their children much further behind in their pursuit of parity with native-born whites and blacks. When we account for hypo-selectivity and reframe our measure of success as intergenerational progress rather than outcomes, our data show that Mexicans are the most successful second-generation group.[2]

The intergenerational progress among second-generation Mexicans is uneven, however, and some attain higher socioeconomic outcomes than others,[3] which raises new questions: For example, how does the hypo-selectivity of Mexican immigration affect the success frames of the second generation? And how do the success frames adopted by 1.5- and second-generation Mexicans influence their educational and occupational outcomes? We find that hypo-selectivity results in culturally heterogeneous success frames among 1.5- and second-generation Mexicans—competing definitions of success and variegated pathways to achieve it. Although second-generation outcomes may be diverse, what is uniform is the perception among the children of Mexicans about how successful they feel.

Hypo-Selectivity, Cultural Heterogeneity, and a Diversity of Success Frames

For 1.5- and second-generation Mexicans, immigrant selectivity matters in a different way than it does for their Chinese and Vietnamese counterparts. As we noted in chapter 2, the double negativity of hypo-selectivity among Mexican immigrants has four notable consequences for their children. First, it drives the general American perception that all Mexicans are poorly educated—an erroneous perception that endures despite the enormous educational gains made by the second generation. Relatedly, it heightens fear that the children of Mexican immigrants are failing to assimilate.[4]

Second, another result of the hypo-selectivity of Mexican immigration is the much smaller size of the Mexican middle class in relation to the U.S. Mexican population. In addition, the Mexican middle class is proportionately smaller than the Chinese and Vietnamese immigrant middle-class populations compared to their overall populations. In fact, the IIMMLA data reveal an inverse ratio in the level of college attainment among Chinese and Mexican immigrant fathers: about 60 percent of Chinese immigrant fathers have a college degree or higher; by contrast, close to that many Mexican immigrant fathers have not graduated from high school. Given their relatively small size as a proportion of the Mexican immigrant population, the Mexican middle class alone, unlike their Chinese and Vietnamese middle-class counterparts, cannot generate the ethnic capital to support a singular success frame.

Third, the hypo-selectivity of Mexican immigrants results in more cultural heterogeneity among second-generation Mexicans compared to their Chinese and Vietnamese counterparts, leading to a diversity of success frames as well as a diversity of pathways to achieve success. Sociologist David Harding laid out three conditions for cultural heterogeneity: cultural models must be truly contradictory, not just diverse; various competing models must receive social support; and different models actually lead to different pathways.[5] To illustrate his point about cultural heterogeneity, Harding shows that poor teens are more likely to hold more diverse frames about the significance of teenage pregnancy in their lives compared to their middle-class counterparts. Middle-class teens almost uniformly agree that getting pregnant or getting someone else pregnant at this time in their lives would be bad, but there is more variation in the views of poor teens. Harding argues that in economically and culturally diverse environments, there is a weaker signal about what frame is best because there is more social support for a diversity of frames, as well as less information that supports only one.

We extend Harding's thesis of cultural heterogeneity by linking the hypo-selectivity of Mexican immigration with the cultural heterogeneity of success frames among the 1.5 and second generation. Given the cultural heterogeneity of the Mexican immigrant population due to their hypo-selectivity, the children of Mexican immigrants recounted a diversity of success frames rather than a singular and precise one, as was common among their Chinese and Vietnamese counterparts.

For some second-generation Mexicans, simply graduating from college—regardless of the type of college—is essential to their success frame. Members of this group do not distinguish between a neighborhood community college, a local college, and a four-year university, though they are more likely to matriculate into the first.[6] Others are more discerning and adopt a success frame that involves graduating from a four-year university, typically California State (Cal State) or University of California (UC), because they know that they need a four-year degree in order to work as a teacher or social worker—the two most popular professions among college-educated second-generation Mexicans. For still others, college is not a part of their success frame at all. Most paramount is graduating from high school and securing a job that will allow them to support themselves and their families and work toward home-ownership. This group charts a different path, one that leads to entrepreneurship, such as owning a gardening, roofing, or electronics business. These three success frames are diverse and even contradictory, yet each has social support, and each marks a different pathway to success.

A fourth consequence of hypo-selectivity is that regardless of which frame they adopt, the 1.5- and second-generation Mexicans feel successful because they recognize that they have attained more than their immigrant parents, as well as more than many of their family members and coethnic peers. Coethnics are the reference group by which the new second generation measure their success, rather than native-born whites or blacks.

Here we provide two case studies that offer insight into the cultural heterogeneity of the success frames and variegated pathways to success that the children of Mexicans pursued in their quest for intergenerational mobility. Both of these interviewees hailed from backgrounds of similar socioeconomic status, but each adopted a different success frame and took a different path to achieve success. Despite their different educational and occupational paths, both feel successful because they recognize how much more they have achieved than their immigrant parents, siblings, cousins, and coethnic peers.

Federico: An Entrepreneurial Success Frame   Twenty-seven-year-old Federico is a second-generation Mexican male who is self-employed and owns a tree-trimming and gardening business. When business is good, he earns anywhere between $2,000 and $4,000 a month, but with the downturn in the economy he makes less. To supplement his income, Federico takes odd jobs, such as helping people move. When asked how much he would like to earn, Federico said that his dream salary is $5,000 a month, which he believes will afford him a comfortable lifestyle. Unlike the second-generation Chinese and Vietnamese, Federico measures his dream salary in monthly rather than annual terms.

Federico's parents came to the United States as undocumented migrants but had since legalized their status through the Immigration Reform and Control Act (IRCA) of 1986.[7] Because Federico and his two siblings were born in the United States, legal status had never hampered their opportunity horizon or mobility, but their parents' low parental human capital did. Neither parent had more than an elementary school education, so neither had been able to help Federico with his schoolwork or advise him on which classes to take. Resources were also thin at his high school, which was located next to a Los Angeles public housing complex. But one experience stands out when Federico recalled his high school years: a mentorship program in which he was paired with a successful entrepreneur, who was also Mexican and also hailed from a disadvantaged background. His mentor's parents were poorly educated, agricultural workers, yet despite their poor human and financial capital, his mentor became an entrepreneur who earned a salary of $500,000. This was a turning point for Federico, who, for the first time in his life, became acutely aware that mobility was possible through entrepreneurship. His mentor became his role model and mobility prototype, and like his mentor, Federico adopted an entrepreneurial success frame, as he explained: "I knew I wanted to have my own business. I knew I wanted something with the business field. I didn't know what, just be my own boss."

Lacking the capital to start his own business immediately after high school, Federico churned from one low-wage job to the next until a car accident left him injured and unable to work for six months. During this downtime, Federico decided to join his father's gardening business. Federico quickly acquired gardening and tree-trimming skills from his father and also used his English-language ability to help his father expand his client base. In a short period of time, Federico had doubled his father's customer base by negotiating with existing clients for more work and by adding new clients, as he detailed:

> We started doing more, bigger projects, commercial places, $5,000 or $6,000 jobs, because I was so good at convincing these clients to spend this money. I would explain to them, I would go in[to] detail. That's when I knew that was my niche. In about a month I probably brought in over $15,000 in extra projects. . . . I'd bring [my father] in $15,000, he only gives me $2,000. So that's when I knew I wanted to do my own tree trimming and landscaping. I didn't want to work with him no more.

Armed with the skills he acquired while working with his father and a new-found confidence that came from recruiting new clients, Federico decided to branch out on his own. Unlike his father, Federico relied on his English-language ability and social skills to build his client base. He explained how his business approach differed from his father's:

> I do it differently in the sense that I advertise. I go out there and talk to clients. I would tell the clients, "If you guys need a tree-trimming service, let me know," or, "If you've got any friends or employees, just let us know." And we've got a lot more business because of that. Because I'm not afraid to go and approach somebody and tell them, "Do you want this, do you want that?"

Another source of motivation to open his own business was seeing that his father's clients (most of whom were self-employed) earned high salaries and enjoyed a comfortable lifestyle that gave them a great deal of personal freedom:

> I started working with [my father], and most of his clients, they're all doctors, lawyers, they're in the entertainment field, fashion. But 90 percent of them, they all have their own business. They're all law firms, they're all insurance companies or CEOs. So I would see that [with] all this freedom they have more time for their kids, for the wife. And they made a nice, comfortable take-home. That's what I kind of knew I wanted to do, have my own business, but at the same time be outside. Not work for someone.

Federico plans to grow his business by attaining a landscaping license, which will allow him to accept larger corporate and government jobs and potentially quintuple his salary. The two licensed contractors he knows earns over $20,000 a month. In his view, success boils down to individual initiative and thinking big. Federico believes that his immigrant father has been held back because he lacks these traits, and that is why, as Federico reiterated throughout the interview, "I do things differently."

When we asked Federico whether he feels successful, he said that he does because he has his own business, owns two trucks for his business, and has no children. Federico compares his success not only to the accomplishments of his father but also to what his cousins and friends have done: many have dropped out of high school, married young, have children at an early age, or are single mothers. When we asked whether he thinks his parents are proud of the level of education he has attained, Federico answered, "I would say they're proud of it. Of all my cousins, I'm the only one that got a high school diploma. I'm also the only one to have my own business. Compared to my cousins, I'm doing a lot better than they are."

There are several points about Federico's entrepreneurial success frame and path to mobility that are worth underscoring. First, given his parents' low levels of education, Federico's graduation from high school represents an enormous jump in intergenerational mobility. Second, Federico achieved intergenerational mobility not only with respect to education but also with respect to income. Although he holds the same occupational status as his father, Federico earns far more, runs a more profitable enterprise, and has expanded his entrepreneurial vision to include licensed contracting.

Measuring what he has now from where he started, Federico recognizes that he has achieved a great deal in a very short period of time; therefore, he feels successful. He also feels successful compared to his cousins and peers because he has attained more education than they have. In addition, he is financially independent, unlike his same-age peers in his reference group, and he is also acquiring wealth. However, if we were to measure Federico's educational and occupational outcomes against those of other second-generation groups or against the U.S. mean, he would fall into the "less successful" category because he has only completed high school and holds a relatively low-status job as a self-employed landscaper.

Danielle: College Was the Expectation   Danielle is a thirty-four-year-old Mexican woman who holds a master's degree and works in her dream job as a kindergarten teacher earning an annual salary of $65,000—more than her parents' salaries combined. Danielle has achieved her success frame: a college education, a job as a teacher, and economic independence. Her achievements are especially remarkable given where she began on the starting line: she was brought to the United States at the age of one by her parents, who crossed the border as undocumented migrants. However, Danielle's parents gained permanent residency status under IRCA when she was in the tenth grade and later became naturalized citizens, as did Danielle. The change in citizenship status for Danielle and her parents was pivotal because it removed impediments on Danielle's opportunity horizon.

After migrating to the United States, Danielle's parents settled in a working-class neighborhood near Los Angeles, and both of her parents held factory jobs. Her father worked in manufacturing, and her mother worked as an assembler. Having witnessed the long hours and physically challenging labor they performed, and how little they earned for it, Danielle decided from a very young age that she wanted to become "a professional."

Ever since Danielle could remember, her parents stressed education and instilled in their children the importance of attending college; from her parents' perspective, college was "just expected" of Danielle and her siblings because a college degree would open doors that had been closed to them. As Danielle explained, "When I was growing up, you had to go to college. Like, there is no ifs or buts about it, like, that was expected from the get-go, like, you were going to go to college." Strongly influenced by her fifth-grade teacher, Danielle decided at an early age to become a teacher, and she knew that she would need a college degree to attain this goal.

Danielle enjoyed school, did well in her classes, and became involved in extracurricular activities such as softball and the drill team. An organized teenager with abundant energy, Danielle wanted to work part-time during high school, and she got a job at a local car dealership to cover her personal expenses. Having witnessed her parents struggle just to make ends meet, Danielle could not imagine asking them for extra spending money. However, before she was allowed to accept the job, her father stipulated that she would be allowed to work only on the condition that she kept up her high grades; if her grades faltered at all, she would have to quit.

Danielle kept her end of the bargain, worked part-time, and graduated with a 3.5 GPA (grade point average). With direction from her school's "College Bound" program, Danielle applied to four-year universities rather than enrolling in the local community college and earned admission to several selective universities, including a UC school. The College Bound program was critical for Danielle because it provided her with information about the college admissions process, including when to take the SAT exam, how to apply to universities, and how to apply for financial aid. This form of institutional support was critical because Danielle's parents (like many Mexican immigrant parents) wanted their children to attend college, but "didn't know very much about how to get a child into college," Danielle explained. "What is it that you should do?" Aware that her parents, as immigrants to this country, did not know how the system worked, Danielle felt that it was her responsibility to get information. "And then I also had a good counselor that, you know, from the get-go I told her what I wanted to do and she kind of directed me to where I needed to go. She was very helpful, very helpful."

Although Danielle earned admission to a UC school, because of her family's limited financial resources, she decided to forgo this option and attend the local community college for a few years to take her general requirement courses. When we inquired whether her parents would have preferred that she attend the UC school, Danielle replied, "It didn't matter, and, like, they didn't really know, you know, which college is better or which college you should go to. I don't think it really mattered as long as I was going to college." Not only was tuition much cheaper at the community college, but Danielle also saved money by living at home. While she had to work part-time during college to cover her tuition, her parents helped as much as they could: they gave her $1,000 so that she could purchase a car to drive to and from school, and they also paid her car insurance.

Danielle excelled in community college and eventually transferred to a four-year California state university, where she received her bachelor's degree. After graduating from college, she earned her teaching credentials and then a master's degree, and she now works as a kindergarten teacher. Although Danielle recognizes that she worked hard to get where she is, she firmly believes that the path to mobility is a simple one: education, which is open to all Americans. In fact, Danielle is extremely critical of coethnics who do not prioritize education, and she is especially disparaging of those who, like two of her sisters, chose to work rather than attend college. Danielle's youngest sister is still in high school, and Danielle is doing what she can to ensure that she follows Danielle's path.

Danielle adopts a strictly individualistic approach to her educational attainment and adamantly maintains that there are "no excuses" in life for not getting ahead, but she has had several important advantages in attaining her success frame. First, like the Chinese and Vietnamese immigrant parents, Danielle's parents placed college in her success frame from an early age and underscored that college was "expected." Second, Danielle's parents prioritized school over work, despite their low income, by stipulating that she could maintain her part-time job only if she kept up her grades. Third, her high school provided tangible public resources to reinforce Danielle's success frame: a College Bound program that helped her with the SAT exam and the college admissions process, as well as an instrumental guidance counselor who helped Danielle navigate the college admissions process. Given her parents' lack of knowledge about college admissions, coupled with her lack of class and ethnic resources, the tangible public school resources were pivotal for supporting Danielle's success frame. Finally, her parents provided some financial support: they were able and willing to financially support her while she attended college, and they helped her purchase a car, which she needed to get to and from college.

Danielle's mobility is similar to that of 1.5- and second-generation Chinese and Vietnamese from working-class backgrounds: a concrete success frame coupled with reinforcement mechanisms that supported it. However, there are four notable differences. First, while Danielle's parents expected her to go to college, they did not specify or stipulate that they expected her to attend a top college. Second, while Danielle wanted to become a professional, her success frame included more professions than the narrow set of only four (doctor, lawyer, scientist, engineer) specified in the success frame of her Asian ethnic counterparts. Third, Danielle relied exclusively on public resources to reach her success frame of attending college, rather than supplementing her education with after-school courses, tutoring, or SAT prep courses in the ethnic community. And, fourth, unlike the high-achieving Asian Americans, Danielle feels enormously successful because she measures her success intergenerationally and against lower-achieving coethnics, including her sisters, neither of whom attended college. With parents who have only a GED (general education diploma) and who work in factories, Danielle has achieved far more than they—a feat for which she is enormously proud. "I consider myself successful because I have accomplished all the goals that I set for myself. I feel successful. So it's like I have accomplished everything that I had desired to accomplish. Now everything else is bonus."

The Success Frame for Whites: Class, Individualism, and Self-Reliance

Along with our interviews of 1.5- and second-generation Chinese, Vietnamese, and Mexicans, we also interviewed twelve third-plus-generation whites who were randomly selected from the IIMMLA survey. The majority of the white interviewees hailed from the middle class—the reference group commonly used by all Americans for measuring social mobility outcomes.

Among the interviewees, none have poorly educated parents; all of the white parents have graduated from high school. Moreover, nine have a father with at least a bachelor's degree, and five have a mother with at least a bachelor's degree. Eight of the twelve white interviewees have earned at least a bachelor's degree (see table 2.3). That the majority of the white interviewees have graduated from college fits the normative pattern predicted by the classic status attainment model: if parents have attained a college degree, their children are likely to attain the same, if not more.

While college may be expected by middle-class white parents, this is not the case for working-class white parents, for whom college is an option. Moreover, the success frame for educated whites diverges from that of educated Chinese and Vietnamese in that an advanced degree is a personal choice rather than a parental expectation. Furthermore, none of the white interviewees mentioned that their parents had directed them toward a narrow set of elite universities or into one of the four professions; by contrast, the middle-class white interviewees exercised greater freedom with respect to college selection and occupational choice.

The middle-class white respondents relied on their parents' class resources to support their educational and occupational pursuits. Employed as doctors, lawyers, social workers, teachers, graphic artists, and engineers, the middle-class, native-born white interviewees feel successful because they firmly believe that they have earned their success through individual effort. They also feel successful because they are self-reliant, they are able to support themselves and their families, and they have never turned to the government for financial assistance—an alternative they equate with economic and moral failure. Unlike the 1.5- and second-generation Chinese, Vietnamese, and Mexicans, they do not measure their success against that of others, but when pressed to compare their success to that of their family, friends, or other Americans, they said that they feel *more* successful. In these ways, the highly educated, middle-class white interviewees diverge sharply from their Chinese and Vietnamese counterparts.

Laura: The Reproduction of Class Advantage   Laura is a forty-year-old white woman who graduated from a University of California medical school and now works as a physician at a premier research hospital in Los Angeles. She is married to a general contractor who has a master's degree in engineering and designs and builds homes. Together they have two daughters, ages seven and ten. Laura exemplifies how the highly educated, middle-class white interviewees frame success and their way of attributing their success to "calculated decisions" and individual effort. Moreover, Laura not only feels successful but feels more successful than most Americans.

Laura's parents are highly educated: her father holds a master's degree in musicology, and her mother has a bachelor's degree in music. Her father works as an elementary school teacher, and her mother works part-time teaching music to preschoolers and also gives private piano and voice lessons. For Laura, college was never a question, and her parents told her that they would pay for all of her college expenses. Graduate school, however, was "an option." Although Laura's parents divorced when she was twenty-one, this did not affect their ability or willingness to financially support Laura during medical school. As she explained, "My father put me through school completely, all expenses. And in the summers, I did research projects that were unpaid, and he supported me."

Unlike the Chinese and Vietnamese immigrant parents who stressed to their children that practicing medicine is one of the four coveted professions for which they should strive, Laura's parents never pushed her into a particular profession:

> I come from a family of ministers and teachers and musicians, so I was out in left field with the doctor thing. They really went out of their way always to not influence me, or to try not to influence me. My mom felt like her mother was very overbearing, so deliberately, she has really taken a backseat. They really went out of their way to let me live my life.

Also unlike the parents of our Asian American interviewees, Laura's parents did not stipulate that she should earn straight A's in high school, nor did they buttress her education with supplementary classes such as SAT prep. As

Laura recalled, she "just went in cold" to take the exam, with no preparation whatsoever.

Starting in her sophomore year of high school, Laura set her sights on one of the most competitive UC schools because it has an excellent medical school. She applied to and was accepted to the UC of her choice based on her 4.2 GPA in high school, which placed her eleventh among her graduating class of four hundred seniors. In college, she majored in biology because she calculated that some of her undergraduate classes would count toward fulfilling the premed requirements. She graduated from college with honors and earned admission to a top UC medical school, which she attended immediately after graduating from college. Laura was offered and accepted a job at one of the premier hospitals in Los Angeles after having completed two rotations there as an intern. With full financial support from her parents, Laura graduated from college and medical school with zero debt.

Laura is successful by normative measures of success, including years of education, occupational status, and income. Moreover, she feels successful and believes that she is more successful than most Americans, regardless of ethnoracial status or nativity. She has had the privilege of growing up with class resources as well as social and financial support from both parents, even after they divorced. Because of her privileged class status, she never had to worry that a lack of resources might prevent her from attaining her success frame, however she chose to define it. As someone who had set a goal to become a doctor and realized it, Laura feels successful because she made calculated decisions and met the "internal standard" that she had set for herself.

When we asked whether she feels successful, Laura admitted that she did, because "I'm able to support myself and my family, and I have never been on government aid or relied on other people, or the population in general for my gain. I take care of myself and my own." For Laura, individualism and economic independence are key to her success frame.

Cathy: Working-Class Whites and Natural Growth   The success frame for the children of working-class white parents differs in critical ways from that for middle-class white children and also from that for the children of working-class Chinese and Vietnamese. For whites whose parents had earned no more than a high school degree, the success frame is far broader and reflects a working-class parenting style that Annette Lareau describes as "the accomplishment of natural growth."[8] As part of their natural growth, working-class white children decide for themselves at the age of eighteen whether to attend college or get a job. College is a choice rather than a requirement for success—a perspective that their children also adopt, as Cathy's case illustrates.

Cathy is a forty-one-year-old white woman who, together with her husband, owns and operates a classic car business. Cathy takes care of the accounting, marketing, website design, and advertising portions of the business, while her husband oversees the rest. Because they have three young children (ages nine, seven, and three), she limits her work to half-time. When we interviewed Cathy, she noted that she is proud of their business since she and her husband earned over $200,000 the previous year, which was enough to pay their mortgage, support their family, and cover their children's tuition in a Christian private school.

Cathy grew up in an agricultural community in northern California in a family in which neither parent attended college. Cathy was an above-average high school student who earned a "three-point-something GPA" and participated in school volleyball, student government, and band. As high school graduates, Cathy's parents did not impress upon their daughter that college was expected of her, nor did they encourage her to apply. The only advice she received was to stay out of trouble and finish high school. "The truth is, that's all they expected of me. Finish high school, and stay out of trouble. There was no parental guidance saying, 'You're going to college, you're going beyond that.' Their expectations were, I guess, you know, 'Do what we did.' I don't think they knew any different. It wasn't important to them."

Cathy's parents were wealthy because of the property they owned, yet they insisted that she work part-time during high school to pay for some of her expenses, including her car and car insurance. Cathy's parents also expected her to pay rent when she reached the age of eighteen, but again, not because they needed her income; rather, they felt that as an adult she should be a financially independent, responsible, contributing member of the family household. Reflecting on her parents' insistence that she begin paying rent, she stated, "You know, they were strange; as soon as I turned eighteen, I had to start paying rent. And they didn't need it." Cathy worked two part-time jobs: the first doing data entry for a car dealership and the second in a movie theater. Cathy candidly admitted in the interview that she still resents that her parents expected her to work to pay for her expenses, especially because she could have easily not worked given her parents' financial status.

Although Cathy's parents insisted that she work during high school and community college, they fully supported her financially when she decided to attend nursing school. They paid her tuition, did not ask for rent, and also paid her living expenses since they considered nursing school a full-time job. "I actually was cut some slack," Cathy noted. "They helped, my parents. My dad helped me with gas and stuff for the car and tuition, and I didn't have to pay rent. School was a full-time deal. There was a lot of studying, you know; there was absolutely no way I could work."

Cathy graduated from nursing school without debt and worked as a nurse for nine years before deciding to leave nursing to help her husband with his classic car business. Although Cathy's parents fully supported her during nursing school, the demand they placed on her at the age of eighteen has made a lasting impression on her. Cathy believes that everything she and her husband have accomplished and accumulated is the result of their individual hard work, determination, and perseverance. To support her point she stated that in no other country but the United States does she see any possibility for the type of mobility that she and her husband have attained. She views U.S. society as offering equal opportunity for everyone to get ahead. Hence, like Danielle and Laura, Cathy does not tolerate excuses, nor does she believe that other people "can hold you down if you really want to make it."

Like Laura, Cathy feels successful because she is financially secure; she elaborated: "We certainly know how to budget, and we don't live beyond our means, no. We're very proud of what we've been able to accomplish financially." Furthermore, like Laura, Cathy does not measure her success against the success of others:

> I don't really compare us to anybody. I think we just feel we're successful because [of] how we've been able to budget. The fact that we own our home, the fact that if we wanted, we could do anything we want, and the fact that we can send our kids to a good school . . . that's enough for us, and that's successful. I don't know what anybody else is doing.

The Success Frame for Blacks: The Quest for Residential and Upward Mobility

Like the native-born white interviewees, the twelve native-born black interviewees hail from middle-class family backgrounds. Among them, all have a father who graduated from high school, and only one has a mother who has not. Furthermore, six have a father with at least a bachelor's degree, and four have a mother with at least a bachelor's degree. Unlike the white interviewees, however, the black interviewees have not reproduced their parental educational attainment: only three have at least a bachelor's degree. Thus, we find a pattern of downward educational mobility among the black interviewees: their college graduation rates are lower than those of their parents (see table 2.3).

However, unlike the more diverse success frames of working-class whites and Mexicans, for whom college is an option, the success frame of our black interviewees includes a college degree regardless of parental education. In this regard, their success frame is more similar to that of middle-class whites, Chinese, and Vietnamese. College is critical to black parents' success frame for their children because they believe that a college degree is the surest ticket to residential and upward mobility, which is what they want most for their children. Although college is an essential part of the success frame for our black interviewees—as it is for the working- and middle-class Chinese and Vietnamese and middle-class white interviewees—they lacked the institutional, class, and ethnic resources that could have helped them. Lacking both tangible and intangible resources, few black interviewees have been able to realize their parents' educational aspirations, and those who did overcame extraordinary odds. Most, like Malcolm, have experienced some form of blocked mobility.

Malcolm: Opportunity but Blocked Mobility   Malcolm is a thirty-five-year-old black male who had recently been promoted to foreman after working as an iron worker for fourteen years. Identified as a "gifted" student in elementary school, Malcolm was bused to a more competitive junior high school in another neighborhood and placed in the gifted and talented program. Despite Malcolm's academic advantages, he did not graduate from high school, nor did he attend college, as his parents had hoped and expected. Instead, he was sentenced to prison for three years during his junior year in high school. In prison, Malcolm earned his GED. Upon his release from prison, Malcolm attended a trade school, from which he earned a certification allowing him to take a job as an iron worker.

Although his parents had expected Malcolm to go to college and had him bused to a more competitive school district to gain the class advantages they could not provide, they did not anticipate how he would feel as the lone black student in his classes. Reflecting on the decisions that he made when he was younger, Malcolm blamed himself for having allowed opportunities to slip by. Like the middle- and working-class white interviewees, Malcolm adopted an individualistic approach to success.

Malcolm's parents believed that busing him to a better school district would provide him with a better education and expand his opportunity structure, putting college within reach for their son. In this way, Malcolm's parents adopted the same strategy that working-class Chinese and Vietnamese employ when they transfer guardianship of their children or move to better neighborhoods so that their children can attend more competitive and resource-rich schools. Unlike the working-class Chinese and Vietnamese, however, Malcolm did not have older siblings, relatives, coethnic peers, or neighbors to use as his proximate role models or mobility prototypes, nor did he have a reference group of high-achieving coethnics with whom he could identify. As the only black student enrolled in the gifted and talented program, Malcolm stood out among his white and Asian peers. He described the visible ethnoracial segregation in his school's academic tracking system and how he felt as the only black student in his gifted classes:

> You don't see very many African Americans in a gifted program. So in that program, in those classes, I felt like, man, not too many of us, and that was hard. And I felt like I come out of my class at break time or lunchtime or what not, I'd go hang with my people, so to speak. They weren't in the gifted program, but those were the people I felt comfortable with.

Malcolm admitted that being the sole black student in his classes was challenging. Although he got along with his peers in his classes, he felt more comfortable with his African American friends and sought to fit in with them: "I didn't fit in with the academic people really. I was in those classes, and I knew them, but it wasn't my clique, so I found a clique. I always made a conscious effort to fit in with African American people. I made a conscious effort to do that."

Although Malcolm felt more comfortable hanging out with his coethnic peers, it was his friendship with a particular group of those peers that landed him in trouble with the criminal justice system. During his junior year, Malcolm began joining friends in a series of robberies. After several successful robberies, Malcolm and his friends were caught and convicted. Because it was Malcolm's first offense, the judge sentenced him to only three years in prison and allowed him to serve part of his sentence in a youth correctional facility.

The time in prison was a game-changer for Malcolm. He spent his time earning his GED, reconsidering his priorities, reflecting on the opportunities that he had let slip by, and vowing not to squander any more. At the time of the interview, Malcolm had become a young man who fully applied himself in everything he did, as he candidly revealed:

> You know what? As crazy as this sounds, I needed prison so bad. I needed it. It just woke me up and made me so wild. I'm not blowing any more opportunities, and when I came home I just didn't. I hated prison, I hated jail, I can't stand it. I hated losing my freedom. Man, what was I thinking? It just really helped me in life.

When he was released, Malcolm immediately followed up on the GED he had earned in prison by enrolling in City College for his trade degree. He earned straight A's in his classes, and after he received his associate's degree his father secured him a job in the iron factory in which he worked. Malcolm had recently been promoted to foreman, which he described as no easy feat for a black man who worked in an industry dominated by white superiors and white and Latino subordinates. With calm resignation rather than anger, bitterness, or indignation, Malcolm maintained that he had to work twice as hard to get halfway ahead of his white peers.

When we asked Malcolm to look back and reflect on what, if anything, he would have done differently, he pointed to the opportunities he squandered by trying to fit in with his coethnic peers rather than trying to adapt to being the only black student on his academic track:

> Looking back, I wasted a lot of opportunity that was given to me. Because I was a black child, I didn't interpret it well and kind of went into a culture shock. I didn't take it in well, and I didn't respond well. So I felt I lost some opportunities there, trying to fit in. And now I'm an adult, I'm like, wow, that's not really what it was about. I should have grasped

the opportunity and really ran with it. That's what I should have done, and just been independent and been myself and been able to fit in with everybody. That's what I should have done.

Malcolm described the "cultural shock" that he experienced as the lone black student in the gifted and talented program among his white and Asian peers and the feeling of being bereft of a coethnic reference group or role models to identify with and emulate. He added that he wished he had had a bright, intelligent, and self-confident black male role model like Tavis Smiley when he was younger:[9]

> You ever heard of Tavis Smiley? Very bright brother. He is very intelligent, and he's black, and he's proud to be black, and he's fine in that he's self-confident, and it's all right. I think that had I saw him when I was a child, I mean, I see him as an adult, and I'm like, wow! This is how you do it: you just be yourself, and be as intelligent as you're supposed to be, and it's all right. And I didn't see a lot of that when I was coming up. I think I needed to see that. The coolest people I know today are very intelligent people. The coolest people that I look up to now and that I aspire to be like are very intelligent.

Rather than considering how the school could have fostered a more accommodating milieu for black students like him, Malcolm blames himself for not having taken advantage of the educational opportunities that were afforded to him. He adopts an individualistic approach to explain his choices and his trajectory, blaming himself for squandering opportunities when he was younger. And like the native-born whites, Malcolm does not measure his success against that of others. He does feel successful, both because he has overcome a number of obstacles and because he has attained his goal of becoming a foreman—a position typically reserved for white males.

Cynthia: Mobility Against All Odds   A thirty-nine-year-old black woman, Cynthia has two daughters and is married to her high school boyfriend. Born and raised in Compton, Cynthia worked her way out of the poor, segregated neighborhood in which she grew up and is now working toward her PhD in biology at a private university in southern California.

However, her pathway to mobility has been anything but smooth and linear. Cynthia was raised by a single mother who supported her family with Aid to Families with Dependent Children payments while also returning to school. Cynthia attended a low-income school riddled with gangs and violence and performed poorly in elementary school owing to her dyslexia, which was not diagnosed until much later. Cynthia was also a victim of rape, which resulted in the birth of her first daughter at the age of nineteen. Throughout the traumas and obstacles of Cynthia's adolescence, she always turned to her mother, who has been her role model and bedrock of support.

After Cynthia's father left her mother when Cynthia was a young child, her mother returned to college to complete her bachelor's degree and receive training as a nurse; she knew she would earn a higher salary as a nurse and be able to provide more support for her children. At the age of nine, Cynthia accompanied her mother to her evening classes and sat beside her, absorbed in the lectures. It was during her mother's anatomy/physiology class that Cynthia developed an interest in biology. "I was learning what she was learning. I guess if they knew how much I was learning," she said with a laugh, "they probably would have charged me!"

Cynthia also witnessed her mother's unyielding determination to complete her degree, despite the inconvenience of having to walk home after her evening classes. The last bus left at 9:45 PM and Cynthia's mother's last class ended at 10:00 PM, so she would walk home, regardless of the weather. "I went to her classes with her," Cynthia said, "and I remember her not ever missing class—even when it was cold, even when she had to walk."

From an early age, Cynthia wanted to become a doctor, but she lacked the institutional resources and reinforcement mechanisms to help her achieve her success frame. Rather than encouraging Cynthia's aspirations, her high school teachers, counselors, and even community college professors tried to redirect her toward an occupation that would require far less education, even though she had been identified as a "gifted" student.

> If you say, "I want to be a doctor," they have no resources. They have nothing to tell you [about] how to do that. They have no internship programs. You don't even know what it would possibly take. You don't have a list of the classes you have to take; you have nothing. And if you tell somebody you want to be a doctor, they tell you, "Maybe you think about being a CNA, you know—a certified nurse's assistant or something."

Unlike Laura, Cynthia lacked the institutional and financial support that would have helped her carve a pathway to achieve her success frame, but fortunately Cynthia was able to turn to her mother as a role model. As a single mother who was determined to graduate from college, Cynthia's mother pushed her beyond the expectations of her teachers and counselors and provided a concrete example of what was possible, expanding her daughter's opportunity horizon.

After graduating from high school, Cynthia attended a local California State school. Even after having been raped and subsequently learning that she was pregnant, she refused to relinquish her goal of graduating from college—she returned to school just two weeks after giving birth to her daughter. When we asked how she was able to return to school so shortly after giving birth, Cynthia explained that she had no choice; in her view, she could either have returned to school or gotten stuck in Compton. "I'm from Compton," she said, "so you do things or you don't do things like drugs, and don't do things like have a million babies, or you'll get stuck there. So I guess like two weeks after I had her, I went back to school. Unless you want to get stuck, there is no choice."

Because she had made a conscious choice to get out of Compton, Cynthia is critical of her childhood friends who had gotten stuck and resorted to prostitution, selling and using drugs, or welfare dependency. Although both Cynthia and her mother had relied on welfare at various points in their lives, Cynthia clearly differentiated between temporary use of Aid to Families with Dependent Children and a lifetime of reliance. For both Cynthia and her mother, welfare receipt was temporary; they used it only while returning to school in order to secure a better-paying job and career.

Although Cynthia has no tolerance for her childhood friends who use race and class as a crutch, she is not blind to the barriers she faces because of her racial status. Candidly and calmly, she recounted the assumptions that nonblacks (and whites in particular) routinely make about her ability, her attitude, and her work ethic:

> They expect you to be proud, they expect you to be belligerent, they expect you to talk back, they expect you're lazy, they expect that you know less than everyone else. They expect that you're late, you know? They expect these things. You have to be twice as good at anything that anybody else is doing, or you're being lazy.

Yet despite her recognition of the negative stereotypes she routinely has to combat, Cynthia believes that the onus is on blacks to "get over it" and forge ahead.

Cynthia is the most educated of our black interviewees and is living her dream because she is doing what she loves, but she does not yet feel successful. Exemplifying a strong sense of collective identity and "linked fate," Cynthia explained that she will feel successful when she is able to serve as a visible role model for blacks who grow up in poverty: "Success for me would be to get into a position, the highest position possible, and be able to be a positive role model for black people who grew up in poor [circumstances]—abject poverty—and let them know that I'm not doing anything that they can't do. That's success for me."[10]

Although Cynthia has already become far more educated than her mother and her peers, she does not feel successful, at least not yet. Her definition of success is more collective than individualistic and reflects her sense of her fate being linked to that of poor coethnics; her success frame entails attaining even more mobility so that she will have a visible platform from which to serve as a role model and mobility prototype for disadvantaged black youth. Cynthia also exemplifies the achievement paradox that we find among many of our high-achieving Chinese and Vietnamese interviewees, but hers differs in a critical way: while Chinese and Vietnamese interviewees do not feel successful because they compare themselves to even higher-achieving coethnics, Cynthia does not feel fully successful because she embraces the additional responsibility of achieving more in order to broaden the opportunity horizon for all poor black youth.

Summary

By employing the subject-centered approach and comparing the Chinese and Vietnamese success frame with those of 1.5- and second-generation Mexicans and native-born whites and blacks, we highlighted several findings that illustrate the uniqueness of the success frame that the two Asian ethnic groups adopt.

First, the success frame adopted by the Chinese and Vietnamese interviewees is far more exacting than those of the other groups, regardless of class or nativity. For no other group is the success frame defined as getting straight A's, gaining admission into an elite university, getting a graduate degree, and entering one of the four coveted professions: doctor/pharmacist, lawyer, scientist, or engineer. Second, only the Chinese and Vietnamese interviewees mentioned their use of ethnic resources to support their success frame. Third, the interviewees feel differently about how successful they are depending on the success frame they adopt and also depending on the reference group they use when measuring their success.

While the 1.5- and second-generation Chinese and Vietnamese interviewees described a single, narrow frame for success, the Mexican interviewees described a diversity of success frames, reflecting the cultural heterogeneity of the Mexican immigrant population. For the 1.5- and second-generation Mexicans, there is no singular success frame and therefore no single pathway to achieve success. Moreover, in the absence of ethnic resources, they relied exclusively on the resources that were available in their public schools, including College Bound programs, zero periods, and instrumental teachers, guidance counselors, and coaches who shepherded them through the college application process. But regardless of how they frame success, most of the Mexican interviewees feel that they achieved an extraordinary level of success, even when they had just graduated from high school, because they measure their success both intergenerationally and against lower-achieving coethnics.

The success and mobility of the second-generation is especially impressive given their starting point, which is far behind that of their Chinese and Vietnamese peers, as well as that of native-born whites and blacks. However, if we were to measure their success through conventional indicators, such as educational and occupational scales, we would rate Mexicans as less successful than their Chinese and Vietnamese counterparts, and also as less successful than native-born whites and blacks, because they exhibit the lowest educational outcomes in this type of cross-sectional comparison.

The Mexican interviewees are not unique in the cultural heterogeneity of their success frames. The native-born white and black interviewees also adopt success frames that are far less exacting than those of the Chinese and Vietnamese, and they follow a diversity of pathways to attain success. For the native-born white interviewees, parental education is critical in their construction of a success frame: it determines whether college is an expectation or a choice on the part of the children. College is essential to the success frame of native-born blacks, however, regardless of parental education: black parents uniformly want their children to go to college. However, unlike their Asian ethnic peers, most of the black interviewees lack the institutional resources that would have helped them go to college. Moreover, ethnic resources are absent not only for blacks but also for whites and Mexicans. For native-born blacks, the limited opportunity structure blocks their own and their parents' educational aspirations for them to attain their success frame and graduate from college. However, what separates both native-born whites and blacks from their second-generation Asian and Mexican peers is that the former do not compare themselves to a reference group at all; for both native-born groups, success is an individual measure.

Comparing the Chinese and Vietnamese success frame with those of native-born whites and blacks provides even more fodder for analysis and underscores the uniqueness of the Asian American success frame. Native-born whites also evince cultural heterogeneity in their success frames and follow a diversity of pathways to achieve success. Because they have multiple success frames and also because they follow no singular pathway to attain success, native-born whites can feel successful in multiple domains and take multiple pathways to achieve success. They have more leeway to adopt a broader success frame because they feel that success, however they frame it, is accessible. Moreover, they exercise greater freedom because they and their parents are confident that whatever pathway they choose, they will be "just fine"—a privilege that stems from their dominant ethnoracial status in the United States.

Unlike working-class Chinese and Vietnamese, working-class whites specify that education does not define success; rather, education is useful only if it serves as a vehicle to achieve a higher-paying job. Education, therefore, is not an essential ingredient of the success frame for working-class whites, nor is it the sole pathway to attain success. That the success frame of working-class whites departs from that of working-class Asians in this regard and is more similar to that of the 1.5- and second-generation, working-class Mexicans reveals the centrality of class in the construction of success frames for whites and Mexicans.

The white interviewees firmly embrace individualism and feel that they have made it on their own, even middle-class whites who relied on their parental class resources. Lacking the luxury of parental class resources to buttress their educational and occupational pursuits, working-class whites cherish individualism even more strongly—a mind-set that makes them unable to understand why others, regardless of ethnoracial, class, nativity, or citizenship status, are unable to make it on their own. For both middle- and working-class whites, a central component of the success frame is supporting oneself and one's family and never having to rely on others for financial assistance, which they perceive as both an economic and a moral failure.[11] Because both middle- and working-class whites embrace individualism, they do not measure their success against others. Unlike the Chinese and Vietnamese interviewees, they do not compare themselves "vertically up" to coethnic high-achievers. Consequently, they feel successful.

Like their white counterparts, the native-born black interviewees embrace individualism, despite the institutional barriers they identified and the institutional obstacles they traversed. Their success frame diverges from that of whites, however, in that it includes not only self-reliance but also the perseverance to overcome obstacles and the willingness to give back to family, friends, and coethnics in need.[12] And critically, the black success frame includes a college education. Black parents firmly believe that college is the surest ticket to upward mobility with respect to income, occupational status, and neighborhood of residence. What native-born black parents want most for their children is for them to move out of their neighborhood and "do better" than they had done themselves. In short, upward social mobility is a key component of the black success frame, and college is the ticket out and up.

Unlike their Chinese and Vietnamese counterparts who benefit from reinforcement mechanisms to support the success frame, the black interviewees lack proximate coethnic role models and mobility prototypes and also lack the institutional and ethnic resources that would have helped them meet their parents' expectations. As we have shown, resources are critical to educational attainment and mobility. The differential availability of access to resources helps to explain why the working-class children of Chinese and Vietnamese immigrants are better able to override their disadvantaged class background in ways that other groups can not, including native-born blacks and whites as well as second-generation Mexicans.

We discuss additional implications of success frames in the chapters ahead. Success frames affect not only educational outcomes but also the formation and perpetuation of ethnoracial stereotypes and the racial coding of achievement. Furthermore, we show that adopting a strict success frame comes at a high cost, especially for the 1.5- and second-generation Chinese and Vietnamese who are unable to or choose not to attain it, as we detail in chapter 8.

~ Chapter 6 ~

Symbolic Capital and Stereotype Promise

Jeremy Lin catapulted into the American spotlight in February 2012 when he led the New York Knicks to an improbable and fantastic seven-game winning streak, generating the global phenomenon "Linsanity."[1] As one of only a few Asian American athletes in the history of the National Basketball Association (NBA), the first American-born player of Chinese descent, and the first Harvard graduate to play in the league for almost sixty years, Lin has tackled many firsts and, in the process, broken many barriers. *Time* magazine put Lin at number one on its list of "100 Most Influential People in the World" in 2012.[2] According to *Time*, Lin achieved success the "old fashioned way": through hard work, humility, discipline, grit, integrity, and living and playing "the right way." Undoubtedly, Lin works hard and is disciplined, but the same could have been said of his NBA teammates, most of whom are not Asian. In fact, it is hard to imagine any elite professional athlete who does *not* work hard and is *not* disciplined.

While Linsanity may have caught many Americans by surprise, the narrative of Jeremy Lin achieving success "the right way" did not. The attributes used to explain Lin's success have been employed to describe Asian Americans' exceptional academic achievement. With Lin's ascendancy, the cultural values associated with Asian Americans—hard work, discipline, grit, humility, and perseverance—have now moved beyond the domain of education into professional sports. Americans of all ethnoracial backgrounds were captivated by Linsanity, but the appeal for Asian Americans was more multifaceted. In spite of his Harvard degree, Lin broke the classic model minority stereotype because he made his mark in professional basketball, where he was most noted for his athletic skills and prowess rather than his academic record.

Although the values and attributes associated with Asian Americans may be positive today, it is worth remembering that less than a century ago Asian Americans were described as undesirable and unassimilable immigrants, full of "filth and disease." As culturally inferior and socially marginal members of the human race, they were denied the right to naturalize, denied the right to intermarry, and residentially segregated in crowded ethnic enclaves.[3] Yet despite decades of institutional discrimination and racial prejudice, Asian Americans have seen their racial status change from unassimilable to exceptional, most notably in the domain of education.[4] Asian American students outperform their peers, including native-born whites, and are overrepresented in the country's elite high schools and universities as a proportion of their population. The overrepresentation of Asian Americans in education has not gone unnoticed by native-born whites, who now perceive them as a threat—a point to which we return later in the chapter.

How did the status of a group once considered unassimilable, undesirable immigrants and the "yellow peril" change so dramatically in the twentieth century? As we noted in chapter 2, the answer lies in part in the change in selectivity of contemporary Asian immigration. Because of the hyper-selectivity of Chinese immigrants and the high-selectivity of Vietnamese immigrants, immigrant parents and their children construct a strict success frame, which they support with institutional and ethnic resources and strategies. And because ethnic resources cut vertically across class lines, second-generation children from working-class backgrounds are able to access them; that ethnic resources can mitigate the impact of the low socioeconomic status (SES) backgrounds of coethnics helps to explain the Asian American achievement paradox.

In this chapter, we bridge the research in sociology and social psychology in a novel way to provide the flip-side explanation of the Asian American achievement paradox: we illustrate how the success frame is validated and reinforced outside of the family and the ethnic community. The frame is also supported in gateway institutions such as schools, workplaces, and even the criminal justice system by gatekeepers who racialize achievement and positively stereotype Asians as smart, disciplined, high-achieving, and promising. The stereotypes of Asian Americans affect not only how non-Asian Americans perceive Asian Americans, but also how Asian Americans perceive themselves. These positive stereotypes have become a form of symbolic capital for Asian Americans that gives them access to invaluable institutional resources that are not equally available to all students.

Positive stereotypes can lead to "stereotype promise"—the promise of being viewed through the lens of a positive stereotype, which, in turn, can enhance performance.[5] While Claude Steele and others have found that African American students suffer from "stereotype *threat*," which can depress performance, we find that Asian American students benefit from stereotype *promise*.[6] Regardless of ethnicity, class, gender, and generational status, Asian American students gain an advantage over their non-Asian peers in gateway institutions because they are stereotyped by their teachers and guidance counselors as smart, high-achieving, and hardworking. These processes result in a self-fulfilling prophecy of Asian American exceptionalism and the perpetuation of the model minority stereotype.

Asian American Symbolic Capital in U.S. Schools

Pierre Bourdieu defined "symbolic capital" as an intangible resource that is available to an individual or a group based on prestige, honor, or social recognition and that accrues benefits because of its perceived legitimacy.[7] Because of the racialization that occurs in the United States, Asian ethnic groups tend to be homogenized into the broad racial label of "Asian American," thereby eliding differences in ethnicity, class, generational status, and migration history.[8] One of the consequences of this racialization is that Asian immigrant groups with relatively low levels of education (such as the Vietnamese) benefit from the positive stereotypes associated with those Asian immigrant groups with high levels of education (such as the Chinese). Racialization leads to positive stereotypes of Asian Americans as a group, and those stereotypes become a form of symbolic capital that Asian Americans can leverage to facilitate academic achievement and social mobility.

Positive Perceptions Among Teachers and School Administrators

The 1.5- and second-generation Chinese and Vietnamese interviewees consistently explained that teachers and school administrators assume that Asian students—regardless of ethnicity, class, nativity, or gender—are smart, hardworking, and high-achieving. Critically, the interviewees also described the consequences of these perceptions.

When we asked the Chinese and Vietnamese interviewees whether teachers made assumptions about their academic ability, the majority said that they did, and that those assumptions were routinely positive. For example, when we asked David, a thirty-eight-year-old, 1.5-generation Chinese male who worked for Microsoft, how his teachers viewed him, he answered without hesitation, "I think positively, just because the perception that Asians, Chinese, typically do better in school than the Hispanics and the Caucasians and African Americans." When we asked Julia, a twenty-three-year-old, 1.5-generation Vietnamese woman who recently graduated from a University of California school, the same question, she initially responded, "Oh, actually, I don't know." But after a short pause to consider the question, Julia continued:

> I think just because I was Asian, I think they grouped me in that way. Because even now, when I visited the teachers, they said that we were the best in class. Because all of the Asians at our school, you know, they did well, and we broke academic records and all that.

Both David and Julia recognize that they benefited from their ethnoracial status: because the top students in their high schools were Asian, the perception became widespread among teachers that all Asian students are academically exceptional, break academic records, and outperform their non-Asian peers, including native-born whites. Like David and Julia, most of the Chinese and Vietnamese interviewees, especially those who attended ethnoracially diverse high schools, explained that their teachers made positive assumptions about their academic ability and held high expectations of them.

Sociologists Amy Hsin and Xu Xie confirm that teachers rate Asian American students more highly than their white peers on attributes such as attentiveness, task perseverance, and eagerness to learn.[9] They argue that the differences in perceived attributes among teachers—rather than differences in class or cognitive ability—explain the Asian-white achievement gap.[10] And in their study of Silicon Valley in northern California, Tomás Jiménez and Adam Horowitz also find that teachers and students perceive Asian Americans as hardworking and high-achieving and, correlatively, white students as lazy and mediocre by comparison.[11]

These findings shed light on another critical point. Not only do teachers and school administrators evaluate Asian Americans more highly than other ethnoracial minority groups, but they also rate them more highly than native-born whites—the dominant ethnoracial group in the United States. That Asian Americans are compared to not only other ethnoracial minority groups but also to native-born whites signals the failed logic of the "model minority" construct—a divisive trope that pits one ethnoracial minority group against another (typically Asian Americans against African Americans and Latinos). Furthermore, that Asian Americans are no longer a numerical minority in higher education illustrates just how antiquated the concept of the model *minority* is today. Given this reality, Sean Drake has posits that a more accurate descriptor of Asian Americans is "the model majority."[12]

Unequal Access to Institutional Resources

The positive perceptions of Asian American students by their teachers, guidance counselors, and school administrators manifest as a form of symbolic capital that positively affects the grades they receive, the extra help they are offered with their coursework, and the encouragement they receive when they apply to college. The symbolic capital afforded Asian American students also increases the likelihood of their being placed in competitive academic programs like GATE (gifted and talented education) and Advanced Placement (AP) and on the honors academic track. Asian American students thus gain greater access to invaluable institutional resources that are not equally available to all students, especially to Latino and African American students.[13]

Patrick, a thirty-six-year-old, second-generation Chinese male, is a prime example of how the symbolic capital accorded to Asian American students provides them with access to invaluable institutional resources. Patrick explained that his high school teachers assumed that he was an A student and routinely graded his assignments accordingly. When we asked Patrick whether he could provide a specific example, he recalled having received an A for a paper that he submitted late and was certain that his teacher did not even read:

> If there were ever any assumptions made, it was usually beneficial to me. I did have a teacher or two who—and I never thought it had anything to do with ethnicity—but I think they just assumed that I was an A student. And they probably never bothered to read any of my papers and just stamped an A on [them] because I remember writing a paper when I was half-delirious with the flu, and I still got an A. And the teacher—I had to hand it in late because I was out sick with the flu, and so I handed it in at the beginning of class. By the end of the class, he handed it back to me with an A. There was no way he could have read it during class. I think he just assumed, well, you know, he's a good kid. Give him an A. But honestly, I don't know if it had anything to do with ethnicity.

Although Patrick admitted that his teachers routinely graded him favorably (even when there could not have been enough time to read his paper), he does not believe that his ethnicity influenced the assumptions that his teachers made about his academic ability. Rather, he suspects that teachers liked him because he was "a good kid." Even if Patrick believes that the favorable treatment he received was not related to his ethnoracial status, he was not alone in the positive treatment reported by our interviewees.

Robert's case is also illustrative. Robert is a thirty-six-year-old who was born in Taiwan, migrated to the United States at the age of seven, and entered the second grade without speaking a word of English. However, by the third grade he had been placed into the GATE program for gifted students. Initially skeptical, we inquired how this happened:

> INTERVIEWER: How did you get into GATE? I mean, you came here in second grade and knew no English.
>
> ROBERT: They tested me, and at first they put me in ESL [English as a Second Language], and I was like, "Why am I in ESL?" Then somebody tested me again, and they said, "Well, he's really smart." I didn't know what they were talking about.
>
> INTERVIEWER: Do you think your teachers made assumptions about your academic ability based on your ethnic background?
>
> ROBERT: A lot of them thought because I was Asian—because I was one of the few Asians in my classes and stuff—they would think, "Oh well, he's Asian, he must be smart," or something like that. In elementary school, I was the only Asian in my class. In my whole school, I think there were only two or three Asians.

What is remarkable about Robert's experience is that after his initial test, the teachers placed him in ESL, but when he was retested, upon his mother's insistence, he was placed in GATE. Robert recognizes that his teachers made positive assumptions about his academic ability not only because he is Asian, but also because he was one of only two or three Asians in a predominantly Latino school.

Like Robert, Anh was born abroad and also placed on the ESL track when she first matriculated into the U.S. school system in eighth grade. Migrating from Vietnam, Anh's parents did not know anything about the U.S. school system, but her uncle, who had migrated five years earlier, explained to Anh's parents that they should petition the school administrators to have her placed in the AP program in high school. So after only a year in the United States, Anh's parents petitioned the school (whose students were primarily white and Latino) to have their daughter placed in AP classes. Without a hitch, Anh was admitted into all of the AP courses offered in her high school—including civics, economics, math, and science—except AP English.

Robert's and Anh's experiences are not unique. Most of the 1.5- and second-generation Chinese and Vietnamese interviewees were placed in the AP program in high school, even after they had been in the United States for only a short period, and sometimes after their parents petitioned to have them placed in these classes. Even those who were not in AP or honors classes at the start of high school recognized that this was the goal, and most worked toward attaining it.

By contrast, relatively few of the 1.5- and second-generation Mexicans we interviewed were placed on competitive academic tracks. The majority of the Mexican interviewees were placed in general academic classes in high school and placed on the "two-year" track, which geared students toward community college after graduating from high school. The Mexican interviewees contrasted the two-year track with the "four-year" track, which geared students—typically Asians and whites—toward four-year universities. While the 1.5- and second-generation Mexicans noticed that they were not in the same classes as their Asian American peers, most of them did not know the process by which Asian American students were tracked differently, or how they themselves might get onto the more competitive academic tracks. And unlike the working-class Chinese and Vietnamese immigrant parents who learned about the importance of being in AP and honors classes through cross-class learning from relatives, friends, and middle-class coethnics, Mexican immigrant parents lacked anything comparable to this intangible resource, and therefore did not know how to get their children into more competitive academic tracks.

Also unlike their Asian counterparts, Mexican immigrant parents trusted that the authority figures in their children's schools—teachers, guidance counselors, administrators—would make the right decisions for their children. So while Chinese and Vietnamese immigrant parents challenged the decisions of teachers and administrators and routinely petitioned to have their children placed on the school's most competitive tracks, Mexican immigrant parents acted otherwise. Mexican parents did not feel that it was "their place" to challenge decisions made by authority figures who were far more highly educated and experienced than they were. In fact, many of the Mexican interviewees explained that their immigrant parents were too intimidated to go to the school and meet with their children's teachers, even when they were invited to attend parent-teacher conferences to discuss their children's progress.

Hence, even when Chinese, Vietnamese, and Mexican students attend the same school, they have vastly different educational experiences, not only because they are placed on segregated academic tracks, but also because Chinese and Vietnamese immigrant parents interact differently with the authority figures in the school. Within the same school and the same school district, students do not benefit equally from public school resources because academic segregation results in the unequal distribution of these resources. The inequity is even more glaring given that some 1.5- and second-generation Chinese and Vietnamese interviewees are given the benefit of the doubt and placed in honors and AP courses, sometimes without having successfully tested into them.

Although most of the Chinese and Vietnamese interviewees recalled that they passed the test to get into AP and honors classes, others did not remember having taken such tests, and still others admitted that their junior high grades were mediocre, yet they were placed in high school AP courses nevertheless. For example, Trang, a twenty-four-year-old, second-generation Vietnamese woman, was placed in honors classes in high school even though she admitted that she was not an outstanding junior high student; in fact, she recalled having received A's, B's, and C's in her classes. More strikingly, Trang had no idea why or how she was placed in honors classes:

TRANG: I think I just got tracked in actually, because I don't remember being in any honors classes in junior high. And they just kind of put me into honors, and I'm like, "Okay." And it wasn't bad, so I just kind of stuck with it.

INTERVIEWER: Did you have to take a test or anything?

TRANG: I don't think so. I think they just stuck me in there from high school.

However, once Trang was placed on the honors track, she began taking her schoolwork more seriously, spent more time doing her homework, and studied harder for tests in order to keep up with her high-achieving peers. Trang graduated with a GPA above 4.0 and was admitted to all of the University of California schools to which she applied.

Perhaps one of the most egregious cases of the symbolic capital accorded to Asian students is that of Ophelia, a twenty-three-year-old, second-generation Vietnamese woman who described herself as "not very intelligent"; she recalled nearly being held back in the second grade because of her poor academic performance. By her account, "I wasn't an exceptional student; I was a straight-C student, whereas my siblings, they were quicker than I was, and they were straight-A students." Despite Ophelia's mediocre grades, she adopted a success frame that mirrored that of her high-achieving coethnics. "Most Vietnamese, or just Asian people in general, emphasize academics," she said, "and want their child to become a doctor or an engineer or pharmacist." Realizing that a critical step in the success frame is getting into the AP program, Ophelia took the test for the AP program at the end of junior high school, but failed it. Nevertheless, she was placed in the AP program in her predominantly white high school after her mother petitioned the school to do so.

Once she was taking AP classes, something "just clicked" for Ophelia, and she began to excel. When we asked what she meant by "just clicked," she elaborated: "I wanted to work hard and prove I was a good student," adding, "I think the competition kind of increases your [desire] to do better." She graduated from high school with a 4.2 GPA and was admitted into a highly competitive pharmacy program.

Although it is impossible to know how Trang's and Ophelia's academic performances would have differed had they stayed on a general academic track, that they were given the opportunity to realize their potential attests to the symbolic capital that Asian American students are accorded in U.S. schools—even students whose prior academic performance has been lackluster.

A Self-Fulfilling Prophecy

Although Trang and Ophelia admitted that they worked harder on the more competitive academic track, what is missing in their explanation is an understanding of the social psychological processes that help to explain why things "just clicked" for both of them, resulting in their improved performance. Here, Robert K. Merton's concept of the self-fulfilling prophecy provides critical insight. A self-fulfilling prophecy begins with a false definition of the situation that evokes a new behavior that makes the false conception come true. Merton provided a number of illustrative examples of self-fulfilling prophecies, including the way in which a student's worrying about failing an exam can lead to failure: "Convinced that he is destined to fail, the anxious student devotes more time to worry than to study and then turns in a poor examination." Merton also elucidated how self-fulfilling prophecies operate not only at the individual level but also at the group level to reproduce educational inequalities between blacks and whites in the United States:

> [If] the dominant in-group believes that Negroes are inferior, and sees to it that funds for education are not "wasted on these incompetents" and then proclaims as evidence of this inferiority that Negroes have disproportionately "only" one-fifth as many college graduates as whites, one can scarcely be amazed by this transparent bit of social legerdemain.[14]

In Trang's and Ophelia's cases, self-fulfilling prophecies were at work in the precise sense of the term. That is, the prophecy under consideration (that all Asians are high-achieving) was *not* correct, but it became so when these students learned of their teachers' high expectations and changed their behavior, which resulted in a change in their academic outcomes.

Neither Trang nor Ophelia believed at the outset that she was academically exceptional or deserving of being in the AP program, especially Ophelia, who was nearly held back in second grade, earned straight C's in junior high school, and failed the test for the AP program. However, once anointed as exceptional and deserving by their teachers, both Trang and Ophelia changed their behavior; they took school more seriously, put more time and effort into their homework, and changed the reference group against whom they measured their performance to their high-achieving peers in their AP and honors classes. This new behavior resulted in straight A's in high school and admission to top universities.

Critically, because Trang's and Ophelia's outcomes matched their teachers' expectations, the teachers can point to their stellar academic achievement as proof of their initial assessment of all Asian students—that they are smart, high-achieving, and deserving of placement on the most competitive academic tracks—with no awareness of their own role in generating a self-fulfilling prophecy. Not only were these teachers unaware of their role, but Trang and Ophelia were similarly unaware of the social psychological processes that enhanced their performance.

Stereotypes

The role of stereotypes is relevant here. Stereotypes are widely held, oversimplified, fixed images or ideas of particular groups.[15] The social psychology literature has shown ample evidence that stereotypes have varied effects in test-taking situations depending on an individual's group membership.

Stereotype Threat, Susceptibility, Boost, and Lift

Researchers have shown that the effects of stereotypes are in opposing directions, with stereotype threat on one end and "stereotype boost" on the other. Stereotype threat is defined as an individual's fear of performing in a certain way that will inadvertently confirm a negative stereotype applied to the group to which the individual belongs.[16] The threat or fear depresses the individual's performance and leads to an undesirable outcome, though one that is consistent with the negative stereotype of his or her group.[17]

For example, Claude Steele and his colleagues find evidence of stereotype threat when subtly manipulating cues prior to test-taking situations. Stereotype threat decreases the performance of high-achieving African American students on difficult verbal tests when experimenters cue their race prior to the test, as well as the performance of accomplished female math students on difficult math tests when experimenters cue their gender prior to the test, compared to the control group who receives neither cue. Performance also decreases when the tests are presented to the students as a measure of ability, but it improves when the threat is removed—that is, when the tests are presented as problem-solving exercises rather than a measure of ability.[18]

Building on the work around stereotype threat, social psychologists have also examined how positive stereotypes result in desirable performance outcomes that are consistent with positive stereotypes of a group.[19] For example, Margaret Shih, Todd Pittinsky, and Nalini Ambady find that Asian American females who are strong in math perform better on a math test when experimenters cue their ethnic identity and perform worse when they cue their gender compared with a control group who receives neither cue. Test performance is both malleable and susceptible to implicit cues—what they refer to as "stereotype susceptibility."[20]

In further tests, social psychologists have found that by subtly (rather than blatantly) cueing ethnic identities, Asian American women experience a stereotype boost in their math performance.[21] Hence, not only does the specific stereotype matter in boosting a student's performance, but the subtlety with which it is activated also matters. Furthermore, social psychologists find that activating a negative stereotype of an out-group can also improve the performance of the in-group—a phenomenon they describe as "stereotype lift."[22]

Stereotype Promise

Building on this literature, we found evidence of stereotype promise—the promise that one will be viewed through the lens of a positive stereotype, which enhances performance by leading one to perform in a way that confirms the positive stereotype.[23] We found evidence that stereotype promise boosts performance in real-world settings such as schools, workplaces, and the criminal justice system, not just in controlled test-taking environments. The relationship between stereotype promise and performance may be mediated by some of the same mechanisms—anxiety and overcompensation leading to excess effort—that produce stereotype threat, but with the reverse outcome. For example, Ophelia admitted to feeling more anxious about keeping up with her high-achieving peers, overcompensating with more effort, and raising her expectations to meet those of her teachers and peers. Other mechanisms, such as having optimistic rather than pessimistic thoughts or high rather than low expectations, have different effects.

However, a key feature of stereotype promise is that one's ethnoracial identity need not be cued for stereotypes to enhance performance—which is the mechanism that boosts performance in stereotype susceptibility and stereotype boost.[24] Rather, because stereotypes are "in the air," as Steele vividly describes it, simply being placed in a context where others' expectations are elevated can enhance the performance of an individual from a positively stereotyped group.[25] As Trang's and Ophelia's experiences illustrate, Asian Americans are susceptible to reacting to the positive stereotypes that are in the air about them.

Stereotype promise is the social psychological process through which exceptional academic outcomes become a self-fulfilling prophecy. Once Trang and Ophelia were placed in a more challenging setting where teachers' expectations and the performance of their peers were elevated, they enhanced their own academic performance by changing their behavior. Aware of the expectations of teachers and peers in their AP classes, they increased their effort and worked hard to meet the elevated expectations. Both Trang and Ophelia benefited from stereotype promise and rose to the occasion to meet elevated expectations.

Nancy, a second-generation Chinese, is another example of an Asian American student for whom stereotype promise resulted in a self-fulfilling prophecy of exceptional academic performance. By Nancy's own admission, she was not a strong math student in junior high school, but because of the pervasive stereotype that Asian students are good in math, her teachers made assumptions about her math ability. Nancy provided one example:

> Like in math, they [my teachers] would be like, "Oh, Nancy, this should be easy for you." Just like passing tests out, they would make little comments like, "Oh, I expected you to do better." Math isn't my thing, you know. Just because I'm Asian doesn't mean I'm smart in math.

When her parents noticed that Nancy's math grades were dropping, they hired math tutors to improve her grades. And because Nancy wanted to meet her teachers' and parents' expectations, she put in the extra effort required by the after-school tutoring sessions her parents had arranged. The supplemental education paid off when Nancy passed the test for the AP program in math in high school.

Critical to the operationalization of the stereotype promise is the impact of teachers' expectations on students' aspirations, behavior, and outcomes.[26] Nancy was able to realize her teachers' and parents' expectations by drawing on her parents' resources to learn from private tutors who provided supplemental instruction. As a result, not only did she put more effort into her math homework, but she also did additional math assignments in order to meet those elevated expectations, thereby improving her math performance.

It is not only teachers who hold the perception that Asian American students are high-achievers—Asian American students themselves have internalized this perception, as reflected in Julia's earlier comment that "all the Asians at our school, you know, they did well, and we broke academic records and all that." So pervasive is the perception among Asian Americans that the interviewees admitted that they worked hard in order not to disconfirm the perception. In their view, disconfirming the stereotype would set them apart as ethnoracial outliers, as Lilly, a 1.5-generation Chinese woman, candidly explained:

> LILLY: The school that I went to was mostly Asians, and of course this group of Asians was doing so well, and of course they expect me to be part of the big group, so they have high expectations in me doing well and kind of high standards. I felt like it was expected of me to at least do more.
>
> INTERVIEWER: Did that affect you in any way, that you knew that people had these expectations of you?
>
> LILLY: Of course! I didn't want to be left behind. I wanted to be part of the norm, so of course that influenced me quite a bit. I didn't want to be seen as "Hey, she's Asian, and she's not doing well, and she's just lazy." I wanted to be the one that works hard and that wants to achieve a high level of education, so that made me work even harder.

When we asked Lilly to elaborate on what she meant by "high expectations" and "high standards," she explained, "Like, it's expected that every Asian goes to college, gets a college degree or more. It's just, like, they expect you to do well in school. I don't think it's expected much, like, say for Mexicans." Here Lilly pointed out the different expectations that teachers had of the Asian and Mexican students in her school: whereas teachers expected "every Asian" to attain at least a BA degree, their expectations for their Mexican students were far lower. Lilly's perception that her teachers held high expectations of all Asian students, coupled with her perception that all the Asian students in her school excelled, drove her to work even harder to excel academically so that she would "be part of the norm," "wouldn't be left behind," and would not be perceived as "lazy." Lilly's case illustrates how stereotype promise influences attitudes and actions with regard to academic achievement—improving both of which results in positive academic outcomes.

Not only is stereotype promise distinct from stereotype susceptibility and stereotype boost, but it is also distinct from the "Pygmalion effect"—the effect that teachers' expectations alone have on students' performance. In their experimental study, Robert Rosenthal and Lenore Jacobsen told teachers that certain students, who were selected at random, were "special" and had "intellectual competencies that would in due course be revealed." After one year of the experiment, Rosenthal and Jacobsen found that those "special" students were two and a half times more likely to have increased their IQ by twenty points or more compared to students who had not been anointed as "special" (47 percent versus 19 percent). The researchers speculated that the increased IQ may have been the result of teachers giving the so-called special students more attention, which would have enhanced these students' performance.[27] However, unlike the teachers in Rosenthal and Jacobsen's study, Trang's, Ophelia's, and Nancy's teachers were not told that these students had "intellectual competencies that would in due course be revealed." Rather, each of these students exhibited average or below-average academic performance. Yet in spite of their prior mediocre performance, teachers made assumptions about their academic abilities based on their ethnoracial status and the positive stereotypes attached to Asian Americans.

While some Asian American academic outcomes are exceptional, it is not because Asians are intrinsically smarter. Teachers' positive stereotypes of Asian American students can change the behavior of even some of the most mediocre students, thereby producing exceptional outcomes and reinforcing the belief that Asian Americans are intrinsically brighter, more hardworking, more diligent, and more promising than other students. These examples provide a glimpse into the way social psychological processes operate in gateway institutions like schools and through gateway interactions with teachers to reinforce stereotypes about Asian Americans that can enhance their performance.

Positive stereotypes extend beyond the domain of education; Asian Americans encounter them not only in schools but also in the workplace and the criminal justice system.

Stereotypes in the Workplace

Asian Americans benefit from positive stereotypes as students, but what happens when they enter the labor market? In a 2011 *New York* magazine article, journalist Wesley Yang raised a similar question: "What happens to all the Asian-American overachievers when the test-taking ends?"[28] When we asked our interviewees about stereotypes at work, the majority of the 1.5- and second-generation Chinese and Vietnamese reported that at work—as in school—Asian Americans are stereotyped as smart and hardworking by their employers, colleagues, peers, and clients. Many of the interviewees told us that the assumptions that others held about their skills, ability, and work ethic were made even before the point of initial contact. For example, Shirley, a 1.5-generation Chinese self-employed contractor, noted that

> people buy into that concept that if you're Asian, you do well. People actually make an assumption about my work ethic—and I'm fortunate that I do have that work ethic—but there's never a question of, "You're lazy," or, "You're not doing your job," or "You're not putting effort into it." There's never a question of my abilities. Let me rephrase that: there's never a question of my work ethic before I come into a situation. I just work.

Similarly, William, a twenty-nine-year-old, second-generation Chinese male who left college after his third year to start a home-based web design business, explained that he benefited from the stereotypes about Asian Americans and Asian culture. Especially notable about William were his poor class origins. His parents had only completed the eighth grade; his mother worked as a seamstress and his father as a janitor. Despite his family's low-SES status, William believed that his symbolic capital as an Asian American overrode his lack of a college degree and his disadvantaged class background in the workplace. In fact, he freely admitted to profiting from it:

> I always looked at [being Asian] as a strong point. Because I think, not to be biased, but I think the Asian culture has a good stereotype, known as hardworking and smart, and things like that, so I think it's a benefit. So right away, when I go into a meeting, I already have some respect because they know that I'm knowledgeable and smart.

Those traits—being smart and hardworking—resonated throughout our interviews with 1.5- and second-generation Chinese and Vietnamese, who worked in a wide range of fields, including information technology, engineering, medicine, math, business, and education. For example, Kathy is a twenty-four-year-old second-generation Vietnamese who graduated with a bachelor's degree in computer science and recently decided to return to school to earn a master's in education in order to become a math teacher. When we asked why she chose this career path, she replied, "People hold the stereotype that Asian people are good at math, so maybe I would make a good math teacher." Not only is Kathy aware of the positive stereotype of Asians' ability in math, but she chooses to capitalize on it in her career choice.

Angela, a thirty-year-old, 1.5-generation Chinese female, was more blatant about the benefits of being stereotyped as smart in math because of her ethno-racial status. Angela chose to become a junior high school math teacher despite her admission that math had always been challenging for her. Incredulous that Angela would choose to teach math after having admitted earlier that she had always struggled with the subject in high school, we pressed her and asked why she had chosen this career.

ANGELA: They [her students and other teachers] think I'm good at math, and really I'm not. It's good that they think so because I use it to my advantage, you might say.
INTERVIEWER: As a math teacher?
ANGELA: Yes. They look up to you. They're like, "Oh, you're Chinese and you're good in math," and it's advantageous when they think that.

Both Kathy and Angela chose a profession in which the positive stereotypes associated with Asian Americans in the field of mathematics work to their advantage. In addition, neither Kathy nor Angela (nor the other Chinese and Vietnamese women we interviewed) mentioned gendered stereotypes about women in technical and math-related fields. Instead, the positive stereotypes about Asian Americans in fields such as math, computer science, and information technology obliterated the mere mention of the gender frame or the consequences of stereotype threat or stereotype susceptibility in traditionally male-dominated technical fields.[29]

Stereotype Promise in the Criminal Justice System and Second Chances

We also found that stereotype promise spills into another domain: the criminal justice system, as Brian's case lucidly reveals. Brian is a twenty-eight-year-old, 1.5-generation Chinese male who, with two partners, started his own business designing and selling T-shirts. Brian's mobility path is unconventional: unlike the other 1.5- and second-generation Chinese and Vietnamese we interviewed, he was involved with gangs, sent to military school, and arrested for importing and selling guns. Yet, despite his turbulent, violent, and criminal past, Brian had been given second chances that enabled him to graduate from high school and college, land a well-paying job after college, and branch off to start his own apparel business. Although Brian's past is atypical among our interviewees, he also benefited from the symbolic capital associated with his ethnoracial status and from stereotype promise in the same way the other Vietnamese and Chinese interviewees did.

Brian came to the United States at the age of six with his parents, who divorced shortly after immigrating. His mother soon remarried, and Brian was raised by his Chinese mother and white stepfather in an ethnoracially mixed working-class neighborhood in Orange County. What Brian remembered most vividly about his childhood was the tension between the Asian students and white "skinheads," who would routinely taunt him and his Asian friends with racial slurs such as "nip," "chink," and "gook." Brian recalled getting into numerous physical fights in elementary and junior high school to defend himself and his friends. The most severe of his fights, in ninth grade, left him badly injured.

Worried about his safety and concerned about his poor academic performance, Brian's parents decided to pull him out of the local public school and send him to a military academy. What neither his mother nor his stepfather foresaw at the time was that by enrolling Brian in the military academy, they were giving him the opportunity to make new connections with a group of students who were even more deeply involved in gang and criminal activities than he was. "You have to remember," Brian explained, "the kids that get sent to military school, they're not sent there because they get straight A's; they're sent there because they're not doing well. So the crowd, many of them, was affiliated with gangs already. My parents should have known better."

Through the new connections he made in the military academy, Brian began selling and importing guns immediately after graduating—a crime for which he was later arrested. When we asked about his arrest—and more specifically, whether the district attorney pressed charges against him—he replied, "They tried, but I had a really nice judge. The judge saw me, that I was going to school and everything, my grades were up, so he let me off. I was very lucky." Brian was not sentenced to a prison term, and since he was also cleared of all charges, he could return to community college and resume his education.

Although Brian pointed to the judge's leniency ("I had a really nice judge") and attributed his being cleared of all charges to "luck," he also noted that his sentencing differed from that of his Mexican friends, who were not as "lucky" as he was and who were charged with selling and importing guns. We asked Brian what happened to his friends. "All my old friends got deported," he replied. "Some of them had to stay down there by the San Diego Immigration Bureau or something. They were in jail for at least four to five years before they got deported back."

Although it is impossible to know exactly why the judge doled out different sentences to Brian and his Mexican friends—all of whom were charged with the same crime—Brian provided some insight when he mentioned that his status as a college student and his improving grades in college were influential in the judge's decision. Brian's educational profile fit the positive stereotype associated with high-achieving Asian American students; consequently, Brian appears to have benefited from the symbolic capital of his Asian American status.

Regardless of the reason, the judge's decision to drop the charges was a turning point for Brian, who decided to straighten out his life. Brian returned to community college and pushed himself to get straight A's so that he could transfer to a four-year university, which he accomplished. He transferred to a Cal State and eventually graduated with a bachelor's degree in history. However, when we asked Brian what prompted him to strive to excel in his classes, rather than pointing to his arrest or the judge's decision not to sentence him, he reverted to an explanation about his Chinese "culture":

> I think the reason . . . why kids get straight A's, especially the Chinese kids, I think it has to do with culture. Education was always brought up ever since you're born, you know? It's always education equals opportunity in the future. Even the gang members: they'll do crimes, however, the kids that are in gangs get straight A's in school. I thought that was very interesting because the majority of my friends all went to college right after high school, and all had straight A's.

What is remarkable about Brian's explanation is that he had not been a stellar student prior to his court experience, yet he attributed his commitment to education and his straight A's in community college to his Chinese culture. He failed to recognize and acknowledge that his logic could not account for his poor academic performance and disinterest in education prior to his arrest. Like most of our interviewees, he provided an Asian American exceptionalism argument (specifically Chinese exceptionalism in Brian's case).

Brian repeatedly maintained throughout the interview that he did not fit the stereotype of the high-achieving Asian—"I'm not like those people," he proclaimed—but he did not consider how the positive stereotypes of Asian Americans had functioned as symbolic capital that worked to his advantage in the courtroom, in spite of the serious criminal charges leveled against him. Moreover, Brian was unaware that the judge's positive perception of his promise changed his own attitude and behavior and directed him in an upward educational trajectory. Unlike Brian's Mexican friends, and also unlike Malcolm (the African American interviewee who was sentenced to three years in prison for robbery in high school), all of whom are marked with criminal records, Brian was fortunate to have been given a clean slate.[30]

After graduating from college, Brian landed a job at a premier athletic footwear company. While working there, he decided to buy sneakers, paint original designs on them, and then sell them online for a profit. After a slew of successful sales, Brian realized that there was a market for his designs, so he decided to start his own business with two partners. He now designs and sells T-shirts. Although his company is nascent, he is proud that he does not work for anyone and earns enough to support himself. He hopes that his company will continue to grow and that someday he will make six figures.

The Negative Consequences of Positive Stereotypes and the Bamboo Ceiling

The 1.5- and second-generation Chinese and Vietnamese in Los Angeles are still relatively young. The median age of the Chinese respondents in our study is twenty-even, and the median age of the Vietnamese, twenty-five, is even younger. Many had completed their education, and most were in the early stages of their careers at the time of the interview, yet there were others still in graduate school. As they transition from school to entry-level jobs to more senior positions, some are beginning to confront the possibility that the positive stereotypes that worked to their advantage in school and early in their careers might work against them as they become more senior and begin to vie for management and leadership positions.

The Negative Side of Positive Stereotypes

Although the majority of our interviewees believe that the positive stereotypes about Asians in their profession will continue to be advantageous, a minority are more critical. This minority recognizes that they may face new barriers as they climb the occupational ladder, especially in positions or occupational niches that reward certain traits that Asian Americans are perceived to lack. Traits such as hard work, diligence, and quietude could be reframed as passivity, weakness, and coldness.[31] Thus reframed, these positive characteristics could affect Asian Americans' prospects for managerial positions as well as in professions such as law, business, and politics.

For example, Jason, a twenty-five-year-old, second-generation Chinese male who is completing his last year of law school, admitted that he benefited from the positive stereotypes about Asians in high school and college, but also recognizes that those stereotypes might operate differently when he enters the workforce, especially in the legal profession:

> People believe that we're very passive and quiet, and really don't cause much of a ruckus to society. But yet we contribute positively towards society in terms of working hard and not really causing much trouble.
>
> In the legal profession, I think that definitely it could affect us negatively, just simply because Asian males are usually identified as passive and asexual individuals, that we really aren't going to be the best opponent for a case or client.

Jason underscored two critical points about the intersection of race and gender in occupational niches such as law: he speculated that stereotypes of Asians might be especially detrimental for Asian males in professions like law, where clients typically seek to hire attorneys who are perceived as vocal and aggressive—traits that Asian males are perceived by non-Asians to lack. He is cognizant of the overarching stereotype of Asian males as passive and asexual and aware that it might hamper him in his chosen profession. Ironically, law happens to be one of the four coveted professions in the success frame. To extend Jason's reasoning: if clients and employers act on the stereotype of Asian males as passive and meek by choosing not to hire them, then Asian American males like Jason will have little opportunity to refute the stereotype with disconfirming evidence, and their lack of success in the legal profession could become a self-fulfilling prophecy.

Like Jason, Olivia, a twenty-eight-year-old, second-generation Chinese woman, also believes that certain stereotypes of Asians impede their progress, regardless of gender. Olivia, who works as a district director for an assemblywoman, thoughtfully explained the stereotypes of Asian Americans in the workplace:

> One of the stereotypes is that we're taught not to be rabble-rousers. We're taught to be soft-spoken, we're taught to not be very vocal, and that's within our culture. And that's without a doubt. And I feel like that does hurt us, definitely. And that's why we don't see a lot of Asian CEOs and in upper management, because we're looked at as the little quiet Asian that isn't going to cause a lot of trouble, that basically just does her job, clocks out, and goes home. And I don't want that. And I think that we need to start breaking that because, otherwise, we're not going to be looked at as viable candidates to run for office or viable candidates for an upper CEO position.

And I'm not trying to be negative on my people or whatever; it's just that these are the things I see. And I think that, again, the whole stereotype about us being quiet, and stuff, it's kind of true, and I feel like it's perpetuated within how we were born, and how we were in the family structure, because we're all taught to be that way, definitely. Get your good grades, just mind your own business, and that's it.

Several important points made by Olivia about the role of stereotypes differ from Jason's account. First, she explained that while Asian Americans may be perceived as hardworking, they are not considered for upper-management positions or as viable candidates for political office because employers, colleagues, and peers do not perceive them as rabble-rousers; rather, Asian Americans are perceived as soft-spoken workers who are solely focused on completing the task at hand.[32] Second, Olivia agreed with the stereotype and had internalized it in her perception of herself and coethnics. Third, she posited that the tendency to be soft-spoken is a product of how Asian Americans are raised by their families. From Olivia's perspective, Asian immigrant parents direct their children to "get your good grades, just mind your own business, and that's it." Although this advice may be sound in high school and in some college environments, it may be detrimental to Asian Americans as they leave entry-level jobs and move up the professional ladder into positions where creativity, innovation, aggressiveness, and interpersonal skills are rewarded by clients, peers, and employers.

Finally, Olivia admitted that she herself has to consciously act against her upbringing and against the tendency not to ruffle feathers:

I even find myself struggling with that sometimes. Like, if I'm in a meeting and I'm, like, should I say something? And I find myself, like, questioning, like, well, is it going to really add to the conversation? And then, like, five seconds later somebody else says my comment. And I'm just, like, Olivia! And so it's stuff like that where I'm just, like, you know, you're always constantly not wanting to ruffle feathers. And it's just like, no, you can do it, in a very diplomatic way of course. Yeah, you just find that a lot. And I think that does hurt us in certain realms because then we're not looked at as serious contenders, you know, or people that will speak up.

The Bamboo Ceiling

Olivia's concern about the lack of Asian Americans in leadership positions is not unwarranted. The underrepresentation of Asian Americans in upper management is glaring. Asians make up 5.5 percent of the U.S. population and 15 to 20 percent of every Ivy League class. However, while they are overrepresented in the country's elite universities, they are severely underrepresented in corporate and public-sector leadership positions. They make up only 0.3 percent of corporate officers, less than 1 percent of corporate board members, and about 2 percent of college presidents.[33]

Asians' underrepresentation in corporate leadership positions is also evident in occupational niches where they are overrepresented. For example, in the San Francisco Bay Area, Asians make up 50 percent of the high-tech workforce and 23 percent of the region's population, but account for only 8 percent of board members and 12 percent of top executives in the region.[34] At the National Institutes of Health, where 22 percent of tenure-track scientists are Asians, only 5 percent of the lab or branch directors are Asian.[35]

The underrepresentation of Asians in upper management has led to speculation that they may face a "bamboo ceiling"—an invisible barrier that keeps Asian Americans from rising to the upper rungs of the corporate ladder and assuming leadership positions in a way similar to how the "glass ceiling" blocks the progress of women.[36] Wesley Yang first raised the question about the bamboo ceiling in a 2011 *New York* magazine article, "Paper Tigers," and Helen Wan speculated about it in her novel *Partner Track,* which recounts the journey of an Asian American female lawyer whose mobility is blocked when she is unable to break through the bamboo ceiling.[37]

The reasons that have been offered to explain the bamboo ceiling are cultural: Asian Americans' cultural deference to authority suggests that they are weak, ineffective, and unskilled communicators and leaders, as well as poor risk-takers.[38] In short, they lack the traits, values, and skills that would make them capable and effective leaders. Hence, the same positive cultural traits that benefited them in the domain of education and early in their careers become detrimental as they advance in their professional pursuits.

Placing the focus on the perceived cultural traits of Asian Americans ignores the pivotal role of the gatekeepers in leadership positions. Even if perceptions about the cultural traits of Asian Americans were to change, those in leadership positions might respond by seeking to guard their group position by either redefining or shifting the criteria for merit or constructing new criteria for merit altogether.[39] For example, Frank Samson finds that white Californians decrease the significance of students' grade point averages in considering merit-based college admissions when their reference group is Asian American students.[40] However, they increase the significance of GPAs when their reference group is black students. In other words, whites shift the criteria for merit in opposing directions depending on the group that poses the greater threat to their group position. Moreover, as Jerome Karabel has detailed, in the early twentieth century Ivy League universities shifted their application requirements to include personal essays and extracurricular activities to disadvantage Jewish students, whose growing population they perceived as problematic.[41]

Although the existence of the bamboo ceiling is speculative and deserves more careful empirical research, scholarly research has offered empirical evidence of the blocked mobility of Asian American professionals that cannot be explained by their relatively young age, experience, or performance. For example, studies of the career trajectories of Asian American engineers reveal that even after controlling for both job performance and the number of years at a position, Asian American engineers earn significantly less and are also less likely to be promoted to managerial positions compared their white counterparts.[42] Even in occupations that are strongly premised on the principle of meritocracy, such as higher education and medicine, Asian Americans, regardless of gender, are less likely than whites to hold leadership positions at the departmental and university levels.[43]

Although the majority of the 1.5- and second-generation Chinese and Vietnamese interviewees in our study believe that they benefit from positive stereotypes, it remains an empirical question whether they will feel the same when they reach their forties and fifties—the age at which they will be primed for upper management and leadership positions—or whether they will experience the blocked mobility that many Asian American professionals experience. The positive stereotypes that work to their advantage in school and in the early stages in their careers may not operate in their favor as they continue to climb up the professional ladder. They may find themselves bumping up against and trying to break through a bamboo ceiling.

Summary

Although "Asian" is a heterogeneous category, the racialization of Asians in the United States elides differences in ethnicity and class, and as a group, Asian Americans, particularly East Asian Americans, experience positive stereotyping. The positive stereotypes of Asians affect not only how non-Asian Americans perceive them but also how Asian Americans perceive themselves, which is consequential in two ways. First, positive stereotypes become a form of symbolic capital that gives Asian Americans access to invaluable institutional resources that are not equally available to all students. Second, positive stereotypes and symbolic capital lead to stereotype promise, which can enhance the performance of Asian Americans. Studies demonstrate only modest effects of stereotype threat and stereotype boost on performance.[44] Our in-depth interview data, however, provide evidence that positive stereotypes have real-world consequences that can affect the opportunities and outcomes of Asian Americans.

Like other forms of capital—such as economic, cultural, and social— symbolic capital yields rewards in institutional contexts such as schools. The symbolic capital afforded to Asian American students provides them with more opportunities to take advantage of institutional resources (like the AP program and honors classes) and results in their enhanced performance through stereotype promise. The exceptional academic outcomes of previously mediocre students illustrates how positive stereotypes and stereotype promise can lead to the self-fulfilling prophecy of Asian American exceptionalism and the perpetuation of the model minority stereotype. And because teachers, students, and parents are unaware of their role in generating a self-fulfilling prophecy about Asian American exceptionalism, most turn to glib explanations about Asian culture—that Asians value education more than other groups, that they are smarter, and that they work harder.

Just like inequalities at the low end of the educational spectrum—where some students are assumed to be low-achievers, are tracked into remedial classes, and then "prove" their low achievement—inequalities are reproduced at the high end of the educational distribution, where students perceived to be high-achievers (regardless of actual performance) are tracked into high-level classes and then rise to the occasion, thus "proving" the initial presumption of their ability. In this manner, inequalities are reproduced at the high end of the educational distribution just as they are reproduced at the low end.

We would caution, however, that there are two ways in which positive stereotypes and the model minority construct, whether in the classic image of the one-dimensional scientist or the unconventional image of NBA star Jeremy Lin, can adversely affect 1.5-, second-, and later-generation Asian Americans. First, the model minority stereotype places undue pressure on Asian Americans to excel academically, resulting in feelings of abject failure if they do not or cannot fit the narrowly defined success frame. Those who fall outside the Asian American exceptionalism construct respond by rejecting their ethnoracial identity, claiming that they are "not like other Asians" or "not the typical Chinese"—a point upon which we elaborate more fully in the chapters ahead.

Second, a group's expectations are raised by positive stereotypes, and those elevated expectations become the perceived norm, thereby raising the bar for evaluating Asian American candidates for college admissions, entry into the labor market, and promotions within occupations. For example, the significance of an achievement marker—like a perfect SAT score or a 4.0 GPA—is reduced if it is attained by an Asian American. If you are Asian American, according to the expectation, you *should* have a perfect SAT score or a 4.0 GPA. During the college admissions process, Asian Americans may find themselves at a disadvantage because they are held to a higher standard for admission based on objective indicators like grades and SAT scores. The study by sociologists Thomas Espenshade and Alexandria Radford of elite private universities shows that Asian Americans need a nearly perfect SAT score (1550 out of 1600) to have the same chance of being accepted into one of the top colleges as whites who score 1410 and African Americans who score 1100.[45] Moreover, whites are three times as likely to be accepted at a U.S. university as Asian Americans with similar academic records, Hispanics are six times as likely to be accepted, and blacks more than fifteen times as likely.

Although Espenshade and Radford cannot confirm that Asian students face discrimination in the admissions process, this patterns evokes the discrimination experienced by Jewish students when Ivy League schools attempted to solve "the Jew problem" by instituting quotas and other class-biased measures to restrict their admission.[46] Beginning in the 1920s, Harvard, Yale, and Princeton began requiring recommendation letters, in-person interviews, personal essays, and descriptions of extracurricular activities—all of which dissuaded and disadvantaged "the wrong kind" of college applicant. Consequently, Ivy League schools could shroud their admission process in layers of subjectivity and ultimately decrease the number of Jewish students without overtly discriminating against them. When these elite institutions responded to the group threat by constructing new criteria to measure merit, not only was the Jewish out-group disadvantaged but the white Anglo-Saxon Protestant in-group was privileged.[47]

That Asian Americans are held to a *higher* standard compared to other groups, including native-born whites, based on objective indictors like grades and SAT scores alone suggests that all stereotypes hold power and can have detrimental effects on those stereotyped. Although Asian American students are overrepresented in elite colleges given their proportion of the population, rather than asking why there are "so many" Asian Americans in top universities, we should really be asking why there are not more.[48]

This analysis of the impact of stereotypes on who gets in and who does not—with respect to college admissions, career promotions, and executive positions—is a sobering reminder that even positive, seemingly benign, and complimentary stereotypes can be harmful for Asian Americans. Moreover, the positive stereotypes that seem beneficial in the short run can have deleterious consequences in the long run as Asian Americans find themselves trying to break through a bamboo ceiling when they begin to vie for senior leadership positions.

~ Chapter 7 ~

Mind-Sets and the Achievement Paradox

People adopt different mind-sets about talents and abilities. The social psychologist Carol Dweck has identified two main types, a fixed mind-set and a growth mind-set, and found that an individual's mind-set affects performance.[1] Those with a fixed mind-set believe that intelligence, talents, and abilities are innate and fixed traits and therefore that the extent to which an individual's performance can improve is limited. By contrast, individuals with a growth mind-set believe that these traits can be developed through effort, perseverance, and mentoring, which will lead to improved performance. Based on decades of experimental research with adolescent students on how mindsets affect academic achievement, Dweck and her colleagues have found that the way in which teachers praise students affects the mind-set that students adopt, and that mind-set, in turn, affects their performance. In short, the mind-set that students develop has an independent and significant effect on their academic achievement, even controlling for cognitive ability.[2]

In this chapter, we draw on Dweck's research to shed light on Asian American achievement. Focusing on the children of Chinese and Vietnamese immigrants, we examine how their mind-sets affect their academic performance and how they respond to new challenges and obstacles. We elaborate on these points in four steps. First, we show that home and school send 1.5- and second-generation Chinese and Vietnamese contradictory messages about mind-sets. At home their immigrant parents strongly endorse a growth mind-set, believing that their children's performance can continuously improve through increased effort. At school, however, teachers make assumptions about the innate intelligence of Asian Americans, thereby reinforcing a fixed mind-set among Asian American students.

Second, we illustrate how these contradictory messages and experiences have complicated the development of the mind-sets of 1.5- and second-generation Chinese and Vietnamese, resulting in an achievement paradox.

Third, we unveil the negative consequences that high-achieving Chinese and Vietnamese students experience when they suddenly face difficult challenges that they cannot readily surmount. Fourth, we highlight some cases that represent the other tail of the achievement paradox and explain why lower-achieving Chinese and Vietnamese feel successful despite their relatively mediocre accomplishments, unlike many of their higher-achieving counterparts.

Mind-Sets and Achievement

Praising students exclusively for their intelligence, talents, and abilities can affect their motivation, enthusiasm, and performance, and even their assessment of their intelligence and ability.[3] In a series of experimental studies with adolescents, Dweck and her colleagues illustrated the relationship between the type of praise students receive and their motivation to tackle challenging tasks. In one study, they found that students who received praise for their intelligence expressed just as much enjoyment of the task and expressed just as much desire to persist with a new, more difficult task as students who received praise for their effort. That is, after a successful task, neither group lacked motivation to tackle a subsequent, more challenging task.

However, stark differences in motivation emerged between the two groups when they were assigned a more difficult task that they were unable to complete. Students who had been praised for their intelligence interpreted their inability to complete the more challenging task as "failure." In addition, their enjoyment and their persistence plummeted, as did their assessment of their ability—the consequences of a fixed mind-set. By contrast, when students who had been praised for their effort faced a more difficult task, they were more likely to persist despite their inability to complete it, and they were also more motivated to learn new skills in order to increase their ability—the result a growth mind-set. Furthermore, when faced with difficulty, students who had adopted a growth mind-set did not view the setback as failure, nor did they believe that it reflected poorly on their intelligence or ability.[4]

The difference between the children who had adopted fixed versus growth mind-sets stemmed from the type of praise they had received. When children were praised for their intelligence after a successful task, they sought to ensure their success in future tasks and therefore avoided difficult tasks in order to avoid exposing their potential weaknesses to themselves and to others. In addition, when these students encountered a setback, their persistence and enjoyment in future tasks dwindled, their performance suffered, and their belief in their ability plummeted. By focusing exclusively on results rather than on effort, these students attached meaning to their setbacks and negative outcomes and viewed their failure as a reflection of their low intelligence and an indictment of their ability.[5] In sum, while praising students for their intelligence and successful outcomes may give them a boost in confidence while they are succeeding, performance praise can curtail their desire to tackle new and more difficult challenges. Furthermore, performance praise provides no defense against setbacks and failure.

So rather than praising students for their successful results, Dweck proposes that we praise them for their effort, as well as for the strategies they invest in tackling difficult tasks. By encouraging students to take on challenges and stick with them, we teach them that immediate perfection is not the goal, nor is it the marker of intelligence. Instead, they learn that intelligence develops from the willingness and persistence to embrace new tasks that will expand their skill set and knowledge in the long run—markers of a growth mind-set.

Dweck's research has direct implications for high-achieving Asian American students, who, unlike the students in her study, receive contradictory messages about which mind-set to adopt. At home, 1.5- and second-generation Chinese and Vietnamese are raised by immigrant parents who strongly endorse a growth mind-set. Their parents believe that effort rather than ability is the key to improved performance. Hence, parents insist on supplementary education and stress that increased effort will improve their children's outcomes, both in relation to their past performance and in relation to the performance of their peers.[6]

In school, however, Asian American students receive a different message. Teachers praise Asian American students for their academic performance and expect them to excel. Unlike their immigrant parents, teachers laud students for their intelligence and abilities and attribute these traits to their ethnoracial status and culture. In contrast to the growth mind-set of their parents, their teachers adopt a fixed mind-set about the children of Asian immigrants, and consequently they downplay the effort involved to attain their exceptional academic outcomes. The same applies to their non-Asian peers, who similarly believe that Asian American students achieve perfect grades and test scores because they are naturally smarter.

The mixed messages in these contradictory types of praise lead to a conundrum for high-achieving Asian American students about which mind-set to adopt. When those who have been praised for their intelligence are suddenly faced with a new challenge that they cannot immediately surmount, even after increasing their effort they become vulnerable to feelings of embarrassment, inadequacy, and frustration. As a result, they may lose motivation to press forward and may even question their intelligence and ability, despite their prior accomplishments, as revealed in Adam's and Hung's cases.

Adam: The Pressure of Expectations   Adam is a twenty-one-year-old, second-generation Vietnamese male whose highly educated parents provided him with the class, institutional, and ethnic resources to bring the success frame within his reach. Adam's father, a physician, had immigrated to the United States to attend medical school. His father's salary enabled the family to purchase a home in an affluent suburban neighborhood of Los Angeles with a strong school district and also allowed Adam's mother to stay at home full-time to care for him and his younger brother. Adam's parents hoped that both their sons would follow in their father's footsteps and become doctors.

Adam excelled in elementary and junior high school and received straight A's in his classes. Given his stellar grades, his father insisted that Adam take the Preliminary Scholastic Aptitude Test (PSAT) in the seventh grade (three years ahead of schedule), as other high-achieving Vietnamese students were doing. Adam's junior high school performance landed him in the AP program in high school, but to his shock and chagrin, he was academically unprepared for the rigors and demands of his AP classes. Having earned straight A's in elementary and junior high school, Adam found himself struggling to get B's and C's in his high school AP classes. Alarmed by his dropping grades, Adam's parents hired private tutors to help him in his schoolwork, but the tutors helped only minimally and he was unable to maintain his straight-A average. Faced with Adam's plummeting grades, his parents requested that the school administrators remove him from the AP program and place him in general academic classes.

Having been lauded for his intelligence and his academic performance throughout elementary and junior high schools, Adam felt like a failure when he was no longer able to maintain a straight-A average. He also felt like a failure because his parents had to lower their expectations of him, as he explained: "My parents wanted me to do well, but I just couldn't get into it. They ended up lowering their expectations, especially because they knew the classes were hard for me." With a 3.0 grade point average (GPA) and 1200 on his SAT exams, Adam recognized that he would not be admitted to any of the elite private universities that he and his parents had hoped that he would attend, so he applied two University of California (UC) schools and a private college in the Los Angeles area; he was only accepted into the private college.

The pressure that Adam experienced during high school only intensified during his freshman year in college and climaxed in a nervous breakdown during the spring semester. Unable to continue with his freshman year, Adam decided to drop out of college and return home. After a few months at home, trying to figure out his next steps, Adam decided to enroll in the local community college and take classes in graphic design. Now that he is so far afield from the success frame, Adam has decided to pursue an entirely different course.

However, Adam continues to measure his outcomes to those of his younger brother, who squarely fits the success frame. After excelling in all of his high school AP courses, Adam's brother now attends an elite UC school as a biology major. He describes his brother as "everything that I'm not. My brother is very successful. He managed to do everything that I wasn't able to do. He got very high grades in all AP classes. I just think I didn't do well enough. I'm not angry at him, just disappointed I didn't meet those goals and expectations."

Adam's sense of not being as successful as his brother affects his choice of identity: he prefers the racial label "American Asian" rather than the ethnic label "Vietnamese" or "Vietnamese American" because he feels like a failure compared to his coethnics. When we asked Adam how he thinks other people identify him, he answered, "I'm not sure how people see me. If they ask what I am, I say Vietnamese, but I don't consider myself Vietnamese enough." Adam added that his brother is "much more Vietnamese than me"—because he attends a prestigious university and is on the path to medical school. Because his brother fits the success frame, Adam feels that he is a better and more accurate reflection of Vietnamese ethnicity. Feeling like an outlier in the Vietnamese community, Adam feels no connection to his Vietnamese ethnicity and chooses to avoid contact with coethnics whenever possible.

Hung: Setting an Exceptionally High Bar   Hung is a twenty-five-year-old, second-generation Vietnamese male who earned a bachelor's degree from UC Berkeley and a master's from UCLA. According to normative and intergenerational indicators, Hung's socioeconomic attainment is extraordinary: he excelled in high school, earned a prestigious college scholarship, graduated from a top UC school, attained a master's degree, landed a job as a middle-school teacher in a coveted school district, and will soon pursue his PhD with funding already secured through a fellowship.

Hung's level of educational and occupational attainment is even more impressive considering his parents' humble class origins: his mother is a manicurist, his father is a gardener, and neither have graduated from high school. But rather than measuring his success intergenerationally or against the U.S. average, Hung measures his accomplishments against the success frame and against the highest-achieving Asian Americans—that is, he measures his success against an almost impossibly high bar. Hence, despite the accolades and the numerous status markers that Hung has attained, and in spite of the extraordinary intergenerational mobility that he has achieved, he does not feel successful.

Hung attended a low-income, predominantly Latino school in Orange County that was riddled with Latino and Vietnamese gangs. He kept to himself and managed to steer clear of gang members, and they left him alone. But Hung was far from a social isolate; he immersed himself in a slew of high school clubs, such as the California Scholastic Federation, the Key Club, the academic decathlon, the Vietnamese club, a foreign language club, and the science club. He also took on leadership roles in high school as the yearbook editor and editor-in-chief of the school paper.

His extraordinary extracurricular record was matched by his stellar academic record. Teachers began to test Hung for the GATE (gifted and talented education) program beginning in kindergarten and enrolled him in it in the fifth grade. Hung described his teachers as influential because "they all saw potential in me that I didn't see." He remained on the honors track throughout junior high school and was placed in all AP classes in high school. Because he received straight A's in his AP courses, he graduated with a GPA of 4.23. Not only did Hung graduate as salutatorian of his high school, but he was also awarded a prestigious scholarship that covers tuition for his BA, MA, and PhD degrees.

Hung's exceptional high school record led to acceptances into all of the UC schools to which he applied, as well as to the University of Southern California. He chose UC Berkeley for two reasons. First, it was the most competitive academic institution to which he was admitted. Second, by attending Berkeley, he had a reason to leave his parents' home and, consequently, leave behind the filial obligations attached to living with his parents. Not only could he stop helping to care for his parents, but he also was no longer obliged to help provide child care for the infant daughter of his sister, who was a single mother and relied on Hung and both parents for this help.

Excited to embark on his new life in the Bay Area, Hung was soon shocked by the level of difficulty of his college classes at Berkeley. He felt woefully unprepared and was stunned when he earned a C average in his first year of college. Having excelled in all of his classes prior to this point, Hung fell into a state of severe depression. Reflecting back on this time, he openly admitted, "It gave me grief, and I was depressed, and felt worthless." Confronted with his mediocre grades, Hung started to doubt his ability to major in neurobiology. And for the first time he was forced to confront the possibility that he might be unable to realize his dream—and his parents' dream for him—of becoming a doctor.

Hung's friends made him aware of the depth of his depression, prompting him to seek professional counseling, which he never revealed to his family. Hung's recollections of how he felt during this period were candid: "My friends noticed a difference in my behavior and my attitude, and I just got disgusted with myself, and that motivated me [to see the school psychologist]. And to this day my parents still don't know about it." When we asked why he decided to keep his depression and his decision to seek professional counseling from his parents, he revealed, "It's a taboo. The Vietnamese community is not as trustful of Western medicine and is not used to psychological counseling. My parents would probably just tell me to snap out of it."

After much anguish and deliberation, Hung decided to switch majors, from neurobiology to comparative literature. When asked how his parents felt about this decision, he admitted that "humanities is a hard major for Asians to swallow. They want you to be a doctor, pharmacist, or lawyer. My parents saw English as a hobby; it's not going to make you rich. My dad's friends would tell me that I destroyed my dad's dream, but they're supportive now."

Even some of Hung's Asian American friends at Berkeley expressed disapproval at his change from a "hard" major to a "soft" one. They accused him of taking "the easier way out" and "not using his intelligence" when he switched from neurobiology to comparative literature. Not only was he asked difficult questions and criticized by his parents and peers, but Hung also began to question his intelligence and ability and wonder whether he really had taken the easy way out, as he candidly revealed:

> I was thinking I was stupid and, like, not very smart or capable, especially since I dropped out of science, because I do, at times, think that I did take the easier way out. And I don't know if it's because of myself I'm thinking this, or because I was, you know, affected by these expectations that everyone has given me.

Unable to excel at the new and unforeseen challenges that he faced at Berkeley, Hung felt "stupid," "worthless," and "not very smart or capable." Having always received the highest accolades and praise for his intelligence and performance through high school, Hung was unprepared when he failed to perform at the level to which he had become accustomed, even after he increased his effort. After seeking professional counseling and changing majors, however, Hung began to feel better about himself—in large part because of his improved grades.

We asked Hung whether he feels successful now that he had graduated from Berkeley, earned a master's from UCLA, and works as a middle school teacher. He replied:

> Sometimes I do, but sometimes I don't. And I think it's because I have really high expectations for myself that I don't have for others. And I seldom live up to my expectations. I guess, when people are able to tell me, like, "Oh, we're very proud of you," or, "You're doing a great job," that's how I gauge being successful. But I'm very results-driven, so when my students do well on their tests, or when, you know, a lesson went well, that's when I feel like, oh, I am being successful.

Hung's comments about being "results-driven" and feeling successful only when people told him that he is "doing a great job" are revealing. Hung feels successful only when he achieves the high grades to which he had become accustomed, only when he receives praise from others, or only when his middle school students perform well on their tests. Success, in Hung's view, is measured by his performance, results, and external praise, which he believes to be the result of his ability and intelligence. Even Hung's assessment of himself as "worthless" and "stupid" at Berkeley changed only after he sought professional help, and only after he changed majors, which resulted in improved grades. Once again, Hung's self-esteem and self-worth are directly correlated with performance markers.

The Contradictory Messages
of Two Mind-Sets

Both Adam's and Hung's cases highlight how the different social environments at home and at school can complicate the development of mind-sets for Asian Americans. The children of Chinese and Vietnamese immigrants are socialized by their parents to believe in the importance of effort for improved outcomes, as manifested in their parents' insistence on supplementary education for their children. In school, however, they are socialized to believe that their intelligence is innate and that their high academic achievement is the expectation and norm for Asian Americans. In adopting beliefs about Asian American exceptionalism, teachers, guidance counselors, and peers unwittingly endorse a fixed mind-set for Asian American students; they encourage students to believe that their stellar grades and academic achievements are attributable to their intelligence and ability rather than their hard work. Based on our interviews with 1.5- and second-generation Chinese and Vietnamese, we noticed that, in spite of their different mind-sets, both Asian immigrant parents and American teachers prioritize performance over learning.

As Dweck's research shows, exclusively praising students' intelligence and focusing on their successful outcomes can be detrimental for Asian Americans students' motivation, self-esteem, and self-efficacy.[7] Such praise leaves students ill equipped to confront difficult challenges they cannot easily surmount, less likely to be motivated to keep trying, more vulnerable to feelings of failure, and more susceptible to low self-esteem. Furthermore, they quickly lose confidence in their intelligence, self-worth, and self-efficacy, despite their string of earlier successes.

The beliefs of the Chinese and Vietnamese immigrant parents stems from the Confucian philosophy that all individuals are born with similar ability and that outcomes reflect differences in individual effort. Their focus on effort reflects a growth mind-set. The Chinese and Vietnamese immigrant parents maximize their children's opportunities for putting more effort into their schoolwork by relying on institutional, class, and ethnic resources; in addition, they insist that their children are placed on the most competitive academic tracks and supplement their children's education with after-school classes, tutors, and preparatory courses for standardized exams.

From an outsider's perspective, this degree of academic preparation may seem like irrational overpreparation. But from the perspective of Chinese and Vietnamese immigrant parents, this level of effort and preparation is rational for three main reasons. First, they hail from countries of origin that privilege effort—rather than innate ability—as the key to achievement. Second, having been raised with a growth mind-set themselves, they impart to their children the message that extra effort will yield the greatest chance that they will attain the success frame: admission to an elite university and a high-status position. Third, they believe that extensive preparation and effort will best shield their children against potential bias and discrimination in the labor market, and their concerns in this regard are not unfounded. Asian American students may outperform their peers, including native-born whites, the dominant group, but the criteria for evaluating merit often change to protect the dominant group's position.[8] As immigrants and as nonwhites, Chinese and Vietnamese parents believe that the best way to ensure their children's success is to overprepare them in relation to their peers. Although they may be unable to control changes in the criteria for merit, these parents can control how prepared their U.S.-born children will be at the starting gate, irrespective of potential changes.

While Chinese and Vietnamese immigrant parents focus on their children's effort, teachers in U.S. schools, by contrast, focus on students' innate intelligence, abilities, and talents. And based on our in-depth interviews, Chinese and Vietnamese students perceive that teachers have elevated expectations of Asian American students. As a result, teachers promote a fixed mind-set among Asian American students. But exclusively praising intelligence and performance over effort and strategies can have deleterious consequences, as Adam's and Hung's cases vividly reveal and as Dweck's research highlights.

We extend Dweck's research by noting that the children of Chinese and Vietnamese immigrants are especially vulnerable to the negative consequences of the clash of mind-sets they experience at home and at school. Prior to college, both Adam and Hung were repeatedly praised for their intelligence by their teachers and experienced a string of successes in school, including placement in GATE programs in elementary and middle school, followed by the honors track in high school. Hung's successes continued through high school as he held leadership positions in prominent high school clubs, earned a 4.23 GPA, received a highly competitive and coveted scholarship, and was admitted to all the universities to which he applied.

But Hung's successes came to a crashing halt when he entered Berkeley and experienced difficulty in his rigorous science classes. Because Hung's self-esteem rested on performance markers, once he was unable to attain these, his sense of self-worth plummeted, resulting in feelings of inadequacy and the onset of depression. Hung's experience illustrates that when parents or teachers focus on performance praise rather than on learning and the enjoyment of tackling challenges, students may become more susceptible to mental health problems, including anxiety, pressure, frustration, and feelings of failure.

Asian American students are particularly vulnerable to these mental health risks because their achievement mind-set is simultaneously influenced by two different social environments that stress two types of mind-sets. What made Hung especially vulnerable to feelings of inadequacy and to depression was that while he was praised for his intelligence and his performance at school, his immigrant parents believed that Hung's performance was a direct result of his effort. Unable to reconcile the contradictory messages of the two mind-sets, Hung believed that he was inadequate because he failed, even after he put in more effort, to achieve at the level that his parents and his teachers expected of him—and that he expected of himself.

Like Hung, Adam received contradictory messages from two distinct mind-sets. Consistently praised for his intelligence in elementary and junior high school (fixed mind-set), he began to feel anxious when he could not perform at the same level in his AP classes in high school. His parents responded by hiring tutors, believing that the supplementary education and Adam's increased effort would improve his performance (growth mind-set). When Adam's increased effort did not achieve the outcome expected of himself, his parents, and his teachers, Adam became increasingly anxious about his failure, which resulted in a nervous breakdown during his freshman year of college.

As Adam's and Hung's cases underscore, the ideal model for learning is not one that focuses exclusively on performance, but rather one that emphasizes the malleability of ability and praises effort as well as performance. When this mind-set is integrated with a learning-oriented framework in which students strive to achieve while also embracing the challenge of learning, students learn to overcome the fear of tackling new challenges and the fear of failure, and they learn more in the long run.[9] Asian American students in particular would especially benefit from this approach because it would help them reconcile the mixed messages they receive from two different social environments that stress contradictory mind-sets but reward performance.

The Subject-Centered Approach and the Achievement Paradox

Adam's and Hung's cases illustrate another point that resonated throughout our interviews with 1.5- and second-generation Chinese and Vietnamese. Rather than adopting normative assumptions about success, they shared a similar success frame and had similar experiences with academic achievement. Our subject-centered approach revealed that, while these high-achieving Chinese and Vietnamese might have been successful based on middle-class American, normative socioeconomic measures, many did not feel successful because their reference group included those who had far exceeded the average standard for native-born Americans.

While homophilous peer networks for Asian American students may positively affect their academic outcomes, these exclusive coethnic and panethnic peer networks can also adversely affect their self-esteem. In studies of college students at elite private and public universities, researchers have found that Asian students have the strongest academic records and express the strongest commitment to school, yet despite these positive indicators, they exhibit the lowest levels of self-esteem compared to white, black, and Latino students.[10]

This is the achievement paradox that is illuminated by our research. Because 1.5- and second-generation Chinese and Vietnamese turn to high-achieving coethnics as their reference group, those who do not fit the narrow success frame feel like outliers, and in some cases like failures. Furthermore, even many of those who feel successful are not satisfied with their own achievements, regardless of how much education they have attained or how much they earn, because they compare their accomplishments to those of a reference group that includes higher-achieving coethnics—not just peers in school but also siblings, cousins, and friends—rather than those of native-born whites and blacks or other second-generation groups. Regardless of what they have achieved, they (or their parents) know someone who has achieved more, and therefore they measure their achievements by an exceptionally high standard. The status inconsistency between the normative definition of success and their subjective definition of success (which we glean by adopting the subject-centered approach) is at the root of the achievement paradox, as the cases of Carolyn, Michelle, and Sarah illuminate.

Carolyn: Pursuing a Career Outside the Success Frame   Carolyn, a thirty-five-year-old second-generation Chinese, earned a BA in film studies from a Cal State school and works as a visual effects coordinator for movies. Carolyn's highly educated parents hail from Taiwan; her father holds a graduate degree, and her mother a bachelor's.

By Carolyn's account, she did not excel in high school and earned "only" a 3.3 GPA. Despite her "low" GPA, she always knew that she would go to college, not only because her parents are college educated, but also because everyone in her family is college educated; some of her aunts, uncles, and cousins attended elite universities like MIT, Stanford, and Cornell. Carolyn's high school record was not competitive enough to earn her admission to any of the UC schools to which she applied, but it did earn her a spot at a Cal State school. During college, she took a film class "on a whim" and enjoyed it so much that she decided to major in film studies. After graduating, she landed a job as a production assistant—no easy feat in the fiercely competitive entertainment industry of Los Angeles.

Carolyn had worked in the film industry for most of her adult life and had moved up the ranks from production assistant to visual effects coordinator. Having worked on numerous films, she had also traveled extensively—a perk of her job that she relishes. She aspires to make films of her own someday and is acquiring as much knowledge and experience while "paying her dues." Now that Carolyn earns a steady income and is financially independent, her parents are content, but they are not proud enough to brag about her accomplishments to her aunts and uncles. When asked to elaborate on the way her parents feel about her educational and occupational trajectory, Carolyn candidly replied:

> My parents were disappointed in a few things. Because I didn't go to the UC system, they were disappointed. My brother Robert was a golden child. He

got in, even though it was just Irvine, but Irvine's a good school. My parents felt like I could have done better. I tried my best, but it was a challenge.

In terms of the bragging, you'll hear it. So-and-so went to MIT, and so-and-so went to Cornell or Stanford, and you start feeling, as an Asian person, less and less of yourself because you couldn't compete with these people, because you're not bright or smart enough, and you're not at that equal level. I used to feel a lot like that, especially when I was a production assistant and running around and I was already out of college. I should have been happy that I finished college and [had] a degree to show for it, but I [wasn't].

Carolyn is keenly aware that her occupational pursuit falls out of the success frame; she explained that, although she enjoys her work, her career choice is unconventional by Chinese standards. She also candidly revealed that she feels like the "black sheep" of her family, especially compared to her cousins who graduated from elite universities and work as doctors and lawyers. Her sentiments echoed those of other 1.5- and second-generation Chinese and Vietnamese interviewees who admitted to feeling "really behind," "not that smart," and even "dumb" compared to their friends and family members who majored in the life or hard sciences, attained graduate degrees, now hold high-status occupations, and earn higher salaries than they. Because they compare their accomplishments "vertically up" to the highest-achieving coethnics, many feel that they are not successful.

Michelle: Renouncing the Success Frame   Like Carolyn, Michelle described herself as the family's "black sheep," but unlike Carolyn, Michelle was both cynical about and disdainful of the success frame. Born in Taiwan, Michelle immigrated to the United States as a toddler with her parents and two older sisters. Both her parents were college educated, and they expected all three daughters, at a minimum, to excel in high school and attain a bachelor's degree. Michelle's parents often compared their daughters to one another when they were young, hoping that the competitive pressure would make each strive harder to excel. As the youngest of the three daughters, Michelle was constantly compared to her high-achieving sister Kimberly, not only by her parents but also by her teachers:

My sister Kimberly, the second one, when she was growing up, she was the perfect one in the family. All the pressure was on her. She was straight A's and was valedictorian. Me and my oldest sister were constantly being compared to her. It is like, "Oh, Michelle, why aren't you more like Kimberly?" and it was horrible because I was, like, in maybe four of the classes growing up where she was the year before, so now, not only are my parents comparing me, but my teachers are comparing me.

You know, Kimberly is the perfect student, very agreeable, answers all the questions, and does her own work on time, and then here comes me. I didn't do my homework, and I didn't go to class on time. I talked back to the teacher. I wasn't respectful and stuff like that. This was my life growing up with Kimberly being perfect, and Kimberly blah blah blah. This is my sister, and she goes to Columbia and graduates with honors.

While Kimberly graduated from an Ivy League school, Michelle explained that she did "just okay" by gaining admission to UCLA. But Michelle felt so passionate about the martial arts that after graduating from high school she decided to forgo college altogether in order to pursue a career teaching martial arts. Not only were her parents unwilling to support Michelle's decision, but they were so outraged that they kicked her out of their house and proclaimed that she would become a failure:

I got into UCLA, but I didn't go there. It was a big disappointment for my parents. My oldest sister went to UCLA, and my second sister, she got into Columbia. Both graduated with high honors.

When I decided I didn't want to go to college, they [my parents] were really pissed at me for, like, probably three months. They were really pushing me, like, "What are you going to do with your life if you don't go to college?" and, "You're going to be a loser and not be able to get a job." They were very insulting and very derogatory.

When we asked Michelle why she chose not to go to college, she explained that she was not the typical "Asian kid" who likes school and enjoys studying:

I hated school. I'm not one of these Asian kids that go study and then go be part of all these different organizations. My mom is pushing me all the time. We always had extracurricular activities. I loved the extracurricular activities, but I hated studying. I'm like, "Why do I want to go to college?" I may be a little too smart for my own good. I was thinking, "Why don't I just get my GED so I can get on with my life and start making money?"

Michelle racialized her explanation by proclaiming that because she hated studying and did not want to go to college, she was unlike other "Asian kids." For Michelle, "Asian" was synonymous with academic achievement.

In an unforeseen outcome, however, Michelle is now the most economically successful daughter, despite being the only one not to attend college. Although she did not fulfill her dream of establishing a martial arts studio, she is a successful real estate agent in Los Angeles, and her salary exceeds the incomes of her older sisters. Michelle expressed a sense of both pride and vindication that it is she—not her two college-educated sisters—who is able to provide financial support to her parents.

Both Carolyn and Michelle departed from the success frame and feel like the black sheep in their families because they chose to follow a different course. Both feel that they are atypical Asians because they did not excel in school, unlike their high-achieving brothers, sisters, and coethnic peers. But Carolyn and Michelle also differed in a critical way. Carolyn considers herself "not as smart as other Asians," "not driven," and "not as successful," whereas Michelle describes herself as "a little too smart for my own good" to convey how she diverges from the success frame and what she perceives as the typical Asian student. Despite this difference, both equate Asian status with high academic achievement, and both compare their educational and professional decisions and accomplishments to those of high-achieving coethnics who had followed and attained the success frame. This extremely elite group of coethnic high-achievers is the meaningful reference group for the children of Chinese and Vietnamese immigrants, a point underscored by the cases of Sarah and Jesse.

Sarah and Jesse: An Advanced Degree Is the Expectation   Sarah is a 1.5-generation Chinese woman who graduated from a UC school and owns a profitable contracting and design company from which she earned $160,000 the last year before we interviewed her. Sarah's business ownership and success are all the more impressive considering that she considers herself a "double-minority"— female and nonwhite—in an industry dominated by white males. With her earnings, she purchased a home in an affluent suburb of Los Angeles that she shares with her partner.

Despite all of Sarah's markers of success—including owning a thriving business and a dream home—neither she nor her parents view her as successful because she has not attained an advanced degree. When we asked whether she feels successful, Sarah answered, "Not yet." Compared to her older sister, who graduated from law school and works as a lawyer, Sarah feels inadequate because she does not have a graduate degree. Elaborating on this point, she noted, with a touch of embarrassment, "All of my friends in high school went to grad school except me." When we asked why a graduate degree is important, especially given the success of her contracting and design business, she explained, "The perception among Chinese is that education is the key to success."

When we asked Sarah whether she feels successful compared to her friends who are not Chinese, she paused for a moment, as if she had never considered that comparison before. She finally replied, "If I were to look at my white friends of that same age range, yes, I'm more successful. If I were to look at all of my friends, yes, I would say so."

While Sarah does not feel successful compared to her sister and coethnic friends, she does feel successful vis-à-vis her white and other non-Chinese friends, but she had never considered making this comparison before we raised the question. Sarah is not unique in this regard: none of the 1.5- and second-generation Chinese and Vietnamese interviewees consider measuring their success against native-born whites—or native-born blacks for that matter. Rather, they turn to high-achieving coethnics as their reference group—a finding that underscores that native-born whites are not the standard by which today's 1.5- and second-generation Asians measure their success and achievements.

Similarly, Jesse, a 1.5-generation Chinese male who graduated from a UC school and works in a research laboratory for a scientist, said that he feels unsuccessful because he had not been accepted into any of the PhD programs to which he applied. Those rejections have caused Jesse a great deal of anguish and embarrassment because his brother, his friends, and now his colleagues in the lab are either in doctoral programs or had already attained their PhD degrees. For Jesse, pursuing a PhD was the expectation. When we asked to whom he compares himself in assessing his success, he explained, "Most of my family, at least who live close by. They have already gotten their PhDs a long time ago. My brother already has his PhD. Most of my friends already have their PhDs or are on their way to getting it."

Fewer than 1 percent of Americans have a PhD, yet Jesse's reference group includes only those who had a doctoral degree or are on their way to attaining one; thus, because Jesse had not been admitted to any of the doctoral programs to which he applied, he feels like an abject failure because he "only has a BA." However, even by Jesse's own admission not all of his family members and friends have their PhD degrees, he does not compare himself to these family members and friends, nor does he consider measuring his success against the U.S. average. Instead, like other 1.5- and second-generation Chinese and Vietnamese interviewees, Jesse compares vertically up and therefore feels unsuccessful, despite his educational and professional accomplishments.

The Other Tail of the Achievement Paradox

Although most of the 1.5- and second-generation Chinese and Vietnamese interviewees measure their success vertically up against the highest-achieving coethnics, a small minority do not. Those in this group have not attained the success frame—they did not graduate at the top of their high school class, did not graduate from a prestigious university, and do not hold a high-status job—yet they feel successful. These interviewees embody the other tail of the achievement paradox and represent the exception to the norm. Rather than ignoring this divergent pattern, we felt that it merited further inquiry and explanation.

This small group of 1.5- and second-generation Chinese and Vietnamese share similar characteristics: most come from working-class backgrounds; they attended schools with few coethnics; they grew up with and still maintained an ethnoracially diverse peer network; and they had little or no contact with coethnic peers or the coethnic community. They did not take supplemental classes in ethnic academies, nor did they rely on tutors or summer school to boost their academic performance. Consequently, they felt little or no pressure at home nor at school to attain the success frame, and they did not use high-achieving coethnics as the reference group by which they measured their success or progress. Instead, they measured their success against a different standard—their peers from high school, most of whom fared either as well as they did or worse.

Jack: Success Outside the Success Frame   Consider Jack, a forty-one-year-old, 1.5-generation Chinese male who was born in Hong Kong and migrated to the United States with his family when he was eleven years old. Jack's parents are not highly educated; neither have more than an elementary school education. With little human capital, Jack's parents supported their family by running a small restaurant, where Jack and his four siblings worked after school and on weekends.

Jack owns and operates a business with his brother, importing porcelain items from China and selling them to wholesalers and designers, both locally and nationally, through trade shows. Unlike the majority of our Chinese interviewees, Jack feels no pressure to attain the success frame. He explained that he did "okay" in high school, which meant that he typically earned three A's, two B's, and a C. Upon graduating from high school, Jack decided to attend an automotive program at a local community college with the goal of transferring to a four-year college after he earned his associate's degree. But after graduating from community college, Jack landed a job at a repair shop, then moved to another job as a welder, and shortly thereafter was promoted to supervisor—a position for which he earned $11 an hour. Jack never transferred to a four-year university, as he had initially planned; after he began working, he enjoyed earning a steady income and never pulled himself away from work to pursue a bachelor's degree.

He stayed with the same job for ten years until his older brother decided to open a small gift shop, which blossomed into the importing business that he and Jack now operate together. The business is small but profitable, and Jack holds the title of vice president and earns an annual salary of $55,000. Although he and his brother operate a successful business, Jack earns less than other self-employed coethnics his age whom we interviewed, including Sarah, the self-employed contractor who earns $160,000. Moreover, though Jack graduated from high school and has an associate's degree, he does not have a BA and has no plans to attain one. Based on these indicators, Jack falls at the lower end of the educational and earnings spectrum among our interviewees in his age group, yet when we asked whether he feels successful, he answered affirmatively. He elaborated: "I'm good, you know? I have decent work, decent family life, and decent everything, really. I can provide everything for them [my family] and stuff, you know? I think I did a good job."

Then we asked Jack to whom he compared himself when he considered how successful he is. "If I was comparing," he replied, "I would compare with my friends. I still hang out with all my friends in high school." When we asked about the ethnoracial backgrounds of his friends, he mentioned that his friends are "pretty diverse" and that his three closest friends are Japanese, Mexican, and white. Unlike the majority of the 1.5- and second-generation Chinese whom we interviewed, Jack does not have Chinese friends, nor does he have much contact with coethnics or with the Chinese community. In fact, when we asked Jack how much contact he had with other Chinese people while he was growing up, he answered, "Not that much. We went to Monterey Park, but more like just to eat and stuff." Given what little contact Jack had with fellow ethnics, we asked him whether he feels successful in relation to other Chinese people; his response was telling: "I don't compare myself with other people like that." Jack added that he does not feel pressure to be more successful than he is, except when "my wife wants an expensive purse," he said with a smile, "and I'm like, 'Oh no!' That's the only time I feel pressure." In this way, Jack resembles the native-born white and black interviewees who do not measure their success against others and take an individualistic approach to assessing their success instead.

Because Jack has had very little contact with coethnic peers and the coethnic community (other than his family's occasional forays into Monterey Park), he appears to be immune to the weight of the success frame. Moreover, as someone who has not been influenced by the success frame, Jack feels successful, even though he is less successful by objective socioeconomic indicators like educational attainment, occupational status, and income than the coethnic peers his age whom we interviewed. A useful point of comparison that points to another dimension of the achievement paradox among Asian Americans is Sarah, who also owns and operates her own business but earns triple Jack's salary and holds a BA from a UC school. Despite Sarah's higher educational attainment and earnings, she does not feel successful, while Jack does.

The reasons for the achievement paradox in Sarah's and Jack's cases are twofold. First, Sarah's parents have advanced degrees while Jack's parents have only completed elementary school, so Jack has attained more intergenerational mobility than Sarah. Measuring success by intergenerational progress, Jack *is* more successful than Sarah. Second, Jack grew up in a social environment that gave him little contact with coethnic peers, and he did not attend supplemental education classes in the ethnic community. Therefore, his reference group is not composed of high-achieving coethnics, as is Sarah's; instead, his reference group is an ethnoracially diverse group of friends from high school whom he considers "equally successful" as he. As Sarah's and Jack's cases illuminate, those who have attained the most success based on objective indicators may not feel the most successful, and those whose socioeconomic attainment is lower relative to their coethnics may feel very successful. These cases underscore the relevance of the subject-centered approach in the study of second-generation outcomes.

Leslie: Success in the Absence of Coethnics   Like Jack, Leslie feels successful. Leslie is a twenty-nine-year-old Korean-Vietnamese woman who works as a kindergarten teacher. She grew up with few Vietnamese or Korean friends and compares herself to her high school friends who are non-Asian and who have achieved far less than she has. When we asked Leslie whether she feels successful, she apologetically answered, "I do, but I don't want to admit it." We asked why she feels this way:

> Well, I don't know. [*pause*] Because I don't want them [her friends] to think I've changed. The thing is, a lot of my friends are still, like, working hourly, you know? They have hourly jobs. It's hard because you want to go on a vacation; they can't do it, but I can because I have that time off. I have the summers off, and I can afford it.

Although Leslie is a teacher who has earned a BA, her educational path has been far from smooth. She attended a Cal State school immediately after high school, but after an abysmal first year in which she earned a GPA of 0.56, Cal State disqualified her from continuing and she was forced to drop out. It took her seven years, attending three different colleges, to attain her bachelor's degree.

When we asked Leslie why her GPA had been so low during her first year in college, she explained that she had prioritized work over school. When she took her first retail job, having never worked before in her life, she enjoyed earning her own money and the economic freedom that accompanied it. Leslie had started working only part-time, but she slowly increased the number of hours she worked until she found herself working nearly full-time. Without her parents to oversee her time management and school progress, Leslie began skipping classes and forgoing coursework altogether.

When she received notice of her academic disqualification, Leslie decided to keep the news from her parents and promptly enrolled in a community college. Rather than confessing about her academic disqualification, she explained to her parents that she decided to leave the Cal State school because community college was a more affordable option. She also promised her parents that after she graduated from community college she would transfer to a four-year university, which she did.

After a few years in community college, Leslie applied to and was accepted as a transfer student at another Cal State school, where she decided that she would approach college very differently: she "turned the tables and put school ahead of work," which resulted in straight A's. When we asked what had changed, Leslie explained that she no longer took college for granted because she knew that she had been given a second chance. Also, by then she had decided that she wanted to become a teacher and had set her sights on fulfilling the requirements to meet this goal. We also asked Leslie whether anyone had been particularly influential; she pointed to three professors at the second Cal State school she attended who had taken a special interest in her:

> I had three professors, and they had a lot of faith in me. I was even honored with a fellowship from one of the professors from the Historical Society in California back in 2001. So the three professors, I would say, really influenced me. I took a lot of classes with them because I thought they were really good. I really got to know them, and they got to know me, and it motivated me to do well in their classes, as well as the other ones too.

After Leslie graduated with a BA, she quickly landed a job as a kindergarten teacher, and earns an annual salary of $54,000. Leslie is considering returning to school for her master's degree because it would place her higher on the pay scale.

Like Jack, Leslie had an ethnoracially diverse set of high school friends, and also like Jack, Leslie did not have much contact with coethnics, either Koreans or Vietnamese. Leslie's parents were not involved with the Korean or Vietnamese communities in Los Angeles, and Leslie did not take supplemental educational classes in either community. Moreover, Leslie's parents were not involved with their extended families, especially Leslie's father's family, who had not approved of his choice of a Vietnamese wife. In these respects, Leslie's upbringing is similar to Jack's: neither of them spent much time with coethnics or in their coethnic communities.

One difference is that, unlike Jack's parents, Leslie's parents are highly educated: her Korean father graduated from an elite university in Seoul, and her mother completed two years of college. However, even though Leslie has not attained intergenerational mobility, as Jack has, she feels successful nevertheless. The experiences of Jack and Leslie underscore the significance of coethnic contact and involvement in the coethnic community. The 1.5- and second-generation interviewees who have had sustained contact with coethnics are more likely to use high-achieving coethnics as their reference group for measuring their success. Those with little or no contact with coethnics, however, do not use high-achieving coethnics as their reference group but turn to a more diverse set of peers instead.

Justin: Low-Achieving but Feels Successful   Perhaps the most striking case of the achievement paradox is Justin, a twenty-three-year-old, second-generation Chinese male who is in his fifth year of community college and working close to full-time, for $9 an hour, at a retail store in Huntington Beach. Justin's parents have no more than an elementary school education. His father, who worked as a cook in a fast-food restaurant, passed away when Justin was ten years old. His mother continues to work on a factory assembly line and has picked up extra shifts to support her two children. As a single parent, Justin's mother has always been too busy with work to pay attention to Justin's grades or his after-school activities. He did not have household rules, nor did he have a curfew, so after school he would often hang out in parking lots in Little Saigon with his friends. Justin freely admitted that he never really did his homework in high school, which was reflected in his 1.5 GPA. His Vietnamese friends, like Justin, were also below-average students.

Even though Justin was a low-achieving high school student, his mother had always expected him to go to college, so after graduating from high school, he enrolled in the local community college. Currently in his fifth year, Justin still plans to transfer to a Cal State school when he fulfills his requirements. At the time of the interview, he was taking classes that were unrelated to his business administration major, but he hoped to accumulate enough credits to transfer to a four-year university. However, he later admitted that he was unsure of what requirements were needed to transfer. Unaware of the vast differences among U.S. colleges and universities, Justin's mother was satisfied that her son was in college.

When we asked what success means to him, Justin replied, "If I'm doing what I want to do, and what I set out to do, then I would consider myself successful." He admitted to feeling more successful than his parents because he has more education than they have, and he also feels more successful than his friends, all of whom have dropped out of community college. Among his peers, Justin is the only one who is still in college, and the only one who still aspires to transfer to a Cal State school. That he is in college and plans to pursue a bachelor's degree sets him apart from his high school peers, who serve as his reference group.

When we asked what motivated him to continue with his college education, Justin explained, "I want to do something with my life. I don't want to be working little jobs"—like the one he had at the time of the interview. When we asked him to be more specific about what he would like to do and how much he would like to earn, Justin responded, "Something in an office, I guess, and professional," a job in which he would earn "about $50,000." Because Justin has no contact with high-achieving coethnics or the coethnic community more generally, he does not measure his achievements against the strict success frame, and therefore he feels successful vis-à-vis his reference group, who has attained less education and holds lower educational aspirations.

Justin's lack of contact with coethnics and the coethnic community also affects how he chooses to identify. Although he identifies as Chinese American or Asian, he admits that being Chinese does not mean anything to him because he has no attachment to Chinese coethnics or the Chinese community. In fact, Justin feels that his lifestyle is distinctively American, but he identifies as Chinese American because he does not wish to reject his Chinese ethnicity, and also because his distinctive phenotype and features mark him as Asian. However, because all of his friends are Vietnamese, Justin feels that Asian is a more accurate and suitable identifier.

Of our Chinese and Vietnamese interviewees, Justin is one of the lowest achievers with respect to educational attainment, occupational status, and career aspirations. Unlike many of his higher-achieving coethnic counterparts, he had no contact with coethnics, had not been involved with supplementary education, and was not attached to the ethnic community in any way. As a result, he feels successful because his reference group—a diverse group of high school peers—have achieved less than he has. Justin's experience points to the other tail of the achievement paradox among Asian Americans.

Summary

In this chapter, we have shown that mind-sets are only part of the story of Asian American academic achievement. Complicating the relationship between mind-sets and achievement among the children of Chinese and Vietnamese immigrants are the conflicting messages they receive from their home and school environments about the role of mind-sets. At home, their immigrant parents promote a growth mind-set in the belief that increased effort will improve outcomes. At school, however, their teachers, from a fixed mind-set, praise Chinese and Vietnamese students for their intelligence and abilities. The conflicting messages from these two primary social environments can result in a unique achievement paradox among Asian Americans: high academic achievement coupled with low self-esteem, low self-efficacy, and low resilience in the face of setbacks and inability to meet the high expectations.

We have also shown that the constricting success frame is supported by homophilous peer networks among the 1.5- and second-generation Chinese and Vietnamese, which not only push them to excel but also influence their reference group formation, further contributing to the achievement paradox. Ethnoracially homophilous peer networks among Asian Americans may push coethnics to excel because they are more likely to model their behavior after the highest achievers.[11] However, the same networks may raise the attainment bar so high that many feel inadequate when they are unable to meet it, thereby leading to lack of confidence, low self-esteem, low self-worth, and low self-efficacy.

In extreme cases, the failure to meet the bar leads to mental health problems such as severe depression and mental breakdowns. We should add an important caveat. Our method of data collection prevents us from being able to present accurate data about each interviewee's experiences with mental health issues such as depression, nervous breakdowns, and attempted suicide. We did not ask the interviewees questions about mental health issues, so those who spoke about them did so voluntarily, without our having prompted them. Many who did so were openly discussing their experiences for the first time. However, because we saw consistent patterns emerging from the interviews, we felt it was important to shed some light on these cases rather than ignore them altogether. Any bias arising from our data collection methods is likely to be in the direction of underreporting the prevalence of mental health issues among the children of Chinese and Vietnamese immigrants.

We uncovered another facet of the achievement paradox among Asian Americans: the 1.5- and second-generation Chinese and Vietnamese interviewees with more ethnoracially diverse peer networks exhibited higher levels of self-confidence, even when their academic performance and occupational attainment were lower. Making up only a minority of the interviewees, this group tended to measure their success against a more culturally heterogeneous reference group and were thus more likely to feel successful, even when they had attained less than many of their coethnic peers. This facet of the achievement paradox reinforces the centrality of the subject-centered approach, which focuses on the meaning that success holds for the 1.5 and second generation.

The question of meaning brings us back to the point that the way in which parents and teachers praise students affects how they learn and how they feel about learning outcomes. Although praising students' intelligence may make them feel good after a successful outcome, it is worth remembering that no student has a 100 percent success rate; all students face challenges that they may be unable to easily surmount. When students stumble, they choose either to persevere in the face of difficulty or to give up because of fear of failure. And fearing that they may reveal their weaknesses to themselves and to others, they come to doubt their intelligence, skills, and ability.

As many of our 1.5- and second-generation Chinese and Vietnamese interviewees revealed, the meaning of success is both self-defined and other-defined, so the fear of revealing weaknesses to others is especially consequential for Asian Americans, whom others, especially teachers and peers, perceive as innately exceptional. Promoting a growth mind-set that attaches positive meaning to effort rather than merely to intelligence and performance is critical for the progress of all students. It is especially so for Asian American students because they are susceptible to the contradictory messages they receive from their immigrant parents, their teachers, and the ethnic community, and to the racial stereotyping of Asian Americans as the model minority. Those mixed messages can lead to the unique achievement paradox among Asians: high achievement on objective indicators of success does not necessarily go hand in hand with high self-esteem, self-worth, and efficacy.

~ Chapter 8 ~

Success at All Costs

The success frame comes at a cost and has far-reaching, sociologically significant consequences. While Chinese and Vietnamese immigrant parents believe that increased effort improves outcomes, their children's performance does not always match expectations, despite their increased effort. As we showed in the previous chapter, an exclusive emphasis on performance outcomes can undermine students' willingness to tackle challenging tasks, detract from learning, and lower students' confidence when their outcomes fall short of expectations.[1] The children of Asian immigrants are susceptible to these consequences, especially those who aim for but fall short of the success frame. When Asian American students are unable to meet the exceptional expectations of their parents, teachers, and peers, some lose their motivation to persevere, doubt their intelligence, and lose confidence in their abilities. These feelings intensify when their increased effort to attain the success frame does not result in the desired outcomes.

In this chapter, we draw attention to the price of success at all costs—the price that the children of Chinese and Vietnamese immigrants pay when they cannot meet the success frame, or when they reject it altogether. But before turning to the costs, we shed light on another social mechanism through which Chinese and Vietnamese immigrant parents buttress the success frame: in the exercise of what they believe are their "bragging rights," parents circulate exclusively positive, confirming narratives about their children's success. Bragging rights have consequences: by reinforcing the belief that the success frame is both attainable and normative among Asian American children, parents further intensify the pressure on their children to achieve it.

The perception that the success frame is normative and within the reach of those who put in the effort has individual and social consequences for Asian Americans and for other groups. At the individual level, the pressure on some immigrant children to achieve the success frame is so great that they lie about their accomplishments in order to "save face," while others experience intense intergenerational conflict with their immigrant parents. Still others opt out or reject their ethnic identities and distance themselves from coethnics because they link the success frame with ethnoracial status and culture. In extreme cases, some interviewees experienced mental health problems, including severe depression and nervous breakdowns, as we noted in the previous chapter.

The costs of the success frame extend beyond individual cases to Asian Americans as a group, as well as to other ethnoracial groups. We draw on the rich literature in social psychology to elucidate how stereotypes about race and achievement persist in gateway institutions despite disconfirming evidence. Drawing parallels from the research on gender and gender stereotypes, we illustrate how stereotypes about Asian Americans endure through cognitive and social processes, even in the face of disconfirming evidence and changing material realities.

Parental Bragging Rights: Intensifying the Pressure to Achieve

Chinese and Vietnamese immigrant parents reinforce the success frame by supplementing their children's education with after-school programs and drawing on their cross-class networks to acquire educationally relevant information, but they also rely on another strategy—parental bragging rights. While teachers laud students' achievements by praising their intelligence and abilities, Chinese and Vietnamese immigrant parents do so by bragging to other coethnic parents about their children's accomplishments. But these parents are highly selective; their bragging includes only narratives of exceptional achievement and only cases that squarely fit the success frame. Consequently, parents brag only about their children who gain admission to elite universities, attain advanced degrees, work as doctors, lawyers, scientists, or engineers, and earn six-figure salaries. They readily circulate these positive narratives within their families and among coethnic friends, but they keep decidedly mum about the more numerous disconfirming cases. The positive narratives are then passed on to the children, who hear only about the success stories among their coethnic peers.

Parental bragging rights have social consequences: by selectively circulating only the positive, confirming narratives, not only do parents reinforce the success frame in their U.S.-born children, but they also reinforce the erroneous perception that all 1.5- and second-generation Chinese and Vietnamese are exceptional achievers. As a result, both parents and children come to believe that the success frame is not only attainable but normative.

The children of Chinese and Vietnamese immigrants also adopt, however, a more cynical perspective about their parents' bragging rights. Their parents' insistence on circulating only positive narratives makes them feel like pawns in a game of parental competition, with parental bragging rights as the coveted prize. And because their parents' peer networks are ethnically homophilous, they characterize the game of parental bragging rights as an essentially Chinese, Vietnamese, or Asian practice that stems from their ethnoracial culture. David, a 1.5-generation Chinese male, explained:

> DAVID: Asian culture likes to compare. They always want to outdo one another; my kids got to be better than your kids.
> INTERVIEWER: So your parents compared you to their friends' kids?
> DAVID: Always, always. Chinese parents do that a lot. When they get together, they just talk about their kids. "Oh, two of my kids have PhDs," or, "Two of my kids are medical doctors right now," stuff like that. They love that! They put a lot of pressure on their kids. Even within the sort of peer group within the same background, I was the only one that got into Berkeley.

David graduated from Berkeley and now works as an engineer who earns six figures. He said that his admission to Berkeley had given his parents tremendous bragging rights, especially since he was the only child among his parents' friends to gain admission to the top University of California (UC) school.

While boasting about their children's accomplishments may elevate the status of parents, it also intensifies the pressure on their children to give their parents something to boast about. Many 1.5- and second-generation Chinese and Vietnamese interviewees shared the common experience of not only feeling the pressure but also being annoyed that their parents continuously compare them to other children on hard and objective indicators of success such as grades, SAT scores, admissions to elite universities, occupational status, salaries, car brands, and homeownership. For example, Vanessa, a twenty-five-year-old, 1.5-generation Chinese woman who works as a contract administrator and earns an annual salary of $50,000, described her parents' conversations with other Chinese parents:

> All the things my parents talk about with their friends is, "Oh, so where do your daughters work?" and, "How much do they make a year?" That's the first thing they always ask. "What kind of car do they drive?" And, "Where do they live?" That's all they ask. That's what the adults talk about all the time. That's one thing that I don't like in the Chinese community.

Vanessa added that after the parents compare their children's accomplishments, they go home and tell their children about the accomplishments of other children: "So my parents were like, 'Well, Mr. So-and-So's daughter went to Harvard, and then the first job she has, she makes like $100,000 a year,' and blah blah blah. And I am like, 'Thanks, Dad.' That's actually what they talk about."

By circulating only the confirming narratives of children who have attained the success frame, Chinese and Vietnamese parents underscore that the reference group by which their children should measure their success is high-achieving coethnics rather than native-born, middle-class whites, blacks, or other second-generation groups. Consequently, the 1.5- and second-generation Chinese and Vietnamese children learn to measure their success against high-achieving coethnics, regardless of whether they agree with the success frame and regardless of how bothered they may be by the comparisons.

Another interviewee, Julia, a 1.5-generation Vietnamese, pointed to "Vietnamese culture" to explain her parents' constant comparison of her with coethnic children. Julia added that these routine comparisons reinforced the educational and occupational expectations they had for her:

> Well, I'm Vietnamese, so my parents' friends, all their friends' kids, are doctors and lawyers and engineers. So they just don't expect me to have a regular nine-to-five job. They expect me to do something, you know? They always come home with stories like, "Oh, you know, this guy's your age, and do you remember him? Well, now he's a doctor," or, "He's going get his doctorate, his PhD, or medical degree next year."

When parents evaluate their own children by constantly comparing them to others' children, they can effectively influence their children's educational and occupational aspirations. Hence, the circulation of confirming narratives functions as more than parental bragging rights; Chinese and Vietnamese immigrant parents are also reinforcing the success frame to their children and pointing out when they are falling short.

Christopher, a second-generation Chinese male who works as a financial analyst, is another example of how parental comparison of their children to high-achieving coethnics affects their aspirations. While he was growing up, Christopher's parents constantly reminded him that their friends' children were doing much better in school than he was. "My parents, when they get together with their friends, that's all they talk about is what their kids are doing and how well they are doing." Christopher admitted that repeatedly hearing the names and accomplishments of the children of his parents' friends' "piss[ed] the hell out of me. My mom would always tell me something like this, 'This guy's studying for his doctorate.'" However, his parents' consistent message also affected his educational and occupational pursuits: "Subconsciously it starts seeping in, because when they're talking, they say, 'So-and-So's a doctor, So-and-So does engineering.'"

Many parents in the United States may engage in bragging rights, but doing so is especially meaningful for immigrant parents who suffer from status inconsistency—the drop in status that immigrants experience when they leave their country of origin. Status inconsistency results from the linguistic and cultural barriers that block immigrants from transferring their educational credentials, skills, and prior work experience to their new host society.[2] Asian immigrants, because of their hyper-selectivity and high-selectivity, suffer disproportionately from status inconsistency and often find themselves taking jobs that are far lower in status relative to their professional occupations before they emigrated.[3] Hence, they turn to the educational and occupational achievements of their U.S.-born and U.S.-raised children to regain their premigration status. Parental bragging rights are therefore not only about immigrant children but also about immigrant parents. Boasting about their children to fellow ethnics is an acceptable way in which parents can remain humble about themselves while publicly reveling in the status they have regained through their children.

While positive narratives circulate widely among Chinese and Vietnamese immigrant parents, alternative narratives that deviate from the success frame are noticeably absent. Parents do not discuss children who perform poorly in school, do not gain admission to a top college, drop out of college, or work in low-status, low-wage jobs. Nor do they discuss their children who experience severe depression, have nervous breakdowns, or suffer from other mental health problems. They also remain quiet about teenage daughters who become pregnant, children who run away from home, or children who become involved with crime, gangs, or drugs. Because alternative narratives are conspicuously suppressed, both parents and their children accept the positive narratives as the norm for Chinese and Vietnamese children. Those who do not meet the commonly perceived norm appear to be outliers—a perception adopted by the 1.5- and second-generation children as well as their immigrant parents and coethnics.

Furthermore, the perceived norm is bolstered when the positive narratives of success are featured in the ethnic media, in newspapers and on news programs, and when those who achieve it are hailed as local heroes.[4] Through parental bragging rights and the selective depiction of the second generation in the media spotlight, exceptional has become the norm for Asian Americans. The exceptionally high perceived norm has costs for Asian Americans, however, at both the individual and the group level.

Saving Face by Lying About Accomplishments

As discussed in chapter 7, the social psychologist Carol Dweck found from several experiments that some students become so performance-oriented that they prefer to sacrifice learning in order to look smart to others.[5] These students are unwilling to trade a short-term decline in performance for the challenge of learning something new if the new challenge risks making them look like they lack intelligence or ability in front of others. For some students, the risk is so great that they lie about their test scores in order to look better to other students, even students they have never met.[6] The parental and social pressure on the children of Chinese and Vietnamese immigrants to attain the success frame may make them feel that they need to conform to the perceived norm in order to save face in front of others, including strangers.

During the in-depth interviews, we asked the 1.5- and second-generation Chinese and Vietnamese immigrant children questions about their educational history (including their performance in high school and college) among a host of other questions about their educational and life histories. As researchers, we assumed that, as with all interview studies and large-scale surveys, respondents provided honest answers. To put the interviewees at ease and encourage candor, we assured them that we would use pseudonyms throughout our writing to keep their identities anonymous and that their personal information would remain confidential as well. We also let them know before the start of each interview that they did not have to answer all of the questions, and in particular that they were free not to respond to any question that might cause them emotional discomfort or unease.

Fact-checking responses is prohibitively costly, if not impossible, for interview and survey studies. Although we did not fact-check our interviewees' answers about their level of education, we did notice obvious discrepancies in the account of one interviewee, to whom we gave the pseudonym Garrett. Garrett is a second-generation, Chinese-white multiracial male who works as an assistant manager at a retail business. When asked about his educational attainment, he faltered. When we tried to press him to clarify his answers, he began to fidget and get defensive, all the while trying to maintain an air of bravado. In addition, he was inconsistent in elaborating on his responses: he provided rich details about some portions of his educational background, yet quickly glossed over others. He was also unwilling to expand on points that seemed amiss, even when we gently but persistently pressed for clarification.

As Garrett recounted his educational history and aspirations, he noted with pride that he graduated from an exclusive boarding school on the East Coast, was admitted to a high-ranking private university, and now plans to attend law school. Throughout the interview, Garrett expressed his staunch belief in the success frame while underscoring how his educational background squarely fit it, including his attendance at an elite boarding high school, his nearly perfect SAT score of 1560, his stellar high school grades, and his belief that only degrees from elite private universities count. What Garrett neglected to reveal, however, was that he had fallen short of the success frame and in fact was lying about having graduated from a prestigious private university—and possibly about other educational claims he made, as we would later discover.

Garrett's childhood is one of the most privileged among our Chinese and Vietnamese interviewees. His mother hails from an upper-middle-class background in Hong Kong and works as a designer. His father, who is white, works as a surgeon. Garrett's parents held high educational expectations of him and presumed that he would earn a graduate degree. In their view, a bachelor's degree alone was "the contemporary equivalent of a high school diploma" and therefore not enough to propel him into a professional occupation. To give Garrett as many advantages as possible, his parents enrolled him in private schools and had him take the Preliminary Scholastic Aptitude Test (PSAT) in the seventh grade so that he would be well prepared to take the SAT exam in his junior year.

In the eighth grade, Garrett was accepted to an elite boarding school on the East Coast where the educational expectations and performance standards were higher than those he had ever faced. When we asked him to explain what he meant by this, Garrett replied that the school expected its students to attend the most elite universities, especially the Ivy League schools. He added that even strong private universities like Carnegie Mellon were considered "safety schools" for high-achieving students like him. Given his assessment of Carnegie Mellon, we were hardly surprised by his response when we asked whether he had ever considered attending a University of California school. Scoffing, Garrett answered, "Never a UC. That's just a California public school."

To complement his high grades, Garrett earned a nearly perfect score of 1560 on his SAT exam, but nearly perfect was not good enough for his mother, who was disappointed that he did not attain a 1600. In fact, his mother wanted him to retake the exam, but Garrett's guidance counselor assured her that 1560 was strong enough. Armed with high grades and a near-perfect SAT score, Garrett set his sights on admission to an Ivy League school, his first choice being Princeton. But to Garrett's astonishment and dismay, he was not admitted to Princeton, nor was he admitted to any of the Ivy League colleges to which he applied, so he settled for an East Coast private university to which he had applied as his "safety school." While prestigious and highly ranked, the school was not in the Ivy League, which was a grave disappointment to Garrett and his parents.

Because Garrett was so forthcoming about the details of his high school experience, we were surprised that he was reticent about discussing his college experience, which he tersely described as "disappointing," without further elaboration. In addition, when we asked him why he chose to return to southern California, he glibly replied, "Because I missed good Chinese food." During the interview, Garrett also mentioned that he is currently taking classes at a local public California university; in light of his previously stated elitist views on college rankings, we asked him why. He simply answered, "I want to keep my mind active."

Garrett was cryptic about his time in college, as well as his current student status, and when we pressed for clarification, he repeatedly veered off topic to avoid answering our questions. Finally, when we asked Garrett about his current retail job, he stressed that it is only a temporary position until he begins law school in the fall. He said that he had received two full scholarships to local California law schools, but is awaiting news of his admission to a prestigious private law school on the East Coast before deciding which offer he will accept. Garrett became increasingly jittery, anxious, and defensive over the course of the interview, but all the while maintaining an air of bravado that made us suspect he was holding something back.

In no other case did we feel compelled to verify an interviewee's claims about his or her educational background, but Garrett's mannerisms, evasiveness, and inconsistent responses compelled us to question his. We contacted the admissions office of the East Coast private university from which Garrett claimed to have graduated and learned that Garrett had been enrolled for one year (two semesters), took a leave of absence for a semester, and then returned for three more semesters. Other than those five semesters, there was no other record of his attendance there.

During the two-hour interview, Garrett never mentioned his leave of absence, nor did he mention another possibility: that he had graduated early after completing just five semesters of college. When we followed up on Garrett's claim that, after returning to southern California, he took additional classes at a public university to keep his mind active, that university's admissions office refused to verify any student's dates of attendance. Although we cannot know with certainty whether he graduated from the private university, as he claimed, we find it highly unlikely that he earned his BA in only five semesters, especially since he did not mention doing so during the interview. We suspect that Garrett did not graduate from the East Coast private university and that he returned home to complete his BA at the local California public university. We also suspect that Garrett fabricated portions of the interview in order to look better in front of the interviewer, whom he had never met and most likely would never see again.

As outlandish as it may seem that Garrett would have lied during the interview about graduating from an elite East Coast private university, his behavior is in line with Dweck's findings about students who lie about their test scores in order to look better in front of others, even those they have never met.[7] If Garrett lied about his accomplishments in order to save face in front of others, to mask shame about his "failure," and to buttress his self-worth in front of another, he was not unique in this regard. Sara Lee has also found that saving face is important to Korean Americans in New York, but in her study it was Korean immigrant parents—not their second-generation children—who felt compelled to lie about their children's educational and occupational achievements to other parents.[8] For example, a second-generation Korean female who attended a City University of New York college admitted that her mother was so embarrassed that she had not been offered admission to an Ivy League university that her mother lied to her Korean friends and told them that her daughter attended Columbia University instead. In a game of parental bragging rights, children's accomplishments become the weapon of choice, and thus some parents and children lie in order to look better in front of others—especially in front of their coethnic peers, for whom exceptional is the norm.

Disconfirming Evidence and Rejecting the Success Frame

The Asian American success frame is so constricting that only a very small minority attain it. However, the circulation of exclusively confirming narratives of success, the celebration of those narratives in ethnic newspapers and media, and the widespread use of high-achieving coethnics as the reference group who define success support the perception that the majority of Chinese and Vietnamese have in fact achieved it. Based on our in-depth interviews, we found that most 1.5- and second-generation Chinese and Vietnamese did not achieve the success frame and that many did not even come close. Some of our interviewees had not graduated from college and worked in semi-professional or entry-level jobs as technicians and salespersons. Others exhibited educational trajectories that had been far from smooth and direct. Some languished in college, while others churned in and out of college until they finally earned their degree well past the normative time of four years. Still others had dropped out of college altogether. Their stories, while not atypical, go unnoticed and unremarked upon by their immigrant parents, other immigrant children, their ethnic communities, the American mainstream media, and even social scientists.

Because these disconfirming narratives remained behind the veil, the cases of these immigrant children seemed like exceptions to Asian American exceptionalism. So strong is the perception that the success frame is normative for Asian Americans that the 1.5- and second-generation Chinese and Vietnamese who could not attain it, or who chose to forgo it altogether, find themselves at odds with their immigrant parents, their coethnics, and their ethnic identities. For them, the success frame is inextricably tied to their ethnoracial culture and identities, as Patrick's and Leah's cases reveal.

Patrick: "The Whitest Chinese Guy You'll Ever Meet" Thirty-six-year-old Patrick is a second-generation Chinese who works as a freelance artist. Patrick's mother had died when he was fourteen, so he was raised by his single father, who was not only a strict disciplinarian but also physically abusive. Much of the abuse stemmed from the discord between Patrick's desire to pursue a career in art and his father's insistence that Patrick pursue a more traditional high-status, economically stable career as a doctor, lawyer, or scientist. In his father's view, pursuing a career in art represented outright downward mobility because "he didn't see it as prestigious" and it was "nothing he could boast about." Patrick explained that his father "had other friends whose children were going to Harvard, and becoming scientists and doctors and lawyers, and boasting about their accomplishments. Being an artist seemed like too much of a step down."

Unlike his father, Patrick's mother had always supported his passion for art. After she died, Patrick found himself having to stand up to his father alone. His father was so adamantly opposed to his son's desire to pursue a career in art that he threatened not to pay for Patrick's college tuition if he accepted admission to the art academy he wished to attend. The only way Patrick could contrive to get his father to support his college education was to threaten to ask his uncles and grandparents on his mother's side for financial assistance, which would have caused his father even greater embarrassment. Patrick's father yielded and reluctantly agreed to pay for his tuition at the art academy.

In his work as a freelance artist, Patrick earns a six-figure salary, which makes it possible for his wife to stay at home full-time to care for their two preschool-age children. He and his wife have also purchased a home in an affluent Orange County suburb. Despite Patrick's prosperous career and status markers, his decision to become an artist has caused such a severe intergenerational rift that he and his father had not made amends and Patrick rarely speaks to his father.

Patrick attributes his father's reluctance to support his son's career in art to his adherence to Chinese culture, which, according to Patrick, considers it "really bad to choose to be an artist; it's really undesirable." Moreover, Patrick attributes his refusal to buckle under his father's pressure to his "being more American than Chinese." He explained, "I didn't buy into that. I grew up with the mind-set which I attribute to being more American culture, which is, I can choose to do anything I want; it's about individuality of freedom." Furthermore, Patrick racialized his decision to be an artist by describing himself as "the whitest Chinese guy you'll ever meet." Because he rejected and departed from the success frame, Patrick does not feel Chinese but rather like an ethnic outlier.

There are several noteworthy points about Patrick's description of his educational and occupational aspirations, pursuits, and trajectory. First, by claiming that he is "more American than Chinese" and "the whitest Chinese guy you'll ever meet," Patrick conflated national origin with race because, in his view, American equals white.[9] Second, Patrick attributed his willingness to buck the success frame as a culturally American act rather than a Chinese one, thereby essentializing ethnicity, national origin, and culture. Third, because Patrick did not fit the success frame, he distanced himself from his ethnicity as far as he was able by claiming to be the "whitest Chinese guy you'll ever meet." He has even gone to the extreme of changing the spelling of his ethnic surname so that clients would be unable to detect his ethnic identity prior to meeting him in person.

Although Patrick feels no attachment to his Chinese ethnicity, he is unable to completely relinquish it; insightfully, he remarked: "I'm an American at heart, but I'm Chinese, undeniable." Given his phenotype and features, Patrick believes that he cannot claim an unhyphenated American identity because he cannot physically escape his ethnoracial status. Patrick recognizes that while ethnic identification may be optional and symbolic for white Americans, the same is not true for nonwhite Americans, including Asian Americans.[10]

Like other 1.5- and second-generation Chinese and Vietnamese interviewees who reject or do not meet the success frame, Patrick disassociates from his ethnic identity by distancing himself from it. By doing so, however, he reinforces the association between Chinese ethnicity, the success frame, and achievement. Indeed, many of our 1.5- and second-generation Chinese and Vietnamese interviewees who do not fit the narrow parameters of the success frame reacted similarly: they avidly express that they do not feel Chinese, Vietnamese, or Asian because they believe that the success frame and ethnicity are inextricably linked.

Adam, whose case we discussed in the previous chapter, is another example. Recognizing that he cannot escape his ethnoracial status, Adam chooses to identify as "American Asian" rather than ethnically as Vietnamese because he does not consider himself "Vietnamese enough," especially in comparison to his high-achieving brother, whom Adam considers "much more Vietnamese" than he. Leah's case is similar. She too prefers to "opt out" of her ethnic identity and refers to herself as "Asian American."

Leah: Opting Out of One's Ethnic Identity   Twenty-five-old Leah is a second-generation Vietnamese who lives with her parents. She completed four years of community, earned an associate's degree, and described her work status as "self-employed." When we asked her to elaborate on her self-employed status, she explained that she does odd jobs such as babysit children, take care of elderly neighbors, and help people with film and theatrical productions whenever she has the opportunity.

As the only child of Vietnamese immigrants, Leah has carried the weight of her parents' expectations all of her life, and she feels that she has failed them miserably. She did not graduate from a UC school, as her parents had expected, and she does not hold a prestigious job as a doctor, lawyer, scientist, or engineer. Her parents have since adjusted their expectations and are hoping that she will become a teacher, but Leah has no interest in teaching and dreams of working behind the scenes in films. When we asked how her parents feels about her passion for films, she answered, "I'm so far off from what my parents want, so I might as well just make myself happy."

As a second-generation Vietnamese whose accomplishments are far afield from the success frame, Leah chooses to have as little contact as possible with the Vietnamese community, which, in her view, defines success by the "three M's: Money, Motorola, and Mercedes." Like Adam, Leah chooses to identify racially as Asian American rather than ethnically as Vietnamese or Vietnamese American because she conflates ethnicity with achievement. Both Adam and Leah have opted out of their ethnic identities because they do not fit the narrow parameters of the success frame—which they perceive as an essentialized component of their ethnic identity. Like Patrick, then, they feel like ethnic outliers. But in opting out of their ethnic identities, Leah and Adam reify the association between Vietnamese ethnicity and achievement.

This self-selection process of preferring a racial identification over an ethnic one has an unintended consequence: it provides specious support for the association between ethnicity and achievement. Because the 1.5- and second-generation Chinese and Vietnamese who do not fit the success frame are less likely to identify ethnically and are also less likely to engage with their ethnic communities, they become less visible to coethnics, less visible in the ethnic media, and also less visible to non-Asians more generally.

On the other hand, those who fit the frame are more likely to identify with and embrace their ethnic identity and more likely to have contact with coethnics; they are also more visible in their ethnic communities and are hailed as models for other coethnics. Consequently, they are more likely to stand out among coethnics and non-Asians alike. Their visibility is raised even further when Asian immigrant parents circulate narratives about their achievements among other parents—who then pass them down to their own children—and heightened when stories about their success are featured in ethnic newspapers and on ethnic news programs. Hence, the seemingly simple and inconsequential choice of racial versus ethnic identification—and the resultant behavior— can transform a once-specious association into a veritable one and strengthen the link between ethnicity and achievement.

Again, the stories of Adam and Leah resonated with members of other Asian ethnic groups, such as Koreans. Many 1.5- and second-generation Koreans who do not attend an elite university and have not secured high-salaried, professional jobs are embarrassed by their "failure" and, as a result, do not feel authentically Korean or Korean American. Instead, they choose to limit their interaction with coethnics and disassociate themselves from the Korean American community because they feel like underachieving anomalies who do not belong in the ethnic community.[11] Through this self-selection process, the success frame endures and remains entangled with ethnicity, despite the wealth of disconfirming evidence of 1.5- and second-generation Chinese, Vietnamese, and Asians who do not fit the frame or who actively resist it. By opting out of their ethnic identities and removing themselves from coethnic networks and their ethnic communities, the 1.5- and second-generation Chinese and Vietnamese who feel like anomalies, failures, or poor representatives of their ethnic community unwittingly reinforce the specious link between ethnicity and achievement.

Confirming and Disconfirming Stereotypes

When we asked the 1.5- and second-generation Chinese and Vietnamese interviewees about the reasons behind the academic attainment of their coethnics and of Asian Americans generally, the vast majority were quick to evoke culturally essentialist explanations, in spite of ample disconfirming evidence. Disconfirming evidence is ubiquitous among their friends and even more proximately within their nuclear and extended families. There are plenty of 1.5- and second-generation Chinese, Vietnamese, and Asians who are average or below-average high school students, but these students—who disconfirm stereotypes about ethnoracial status and academic achievement—are far less likely to be noticed than those who confirm the group-based stereotype of Asian American exceptionalism and the model minority. As social psychologists have noted, cognitive and social processes enable stereotypes to endure even amid disconfirming evidence.

Cognitive Processes

At the cognitive level, the psychologist Susan Fiske has shown, individuals have powerful, largely unconscious tendencies to remember people, events, and experiences that confirm their expectations.[12] So strong is this tendency that individuals often fail to see disconfirming evidence, or if they do see it, they often reinterpret it in stereotypic-confirming ways, ignore it, or dismiss it altogether as the exception.[13] In short, disconfirming evidence does not dislodge or change an individual's prior expectations; instead, individuals are more likely to reinterpret disconfirming evidence in a way that matches their expectation.

Drawing on Susan Fiske's research, sociologist Cecilia Ridgeway has explained how stereotypes about gender endure in modern society in spite of disconfirming evidence.[14] Ridgeway notes that changes in the content of people's perceptions of what the typical man and the typical woman are like— what Ridgeway describes as "nonmaterial culture" or "shared beliefs"—lag behind changes in their material experiences. So, in spite of evidence that gender stereotypes do not accurately depict the typical man or woman, our shared beliefs about gender continue to affect how we perceive men and women in what sociologists describe as a "cultural lag." Due to the cultural lag, gender stereotypes persist and reproduce gender inequality, even in fields, companies, and domains that lack a history of a gender hierarchy.

We extend Fiske's and Ridgeway's research to make a parallel argument about the persistence of stereotypes of Asian Americans. We find that Americans, both Asian and non-Asian, notice and remember Asian American students who excel in school and they overlook or ignore those who do not. So even when people come into contact with Asian Americans who do not fit the success frame, they tend either to reinterpret the evidence in stereotypic-confirming ways or to dismiss it altogether as the exception. To draw on Ridgeway's terminology, changes in "nonmaterial culture" lag behind people's material experiences; owing to that cultural lag, ethnoracial stereotypes about Asian Americans persist. We provide two examples of the cultural lag.

First, the stellar image of the high-achieving, exceptional student captures only a minority of Asian Americans, but the image reflects favorably on all of them. For example, a second-generation Chinese woman we interviewed admitted that she disliked high school and often cut classes. One day, when a teacher caught her leaving the school grounds and inquired where she was going, she lied and told him that she had to return home for a "family emergency." The teacher readily accepted her explanation and allowed her to leave without questioning her further. She knew that the teacher's willingness to let her go was atypical because her Latina friends were never accorded this benefit of the doubt; when they were caught outside of class, they were peppered with questions by teachers.

The prevailing assumptions that teachers hold of Asian American students as disciplined, hardworking, and high-achieving often lead them to overlook deviant behavior in these students, such as skipping classes and leaving school grounds. The cultural lag in teachers' belief about Asian American students as exceptional, despite their own material experiences, also perpetuates the ethnoracial stereotype of the model minority student.

Second, only a small minority of Asian American students receives straight A's in high school, attain perfect SAT scores, attend and graduate from a top UC school or an Ivy League school, and build a career in one of the four coveted professions: doctor, lawyer, engineer, or scientist. Most Asian Americans do not attain the success frame, and many depart widely from it. Even based on the Immigration and Intergenerational Mobility in Metropolitan Los Angeles (IIMMLA) data, we find that nearly two-fifths of 1.5- and second-generation Chinese do not graduate from college, and half of Vietnamese do not obtain a bachelor's degree. Yet Asians and non-Asians alike tend to overlook those Asian Americans who do not graduate from college, do not attain the success frame, and do not fit the model minority stereotype. These Asian Americans either go unnoticed or are dismissed as exceptions. The cultural lag keeps the association between ethnoracial status and achievement in place, despite the bevy of disconfirming evidence.

Social Processes

Stereotypes about Asian American exceptionalism persist not only through cognitive processes but also through social processes. Turning again to Ridgeway's explanation of the persistence of the gender frame, she notes that it is "the presumption that gender stereotypes are widely shared that allows people to use gender as a frame for coordinating their behavior with others. Doing so, however, also creates as a side effect social process that inhibits the public expression of stereotype-disconfirming behavior or information." These social processes operate in three interrelated ways that contribute to "public gender conformity."[15]

First, people are less inclined to publicly point out evidence that disconfirms a stereotype because they presume that certain stereotypes about gender, age, or race are widely shared. Second, this presumption encourages people to act in accordance with the stereotypes even when their views have begun to change, especially in public spaces or among strangers. Hence, even if an individual no longer believes in a gender stereotype, the presumption that others do leads him or her to act in accordance with presumptions about others' beliefs. So rather than pointing out the disconfirming evidence, people continue to publicly reaffirm the stereotype and behave accordingly. Third, people are less likely to mention disconfirming evidence because they fear that it might elicit negative or uncomfortable reactions from others. Hence, "public gender conformity" is a social process that contributes to the persistence of the gender stereotype, even when people's material experiences and beliefs no longer match the stereotype.

There are three ways in which the social processes that help explain the persistence of gender stereotypes also help to illuminate the persistence and perpetuation of stereotypes about Asian Americans. First, the presumption of widely held stereotypes about high-achieving Asian Americans leads people, including Asian Americans themselves, to fail to notice Asian Americans who do not fit the stereotype. Consider the teacher who caught the Chinese American student cutting class and leaving school grounds; he acted in accordance with the stereotype of the disciplined, high-achieving Asian American rather than in accordance with the student's deviant behavior. Or consider the teachers and administrators who presume that all Asian American students are high-achievers and place them in AP and honors classes, despite the students' past mediocre academic performance. In such actions, teachers publicly confirm the stereotype of the high-achieving Asian American student in spite of the disconfirming evidence before them.

Second, we add to Ridgeway's analysis by noting that the disconfirming evidence is not strong enough to dispel the Asian American exceptionalism construct because it is reinforced in gateway institutions such as schools, workplaces, and even the criminal justice system. Moreover, the model minority stereotype circulates through stories in both ethnic and mainstream American media that laud those Asian Americans who attain the success frame, especially those who start their quest for mobility from humble origins. With attention perpetually drawn to only those Asian Americans who have achieved extraordinary academic and occupational outcomes, even in spite of their socioeconomic disadvantage, the Asian American exceptionalism construct and model minority stereotype endure.

Third, the model minority stereotype and the Asian American exceptionalism construct are buttressed by the continued circulation of the larger narrative of the American Dream—the idea that anyone who is willing to work hard, delay gratification, and persevere can make it in this country.[16] Asian Americans who attain the success frame are heralded in the media as proof that the American Dream remains intact, that ethnoracial minority status does not obstruct mobility, that humble origins do not determine destiny, and that success and failure are the direct result of individual choices, effort, grit, and morality. In these ways, social processes perpetuate stereotypes about Asian Americans in spite of changes in material culture.

Summary

The success frame and success at all costs have sociologically significant consequences, and in this chapter we highlighted four of them. First, Chinese and Vietnamese immigrant parents intensify the pressure on their children to achieve the success frame by selectively circulating positive narratives of their children who attain it. Parents claim that they have bragging rights to these narratives, but in bragging about their children's success, they convey the message that the success frame is not only attainable but also normative. Moreover, by exclusively circulating successful narratives, both parents and children accept the success frame as the group norm and hold up those who attain it as the reference group by which children should measure their success. Those who do not meet the perceived norm or who choose to reject it thus seem like outliers with regard to Asian American exceptionalism.

Second, because the frame is racialized, 1.5- and second-generation Chinese and Vietnamese link the success frame with their ethnoracial identities and their culture. When they deviate from the success frame—either because they reject it or because they are unable to meet it—a host of negative consequences ensue, including intergenerational conflict, rejection of their ethnic identity, and avoidance of coethnics and their ethnic community. Third, because the success frame is exacting, some who fail to meet the perceived norm of success feel like failures, and some even lie about their accomplishments in order to save face and bolster their sense of self-worth in front of others. Fourth, because the dominant narrative about Asian American exceptionalism is buttressed by confirming cases that are lauded both privately and publicly, Asians and non-Asians alike fail to notice, remember, or remark upon the Asian Americans who depart from the success frame.

Most Asian Americans do not attain the success frame, but people tend to notice those who do, thereby reinforcing the model minority stereotype and the Asian American exceptionalism construct. Drawing from the rich literature on social psychology, we have shown how ethnoracial stereotypes persist through cognitive and social processes and how these processes reify the links between ethnoracial status, culture, and achievement. Because people are less likely to notice (cognitive processes) and mention or give credence to (social processes) the disconfirming evidence of Asian American exceptionalism, the Asian American model minority stereotype persists. The stereotype is buttressed even further when individuals reinterpret disconfirming evidence as the exception to the norm. Through both cognitive and social processes, stereotypes about Asian Americans lag behind material realities, and because of this cultural lag, the construct of Asian American exceptionalism endures, in spite of the wealth of disconfirming evidence.

The private and public circulation of positive narratives about Asian American success is an effective means of reinforcing the belief in Asian

American exceptionalism, the model minority stereotype, and the American Dream. The narratives give specious support to the perceived link between ethnoracial status and achievement. That highly selective narratives are publicly circulated in institutional contexts is particularly salient, since gateway institutions such as schools are where the children of immigrants seek to maximize their opportunities for social mobility. For some, the gateway institutions are where opportunities are realized, but for others who must battle negative stereotypes, these institutions are where opportunities are too often denied.[17]

~ Chapter 9 ~

The Asian American Achievement Paradox:
Culture, Success, and Assimilation

How do we explain the Asian American achievement paradox? That is the central question that we address in this book. More specifically, how have the children of Chinese immigrants and Vietnamese refugees attained such exceptional levels of education in spite of the diverse origins of their parents and in spite of the working-class backgrounds from which some of them hail? Understanding the pattern of second-generation convergence is vexing, given the variation among immigrant parents with respect to their immigration histories, educational selectivity, and resettlement patterns. Chinese immigrants in Los Angeles, on average, are a highly selected and highly educated group—what we refer to as "hyper-selected." Vietnamese refugees, in contrast, are highly selected but less educated than average Americans. In spite of these intergroup differences in the immigrant generation, the educational outcomes of the U.S.-born and U.S.-raised children of Chinese and Vietnamese immigrants converge.

Moreover, family socioeconomic status (SES) affects the mobility outcomes of the 1.5- and second-generation Chinese and Vietnamese differently than it does for other U.S. groups, defying the classic status attainment model. Because some Chinese immigrants and many Vietnamese refugees arrived in the United States with only an elementary school education, no English-language ability, and few skills and economic resources, they are relegated to menial jobs in ethnic restaurants and factories. Despite their socioeconomic disadvantages, their children have graduated at the top of their high school classes, earned admission to elite universities, and found work in high-salaried, professional occupations. Further highlighting the Asian American achievement paradox is our finding that the children of working-class Chinese parents achieve higher educational outcomes than their middle-class counterparts.

Unable to explain these outcomes, pundits and neoconservatives point to Asian culture and values: Asian culture values education more than other cultures do and therefore Asians invest more in education and work harder than other groups. In short, they achieve success the right way. Based on in-depth interviews in Los Angeles with 1.5- and second-generation Chinese and Vietnamese, 1.5- and second-generation Mexicans, and native-born whites and blacks, as well as survey data from IIMMLA, we find that culture matters, but not in the essentialist ways that these commentators posit. Culture is not an all-encompassing set of values, traits, beliefs, and behavioral patterns that are fixed and intrinsic to an ethnoracial group. Rather, culture emerges from unique historical, legal, institutional, and social psychological processes that are linked and that manifest in cultural institutions, frames, and mind-sets. Importantly, cultural formation is not static: culture continuously re-forms to adapt to the host-society context, and these adaptations influence opportunity structures, socioeconomic outcomes and assimilation.

We bring culture front and center in our sociological analyses of second-generation attainment and mobility but do not lose sight of the ways in which it is linked to key historical, legal, institutional, and social psychological processes. For example, a significant historical and legal change, the passage of the 1965 Immigration and Nationality Act, led to a major transformation in the educational selectivity of immigrants from East Asian countries, with profound implications for cultural formation. The hyper-selected Chinese immigrants who arrived after 1965 exhibit a dual positive educational selectivity: they are more highly educated than their counterparts who did not immigrate, and they are also more highly educated than the U.S. population. Although Vietnamese immigrants are not hyper-selected, they exhibit high educational selectivity; those who migrated to the United States after 1965 are far more likely to have graduated from college than their counterparts who did not immigrate.

Hyper-selectivity and high educational selectivity affect patterns of immigrant and second-generation adaptation by generating ethnic capital through ethnic resources, which benefit coethnics across class lines. Ethnic resources enable Chinese and Vietnamese immigrant parents to create and support a narrow success frame for their 1.5- and second-generation children. The frame entails graduating at the top of one's high school class, earning admission to an elite university, acquiring an advanced degree, and working in one of four high-status, high-paying fields: medicine, law, science, or engineering. So strict is the success frame that, on an "Asian scale," an A minus is considered an "Asian F."

The success frame is only effective, however, when it is supported by rein-forcement mechanisms in the form of strategies and resources. For example, Chinese and Vietnamese immigrant parents move to neighborhoods based exclusively on the strength of the public school district so that their children can take AP and honors classes in high school and thereby gain a competitive edge in college admissions. Parents also rely on tangible and intangible ethnic resources to support the success frame. Tangible resources include the elaborate system of supplementary education created by middle-class coethnics. The range of prices for these after-school programs in the ethnic community puts them within reach of working-class coethnics. Intangible resources include the dissemination of educationally relevant information that is preferentially available to coethnics, such as information about the ranking of neighborhood public schools, academic tracking, and the college admissions process. For U.S.-born Chinese and Vietnamese children whose immigrant parents have no more than an elementary school education, these supplemental ethnic resources and collective strategies mitigate their class disadvantage and provide them with a roadmap to mobility.

For some neoconservatives, the fact that Asian ethnic groups like the Chinese and Vietnamese create ethnic resources such as after-school academies appears to lend credence to their culturally essentialist argument that Asians value education and therefore create and invest in institutions that promote educational achievement and mobility. We counter that observation with a point that has been missing from the debate: the institutions and frames that immigrant groups import from their countries of origin and re-create in their host societies are not just ethnic institutions but *class-specific* ethnic institutions. The higher the selectivity of an immigrant group, the more likely it is that it will transport middle- and upper-middle-class-specific institutions and frames and adapt them in ways that are most conducive to mobility for group members and their offspring. Hence, cultural institutions and frames cannot be reduced to ethnic values, but instead should be understood as the outcome of the adaptation to the U.S. host society by hyper- and highly-selected immigrant groups.

The Social Psychological Consequences of Asian American Exceptionalism

Hyper-selectivity also has social psychological consequences, one of the most important being the emergence and perpetuation of ethnoracial stereotypes, which affect the performance of individual group members. The hyper-selectivity of Chinese immigrants drives the general American perception that all Chinese Americans are highly educated. In addition, because the Chinese are the largest Asian immigrant group and also because ethnic groups are racialized in the United States, this perception extends to Asian Americans as a group—and specifically to East Asians—who are stereotyped as smart, high-achieving, and hardworking. Asian American students thus benefit from stereotype promise—the promise that they will be viewed through the lens of a positive stereotype, which can enhance their performance.

We unveiled evidence of stereotype promise in gateway institutions such as schools. For instance, teachers and guidance counselors routinely perceive underachieving Chinese and Vietnamese students as smart and high-achieving, anointing them as deserving of placement on the most competitive academic tracks. Despite their prior lackluster academic performance, some Chinese and Vietnamese students subsequently rise to the occasion and work hard to meet the expectation of the exceptional model student, confirming their teachers' initial assumption about all Asian American students. Each instance of stereotype promise generates a self-fulfilling prophecy about Asian American exceptionalism and reproduces ethnoracial hierarchies at the high end of the educational distribution.

A second social psychological facet of the Asian American achievement paradox is that although 1.5- and second-generation Chinese and Vietnamese can skillfully navigate the rules of the American mobility game and achieve beyond normative measures of success, many do not feel successful. Many are dissatisfied with their achievements regardless of how much education they have attained or how much money they earn because they measure their success against higher-achieving coethnics. That they measure their achievements against high-achieving coethnics indicates that 1.5- and second-generation Chinese and Vietnamese do not turn to native-born whites as their reference group, as classic assimilation theories posit. Instead, they measure "vertically up" against higher-achieving siblings and coethnics, whose achievements far exceed native-born white standards.

We also learned that 1.5- and second-generation Chinese and Vietnamese experience tremendous pressure from their family and coethnic peers to attain exceptional outcomes, which they perceive as the norm. Regardless of how much they have achieved, most of the 1.5- and second-generation Chinese and Vietnamese are continually reminded of a coethnic sibling, cousin, or peer who has achieved more. The reminders come from parents who brag about children's achievements, from teachers in their schools, from instructors and tutors in after-school programs, and through accounts in the ethnic media that hail those who have attained the success frame as local heroes. The circulation of exclusively positive, confirming narratives leads immigrant parents and their children to believe that the success frame is not only attainable but also normative, and that any deviation from it is failure. Consequently, although high-achieving Chinese and Vietnamese are successful based on objective, normative indicators, they may not feel successful because their reference group is even-higher-achieving coethnics whose success far exceeds the standards of native-born Americans.

By contrast, as we learned from our interviewees, most 1.5- and second-generation Mexicans feel that they have achieved an extraordinary level of success, even though their educational and occupational achievements pale in comparison to those of their Chinese and Vietnamese counterparts. Employing the subject-centered approach, we discovered that 1.5- and second-generation Mexicans, who are less successful according to objective socioeconomic attainment indicators (such as years of education, earnings, and occupational prestige), feel successful because they compare their achievements "vertically down." Indeed, in comparing their achievements to those of their Mexican immigrant parents and of hypo-selected Mexican immigrants more generally, many 1.5- and second-generation Mexicans feel enormously successful. This finding from the subject-centered approach illuminates the flip side of the Asian American achievement paradox and highlights the importance of immigrant hyper-selectivity and hypo-selectivity to our understanding of the second generation's assessment of their progress. While they may differ with respect to their subjective assessment of their progress, neither second-generation Asians nor second-generation Mexicans measure their success against native-born whites revealing that native-born whites are not the reference group by which today's second generation measures their success.[1]

Third, those who do not, cannot, or choose not to meet the success frame feel like ethnic outliers.[2] Some even reject their ethnic identity because they do not feel like they are suitable representatives of their ethnic group: instead, they opt to identify racially as Asian American. Because of their phenotype and ethnoracial status, however, they do not feel that they can claim an unhyphenated American identity. The divergent patterns of ethnic versus racial identification can have unintended consequences. If those who meet the success frame are more likely to identify ethnically and those who do not are more likely to identify racially, then the specious link between ethnicity and achievement could become a veritable one. We may also find that the links between ethnicity and achievement and between race and achievement are not the same. Given this ethnoracial pattern, we should pay attention to the identity choices of Asian Americans on surveys and in-depth interviews since academic achievement may affect the racial and ethnic identification of Asian Americans. More research is needed if we are to fully understand the causal links between achievement and ethnic or racial identification.

A final social psychological consequence relates to mind-sets and what we refer to as an "achievement mind-set" among second-generation Asian Americans. Unlike their native-born white and black peers, Asian Americans receive contradictory messages about mind-sets at home and in school. At home, their immigrant parents stress a growth mind-set and believe that their children's outcomes can improve with increased effort. At school, however, teachers and peers make assumptions about Asian American students' innate talents and abilities based on their ethnoracial status, thereby emphasizing a fixed mind-set. The clash of mind-sets, coupled with the high expectations of parents, teachers, and both Asian and non-Asian peers, can result in low self-esteem and efficacy among 1.5- and second-generation Chinese and Vietnamese when they are unable to meet the high expectations and the perceived norm. Furthermore, low self-esteem and efficacy can afflict even those who have achieved extraordinary educational and occupational levels that far exceed what would have been predicted based on the status attainment model. For these high-achievers, the achievement mind-set can induce feelings of shame, embarrassment, and depression when they are unable to easily surmount new and unforeseen challenges.

Race and Achievement: Coupling, Decoupling, and Recoupling

In an ethnoracially diverse country like the United States, socioeconomic outcomes vary widely by group, and historically the benchmark used to determine a group's success or failure was that set by non-Hispanic whites and the extent to which groups converged to the non-Hispanic white mean. Whether measuring success by years of education, occupational status, income, or homeownership, non-Hispanic whites have been the reference group, and consequently achievement has been racially coded as white.

Earlier researchers argued that African American and Latino students who excel in school are accused of "acting white," labeled as "turnovers," and excluded by their coethnic peers.[3] Anthropologist Signithia Fordham reasoned that the phrase "acting white" is a subordinate group's derogatory response to resistance to conformity and a rejection of "the negative claims of the larger society."[4] Fordham and other scholars argued that it is the willful refusal to learn—rather than the inability or failure to learn—that adversely affects the academic outcomes of African Americans and Latinos.[5]

Later research by sociologists discredited the argument that acting white is an anti-achievement ideology that reflects a willful rejection of mainstream values and norms.[6] Most prominently, through her extensive research on low-income African American and Latino high school students, the sociologist Prudence Carter found that ethnoracial minority youths do not equate academic achievement with acting white but rather with certain cultural styles and tastes in music, dress, food, and speech patterns.[7] Moreover, these youths held the same aspirations as their middle-class counterparts; however, they lacked the publicly available institutional resources and the dominant cultural capital to realize their aspirations for upward mobility. Their low family socioeconomic status affected their opportunities for mobility in a way that differed from how low SES affected 1.5- and second-generation Chinese and Vietnamese in our L.A. study.

Despite sociologists' efforts to decouple race and academic achievement, the pairing has endured. Today, however, academic achievement has been decoupled from acting white and recoupled and re-racialized as "acting Asian" or "the Asian thing."[8] The "hard" facts about Asian Americans' educational attainment—from their academic achievement to their overrepresentation in the country's elite high schools and universities—have contributed this recoupling of race and achievement. That they have attained successful outcomes despite their nonwhite status has led neoconservatives to hail Asian Americans as the model minority that has achieved success in spite of their minority ethnoracial status. This assessment is even more widely popular than we had suspected:

most of our 1.5- and second-generation Chinese and Vietnamese interviewees agreed with the Asian American exceptionalism argument and attributed their academic achievement to their ethnoracial culture. They too believed that "Asians value education" more than other groups.

The recoupling of race and achievement has consequences for Asians as well as for other groups; racializing achievement as Asian serves as the antithesis to coupling anti-achievement with blacks and Latinos. It is worth remembering that the model minority trope emerged in tandem with the "culture of poverty" thesis in the mid-1960s. Juxtaposing the "success" of one ethnoracial minority group against the "failure" of another generated the question: if Asian Americans can get ahead in spite of their ethnoracial minority status, then why are African Americans unable to do the same? Culture became the facile answer. However, as we have discussed, culture takes the form of institutions, frames, and mind-sets, emerges from immigrant selectivity, and adapts to fit the host-society context. We underscore this point by noting that, if culture—divorced from immigrant selectivity in a host society—can explain the exceptional academic outcomes of ethnoracial groups, then we should expect similar outcomes in different host-society contexts. However, this is not the case.

The global comparative perspective we adopted reveals that Koreans in the United States exhibit high levels of educational attainment while academic outcomes are abysmal for their counterparts in Japan, who fall far behind their Japanese peers.[9] Unlike the hyper-selected Korean immigrants to the United States, ethnic Koreans in Japan share a history of involuntary migration. As a population that is not of Japanese lineage, ethnic Koreans experience institutional discrimination that blocks their opportunity structure, regardless of their native-born status or how many generations they have lived in Japan. Similarly, the children of Chinese immigrants in the United States are among the highest achievers, but their counterparts in Spain exhibit the lowest educational aspirations and expectations of all second-generation groups, including Ecuadoreans, Central Americans, Dominicans, and Moroccans. In Spain, nearly 40 percent of second-generation Chinese expect to complete only basic secondary school—roughly the equivalent of tenth grade in the United States.[10]

Employing a global comparative perspective illustrates that culture is not essential to a particular group, nor is it fixed; rather, it emerges from the structural circumstances of migration (such as immigrant educational selectivity) and adapts to the migrant-receiving context (including perceptions about mobility and group position in an ethnoracial hierarchy). Chinese immigrants in Spain are selected from a less-educated peasant group, in stark contrast to the hyper-selected Chinese immigrants in the United States. Their lower level of educational selectivity places Chinese immigrants in Spain at a disadvantage out of the starting gate. Moreover, given Chinese immigrants' perception of a closed opportunity structure in Spain—especially for visible minorities—they have no faith that a postsecondary education or university degree will guarantee a professional occupation in the mainstream labor market, so they have turned to entrepreneurship as the route to upward mobility and encourage their second-generation children to do the same. Hence, Spain's Chinese immigrants adopt an entirely different success frame whose mobility strategy is entrepreneurship rather than education. Their frame is supported by ethnic hometown associations and transnational business networks in much the same way the U.S. success frame is supported by an ethnic system of supplementary education and educational networks that are transported from the country of origin and recreated to best fit the host society context.

The global comparative perspective highlights counterfactuals that underscore that it is not Chinese, Vietnamese, or Asian culture that promotes exceptional educational outcomes. Instead, Asian Americans' exceptional outcomes result from their hyper-selectivity and high immigrant selectivity and the cultural institutions, frames, and mind-sets that they construct and reinforce as a consequence. That these emerge in a favorable host society context is key; mobility through educational attainment thus becomes possible for Asian Americans in a way that it is not similarly possible for second-generation Asians in other countries and for other second-generation groups in the United States. These linked processes have raised the status of Asian Americans from unassimilable in the early twentieth century to exceptional in the twenty-firsts reflecting their "racial mobility."[11]

The Double-Edged Sword of Positive Stereotypes and the Racialization of Achievement

Given the positive connotations of Asian American exceptionalism and the model minority stereotype, skeptics have asked: What is wrong with positive stereotypes? How can it possibly be disadvantageous to be perceived as smart, hardworking, and high-achieving? Even the majority of our Chinese and Vietnamese interviewees embraced the positive stereotypes, which they felt worked to their advantage in school and in the workplace. In this section, we reiterate our argument about the negative consequences of positive stereotypes and the racialization of achievement. These are "double-edged swords" that may appear to be complimentary and advantageous but in fact are dangerously fallacious and disadvantageous for not only Asian Americans (including those who are high-achieving) but also other ethnoracial groups.

First, not only is it specious reasoning to make group-based claims from partial data on only a segment of the population, but it is also fallacious because such claims homogenize and essentialize all members of an ethnoracial or immigrant group without considering individual or within-group variation. Not all Asian ethnic groups are high-achieving, and not all members of even the highest-achieving Asian ethnic groups attain exceptional educational outcomes. On the first point, and underscoring the enormous heterogeneity within the Asian American population, Cambodians, Hmong, and Laotians are Asian ethnic groups that exhibit lower educational attainment than the U.S. average, and these groups also have higher high school dropout rates than blacks and Latinos in the United States.[12] On the second point, it is critical to remember that while more than three-fifths of 1.5- and second-generation Chinese in Los Angeles have attained a college degree or higher, two-fifths have not graduated from college. The variation in outcomes within second-generation groups is just as critical as the variation among them.

Deracializing and de-ethnicizing achievement would provide space for the recognition that most Asian Americans are not exceptional and that most do not achieve extraordinary educational and occupational outcomes. When the disconfirming evidence of Asian American exceptionalism and the vast heterogeneity within the Asian American population are acknowledged, Asian Americans whose outcomes do not fit the success frame's narrow parameters might no longer feel like failures or ethnoracial anomalies. Such acknowledgment, however, is a two-way street: coethnics must be willing to acknowledge those who do not fit the strict parameters of the success frame and accept alternative frames for achievement.

Second, the success frame and stereotype promise are double-edged swords. On the one hand, Asian Americans' overrepresentation in elite institutions and in select professional occupational niches appears to validate the effectiveness of their success frame and lend credence to the belief that positive stereotypes only enhance outcomes. However, the stereotypes can also constrain Asian Americans from breaking out of the success frame. Despite the positive qualities associated with Asian Americans as students and employees, they are also perceived to lack the creativity, innovation, and social skills that would make them strong leaders, even in occupational niches in which they are overrepresented as employees. Moreover, the stereotypes may reduce the number of opportunities Asian Americans have to develop their creativity, innovation, and social skills. Both sides of this double-edged sword—others' perceptions of Asian Americans combined with blocked opportunities—can hinder Asian Americans from developing their leadership potential and perpetuate the severe underrepresentation of Asian Americans in leadership positions. The unique disadvantages of Asian Americans stemming from their positive stereotypes may have created a "bamboo ceiling" that is difficult for them to crack as they vie for management and leadership positions, not unlike the glass ceiling faced by women.

Third, positive stereotypes raise the expectations of a group, and those elevated expectations become the normative standard by which we judge the attainment of individuals from that group. We reduce the significance of achievement markers like a perfect SAT score, a grade point average (GPA) of 4.0, or admission to an Ivy League university if they are attained by an Asian American. If you are Asian American, we now expect that you *should* have attained a perfect SAT score, perfect grades, and admission to an elite university. Decoupling ethnoracial status from achievement would enable us to recognize the effort that accompanies the high educational outcomes of some Asian Americans (growth mind-set), rather than continue attributing these outcomes to the innate characteristics of all Asian Americans (fixed mind-set).

Fourth, decoupling ethnoracial status and achievement would have significant implications for mental health, including self-esteem. In a study of college students at elite universities, Douglas Massey and his colleagues found that while Asian college students had the highest academic outcomes, they exhibited the lowest levels of self-esteem compared to their white, black, and Latino peers. Moreover, despite their higher GPAs, Asian American students were the least likely to see themselves as good students.[13] As we have shown, this is because Asian Americans use high-achieving coethnics—rather than whites, blacks, or Latinos—as the reference group by which they measure their success. This exceptionally high-achieving reference group often makes Asian Americans feel inadequate and "not good enough." Decoupling ethnoracial status and achievement might provide more room for Asian Americans to boost their self-esteem in this regard.

Furthermore, if academic achievement is no longer racially coded as acting Asian and an Asian thing, Asian Americans might be more willing to measure their success against a more reasonable barometer, as some of our interviewees did, and follow different pathways to achieve success. They and their parents might learn to relinquish their exclusive focus on performance-based measures of success; if doing so helps Asian American youth to see themselves as good students, their confidence might be enhanced. And enhanced self-confidence might help reduce the rates of depression among Asian American students who, like Hung and Adam, feel like failures because their performance does not meet the perceived norm.

We highlighted the cases of Adam and Hung, both of whom experienced depression and admitted to feelings of low self-esteem, but more than four times as many interviewees told us that they had experienced severe depression, and a few even revealed that they had had a complete nervous breakdown at some point in their young lives. We should note that speaking with us was the first time that most of our interviewees had publicly admitted their experiences and feelings. We were both surprised by and grateful for their openness and trust, and because of their willingness to come forward, we felt compelled to shed light on these issues rather than ignore them as outlying cases. We should add that it is entirely possible that other interviewees had suffered from depression at some point in their lives but did not reveal this experience in the interview. After all, not only did we not ask about depression directly in our in-depth interview questionnaire, but the stigma associated with depression and mental illness, especially among the foreign-born, makes it likely that some interviewees would have been reticent to discuss these issues.

Fifth, the decoupling of ethnoracial status and achievement among Asian Americans has implications for other groups, especially for blacks and Latinos, who are often juxtaposed in direct opposition to Asian Americans and stereo-typed as low-achieving. It would also benefit white students, who are deemed less academically inclined than their Asian American counterparts, especially in metropolitan areas that have experienced high rates of Asian immigration, such as Los Angeles and the San Francisco Bay Area.[14]

In spite of the cultural lag between people's material experiences and their stereotypical perceptions of out-groups, our conscious efforts to acknowledge disconfirming evidence, both cognitively and socially, may begin to break the specious link between ethnoracial status and achievement. These efforts must go beyond the individual, and must also be reinforced in gateway institutions where opportunities to maximize potential is unequally distributed.

Theoretical Implications

We draw four theoretical implications from our research. First, class and cul-ture should not be studied as discrete variables. Sociologists have paid ample attention to the role of class—as measured by markers of family socioeconomic status such as parental education, occupational status, and family income—in influencing intergenerational mobility outcomes. Family SES reproduces inter-generational advantages and disadvantages because it determines the level and type of resources that parents are able to mobilize and invest in their children's human, social, and cultural capital.[15] In its impact on parenting styles and practices, family SES also benefits middle-class children, since the dominant cultural capital is favored in mainstream gateway institutions such as schools.[16]

But for the children of immigrants, another dimension of class is critical: the educational selectivity of their immigrant group, which has three unique consequences for them. First, it affects the group's mode of incorporation. Whether the group is hyper-selected or hypo-selected will determine how the group (not just an individual group member) is received by the host society's government, how it is perceived by the native hosts, and how it is supported by the preexisting ethnic community. Second, immigrant educational selectivity affects which cultural frames, institutions, and mind-sets an immigrant group transports from its country of origin and re-creates in its host society. Third, educational selectivity affects the development of ethnic capital and the type of ethnic resources that a group generates to support cultural frames. Ethnic resources differ from class resources because they extend beyond the family, cut vertically across class lines, and become available to all coethnics. In these three ways, immigrant groups like the Chinese and Vietnamese can circum-vent class disadvantage and buttress their children's educational attainment in ways that defy the classic status attainment model.

In stressing that cultural frames are not intrinsic to an immigrant or ethno-racial group, we take an emergent approach to the role of culture and argue that cultural frames, institutions, and mind-sets emerge from the unique historical, legal, and structural circumstances of a group's migration and adaptation to the host society. Hence, whether a group is hyper-, high-, or hypo-selected educationally affects its ability to develop ethnic capital, which in turn influences its incorporation at the macro level (through the group's mode of incorporation), at the meso level (through institutions, both public and ethnic), and at the micro level (through social psychological processes, including stereotype promise and mind-sets).

The second theoretical implication of our research is that an immigrant group's educational selectivity also affects social psychological processes, including the formation and persistence of ethnoracial stereotypes. Hyperselected immigrant groups are more likely to be positively stereotyped by members of the host society, while hypo-selected immigrants are more negatively stereotyped. As previous research has shown, negative stereotypes can affect the behavior of negatively stereotyped groups. Our research shows that the opposite is also true: positive stereotypes can affect the behavior of positively stereotyped groups like Asian Americans. But as we have cautioned, those positive stereotypes come with high costs and can constrain Asian Americans. There are also other costs associated with positive stereotypes; for instance, while the 1.5- and second-generation Chinese and Vietnamese have attained exceptional educational outcomes and are entering professional fields in disproportionately high numbers, many do not feel as successful as other Americans with similarly high levels of educational and occupational achievement.

This dovetails with the third theoretical implication of our research: there is no disputing the value of the subject-centered approach in the study of success and mobility among the second generation. Employing a subject-centered approach with our interviewees enabled us to look beyond normative attainment measures to identify the sources of one facet of the Asian American achievement paradox—why some high-achieving Asian Americans do not feel successful, despite their high socioeconomic outcomes. Relying on large-scale survey data and using conventional statistical models would not have captured the immediate and delayed effects of a narrow success frame. By employing a subject-centered approach, we were able to provide a more sophisticated understanding of the meaning of success for the 1.5- and second-generation Chinese and Vietnamese in Los Angeles and the pathway they are likely to pursue to achieve it. We are certainly not suggesting that researchers abandon conventional measures of success and mobility; rather, we propose that using a dialectical approach to measuring success and mobility can enrich our findings by unveiling sources of the seeming paradox and help us draw a more multi-faceted portrait of the new second generation's mobility trajectories.

Finally, our study contributes to the concepts of segmented assimilation and minority cultures of mobility. The classic means of status attainment is class reproduction, which leads either to upward mobility (becoming acculturated and economically integrated into the normative structures of mainstream middle-class America) or to downward mobility (becoming stalled or trapped in the margins of American society). A third possibility is socioeconomic integration into the white middle class by relying on ethnic norms, social ties, and institutions.[17] And a fourth possibility—theorized by the minority culture of mobility—is integration beyond the white middle class by utilizing ethnic strategies and resources.[18]

From a segmented assimilation perspective, outcomes vary based on the interaction between group-specific contexts of exit and reception. The context of exit entails a number of factors, including the social class status already attained by the immigrants in their homelands, the premigration resources that immigrants bring with them (such as money, knowledge, and job skills), and immigrants' means of migration, motivation, aspirations, and practices. The context of reception includes the national-origin group's position in the system of ethnoracial stratification, the government policies that affect the group, labor market conditions, public attitudes, and the strength and viability of the group's ethnic community in the host society. Both sets of factors are influenced by immigrant selectivity, which can facilitate upward mobility and reinforce social inequality.

As we have shown, the hyper-selectivity of Chinese immigrants enhances the capacity of the ethnic community to generate ethnic capital by generating ethnic strategies and resources to support a specific success frame. Thus, it is not the case that the success frame of Chinese immigrants and their children is superior to that of their Mexican counterparts, but rather that the Chinese have greater access to supplemental strategies and resources to support their narrow success frame. Hyper-selectivity enables groups to create distinctive ethnic institutions and adaptation strategies that support a strict success frame across class lines for group members, who thereby gain mobility opportunities independent of individual and family socioeconomic characteristics.

We extend segmented assimilation theory by noting that while the children of Chinese and Vietnamese immigrants attain mobility by using ethnic institutions and networks, the reference group they use for measuring their success is not native-born, middle-class whites. Instead, they turn to high-achieving coethnics, and they measure their successful assimilation and model their mobility trajectories after coethnics. Hence, the children of Chinese and Vietnamese immigrants employ a distinct "minority culture of mobility" to attain exceptional educational and occupational outcomes.[19] Using coethnic mobility prototypes, they pave a uniquely Asian American mobility trajectory that takes them beyond the achievements of middle-class whites, who are the reference group in both the classic and the segmented assimilation models, and against whom group progress is typically evaluated.

Practical and Policy Implications

We have identified five practical and policy implications of our research findings. First, the educational outcomes of the 1.5- and second-generation Chinese and Vietnamese underscore the significance of supplemental resources, both tangible and intangible, beyond those available within the family and in public institutions to boost the outcomes of the children of immigrants. Institutional resources in U.S. public schools—especially those in poor and working-class communities—are dwindling and are spread too thin to adequately service all students. Furthermore, schools are not equally equipped with the institutional resources that are vital to academic success—such as AP and honors classes, zero periods, College Bound programs, seasoned teachers and guidance counselors, and extracurricular activities.[20]

Exacerbating class-based inequalities is the expectation on the part of schools that parents will help to fill the resource gap, even though poor and working-class parents are ill equipped to do so given their lack of human, financial, and cultural capital. Middle-class parents, by contrast, are doing exactly that: they have the economic resources to boost their children's educational outcomes by paying for supplementary education, including tutoring, SAT prep courses, and summer school. And those who can afford to do so also provide their children with private lessons in tennis, lacrosse, ballet, and so on, to give their children a well-rounded, competitive profile when they apply to college.[21] Poor and working-class parents (native and immigrant alike) lack the class resources to enroll their children in supplemental educational programs and extracurricular activities, leaving their children acutely disadvantaged.

Some hyper-selected immigrant groups, such as the Chinese and Koreans, are able to create ethnic resources, thereby extending supplemental resources to both middle- and working-class coethnics, and mitigating the class disadvantage of the latter.[22] We find that supplemental educational resources—whether class- or ethnic-based—are necessary to give children the educational boost to help them get ahead. Although Asian immigrant parents may appear to "overly cultivate" their children, they do so because they strongly believe that their approach to supplementary education gives their children the best chance to attain the success frame and also increases the odds that they will be shielded from potential bias and discrimination in the labor market.

Before proceeding, we add an important caveat and word of caution. Our study focused on the children of Chinese and Vietnamese immigrants in Los Angeles, where ethnic communities are sizable, ethnic capital is abundant, and strong ethnic economies create tangible and intangible resources. Those who do not live in metropolitan areas with strong coethnic communities lack access to comparable ethnic resources to enhance their educational and mobility outcomes. Lacking ethnic capital in their communities (or lacking ethnic communities altogether), poor and working-class Asian immigrants and their children must rely exclusively on publicly available resources in nonmetropolitan areas. With no access to ethnic resources, their prospects for mobility may be just as precarious as those of working-class children from non-Asian and non-hyper-selected ethnoracial backgrounds. We should not turn a blind eye to this segment of the Asian American population, nor can we ignore poor Asian American groups like Cambodians, Laotians, and Hmong, who drop out of high school at higher rates than African Americans and Latinos. Public policies should not ignore the children of Asian immigrants for whom supplemental resources are out of reach, especially in those environments where these additional resources are critical to attaining intergenerational mobility.

Second, our study calls attention to multiple measures of success. Success should be measured by more than just outcomes; we must also consider "starting points" and the degree to which the children of immigrants attain intergenerational mobility, which is especially relevant for hypo-selected immigrant groups like Mexicans. If we measure success as progress from one generation to the next, Mexicans are the most successful. Without question, the educational gains made by 1.5- and second-generation Mexicans in Los Angeles are extraordinary; they have nearly doubled the high school graduation rates of their immigrant parents, more than doubled the college graduation rates of their fathers, and more than tripled the college graduation rates of their mothers. In mathematical terms, we should pay attention to the delta (the incremental change from one generation to the next) rather than just the sum (the outcome).[23] For a child of Mexican immigrants who was raised in East Los Angeles with immigrant parents who have no more than an elementary school education, graduating from high school or earning an associate's degree from a community college is an enormous accomplishment because it denotes intergenerational mobility.

The way in which we measure success—the absolute sum or the delta—has public policy implications. If we focus exclusively on the absolute sum, it is easy to paint a pessimistic portrait about immigrant assimilation, especially Mexican immigrant assimilation. That Mexicans and their second-generation children have not reached parity with native-born whites gives nativists cause to fear that they will never catch up and may soon become a perpetually poor underclass. This fear could reduce support for immigration reform and discourage support for policies that would aid immigrant adaptation. If we focus on the delta, however, the portrait of progress changes, as does our ability to reframe immigration reform debates. By focusing on intergenerational mobility, we can illustrate just how far the children of Mexican immigrants have come from their parents and perhaps dispel fears about Mexican immigrants' failure, inability, or refusal to assimilate.

It is worth underscoring that these educational gains made by the second generation are based entirely on their use of public school resources, including College Bound programs, zero periods in which students learn about the college application process, and instrumental teachers, guidance counselors, and coaches. It is also worth asking how much more they would have attained had they had additional resources at their disposal. In other words, would the children of Mexican immigrants have made even greater educational gains with the type of supplemental resources and strategies available to the children of Chinese and Vietnamese immigrants? This question is particularly relevant because despite the impressive gains made by the second generation, the lack of supplemental resources may impede the mobility of the third and later generations. If we do not wish to see the children and grandchildren of hypo-selected immigrants stall in their progress, we must consider policies that would provide additional resources for them so that the descendants of Mexican immigrants may continue their pattern of upward mobility.[24]

Third, the hyper-selectivity of an immigrant group is consequential not only because it helps create supplemental educational resources and strategies for their second-generation children, but also because it helps to generate businesses in the ethnic community and beyond.[25] Although ethnic entrepreneurship exists in all immigrant groups (including those that are hypo-selected), the role of entrepreneurship in community building and neighborhood development has not been formally incorporated into local planning and development processes.[26] This is an area that would also benefit from public policy intervention.

Fourth, while our study has underscored the importance of subjective assessments of success, we recognize that objective indicators of achievement—college education, income, occupational status, homeownership—will continue to be used by social scientists, policymakers, and the American public as markers of success. This is why we have emphasized policy interventions that would provide supplemental resources for both Asian and non-Asian groups. Nevertheless, as we have shown here, the subject-centered approach and subjective evaluations of success or failure, especially given the unique mental health problems that some high-achieving Asian Americans face, lead to important insights and findings. High schools and universities should pay special heed to subjective patterns and trends, especially given the over-representation in the country's most competitive elite universities of Asian American students, many of whom feel compelled to meet an exceptionally high perceived norm that may not be realistic.

By offering professional counseling services in high schools and colleges that target the needs of the children of immigrants, and particularly the children of Asian immigrants, we may be able to more adequately address this population's problems with depression, low self-esteem, and low self-efficacy, which often go unreported, undiagnosed, and untreated. For example, Asian American children under the age of eighteen were less likely than white, African American, and Latino children to receive mental health care, despite their higher levels of depression. We also note that the onus must not fall exclusively on institutions; the responsibility must also be shared with Asian immigrant parents and their adult children, who must become more receptive to utilizing these services rather than stigmatizing mental health issues as a sign of weakness and deficiency or a cause for shame. This change of attitude will not happen immediately, but at the very least, cohort change should lead to more openness about and receptiveness to professional counseling.

On a related note, we should pay attention to the number of suicides among young Asian Americans—the rate is alarmingly high, especially at elite universities. For example, between 1996 and 2000, the University of

Michigan had sixty-nine student deaths due to suicide, and sixteen of those students (23 percent) were Asian. Most troubling is that the number of suicides of Asian students has been rising while the number of suicides among white, African American, and Latino students has been declining. Among high school students, thoughts of suicide are higher among Asian American students: in 2012, 19 percent had seriously considered suicide in the previous year, compared to 16 percent of all high school students.[27] Moreover, about 4 percent of Asian American students reported a suicide attempt that required medical attention within the previous year, compared to 2 percent of all high school students. To emphasize, making counseling services readily accessible in high schools and universities will help high-achieving Asian American students cope better with the stress and pressure they may feel to meet performance goals and attain the success frame.

Fifth, our study has shown that many of our interviewees uncritically embraced the model minority stereotype and felt that it worked to their advantage in school and in the workplace. We cannot emphasize strongly enough that the same positive stereotypes associated with the model minority construct that may have worked to their advantage as students or early in their professions will become disadvantageous for them as they advance in their professions. Even second-generation Asian Americans who have attained the success frame may find themselves bumping up against the bamboo ceiling as they face ethnoracial marginalization in a new domain. For example, a study of bias in science, technology, engineering, and math fields shows that the stereotype of Asians as good at science helps Asian American women with their students but not with their colleagues. Asian American women also felt more pressure to act "feminine"— demure and passive—and received more push back from colleagues when they did not.[28] Moreover, as the second generation comes of age and has children, they may find that the success frame and the ethnic strategies and resources that they have relied upon to attain mobility are no longer relevant for the third and later generations. Just like their immigrant parents, who struggled to ensure that their children would attain middle-class status, the second generation will need to find new ways to organize ethnically and panethnically to respond to ethnoracial stereotypes—including the model minority stereotype, which both expects and discounts exceptional achievements from Asian Americans.

Looking Ahead: The Evolving Meaning of "Asian American"

We close by looking ahead and pointing to the most pressing, promising, and fruitful lines of empirical and theoretical inquiry that could guide future research.

First, we advocate for more comparative research on ethnic groups in different receiving contexts across countries and across metropolitan areas within the United States.[29] As we have shown in our study, contexts matter. The

United States has attracted very different streams of international migration in the past fifty years, in comparison to countries such as Britain, France, Germany, Sweden, Spain, Italy, Japan, and Singapore. Within the United States, metropolitan contexts also differ vastly, even in cities with large Asian immigrant populations like Los Angeles and New York. Moreover, research could compare second-generation outcomes in traditional destinations and in new destinations, which may not yet have a strong ethnic community to buttress their educational outcomes.

As we have noted, to remain intact the success frame must be supported by reinforcement mechanisms beyond the family, in the absence of which it will change. If Asian immigration continues to be hyper-selected in the United States, then it is likely that the success frame will continue to be buttressed by newcomers who will replenish it with the ethnic strategies and resources needed to sustain it. Elsewhere, however, success frames face different challenges. For instance, Chinese immigrants to Spain and Italy are neither highly educated nor highly selected, and therefore they and their second generation adopt a different success frame and mobility strategy; moreover, host-society reception in these European countries differs from that in the United States. As a result of these conditions, educational outcomes among the Chinese second generation in Italy and Spain are much poorer. In Spain, a longitudinal study of second-generation immigrant children showed that the children of Chinese immigrants have lower educational ambition and lower attainment than youths of every other nationality.[30] In Prato, Italy—the city with the highest concentration of Chinese immigrants—only 60 percent of the Chinese children completed middle school, which is the end of compulsory school attendance in Italy.[31] Studying the same ethnic groups in different national and local contexts will help to identify the mechanisms that produce particular educational, occupational, and political outcomes in different host-society contexts.[32]

Second, while we have used the broad panethnic label "Asian American," we recognize that it encompasses a diversity of ethnic groups—from fourth-generation Japanese Americans to first-generation Cambodian Americans—whose immigrant backgrounds, experiences, and socioeconomic outcomes diverge markedly. Although we found convergence in the experiences of 1.5- and second-generation Chinese and Vietnamese, experiences differ among other Asian ethnic groups, such as Cambodians, Hmong, and Laotians. These groups arrived in the United States with much lower levels of human capital than the U.S. average and have very high poverty rates. Their extremely disadvantaged economic status, combined with their distinctive features and darker skin, may deny them the type of symbolic capital from which lighter-skinned, more privileged East Asian ethnic groups benefit. It is entirely possible that poorer and darker-skinned Asians suffer from stereotype threat rather than benefit from stereotype promise. Future research could focus on whether and how social psychological processes differ among Asian ethnic groups and whether these result in variegated outcomes.

Third, demographic trends, including intergenerational succession, may alter the success frame. As the second generation comes of age and has children, how likely is it that the success frame will remain the same? Will third-generation Asians partake in and benefit from the ethnic strategies and resources that have propelled their second-generation parents to attain exceptional outcomes? As research has shown, with intergenerational succession comes a waning attachment to the ethnic community, reduced reliance on ethnic resources, and a weakening ethnic identity.[33] Hence, it remains to be seen how durable the success frame will be for third- and later-generation Asian Americans or whether it will remain the province of the children of immigrants. Comparative research of parenting practices among second-generation Chinese in the Netherlands and the United States shows a waning of the success frame, especially among Chinese-Dutch parents, who have lower educational aspirations and expectations of their third-generation children.[34] Relatedly, it remains to be seen whether later-generation Asians will be as likely to retain the growth mind-set that foreign-born parents have imparted to their second-generation children. Third- and later-generation Asians may be less willing to put in the effort necessary to garner exceptional academic outcomes; such reluctance would also change the success frame.

Fourth, not only is it possible that the success frame will diversify and evolve to accommodate later-generation Asian Americans, but the very meaning of Asian American will evolve as well, owing to the increasing ethnic heterogeneity of this broad category, the high rates of intermarriage rates among Asian Americans, and the growing Asian multiracial population. Intermarriage has increased twentyfold since 1960, when only 1 percent of American marriages were interracial. Today one in every thirteen American marriages is interracial and among new marriages the ratio rises to one in seven, which has led to a visible and growing multiracial population.[35] Asian Americans are at the vanguard of these demographic trends: about one-third of Asian marriages are interracial, and in most of them the partner is white. Currently, 12.4 percent of Asians identify as multiracial—a rate that will continue to increase with the rise in intermarriage, especially among young native-born Asians.[36]

Will multiracial Asians partake in ethnic resources, and will they benefit from stereotype promise as monoracial Asians have, especially when they lack distinctive ethnic identifiers such as features and phenotype? Moreover, the highly gendered nature of Asian intermarriage matters: because Asian women are twice as likely to outmarry as Asian men, Asian multiracial children tend to have Anglo surnames.[37] Will the stereotypes of Asian Americans extend to Asian multiracials who have Anglo surnames and are not readily identifiable to others as Asian? Or will stereotypes of Asian Americans change to reflect the changing Asian American population, including the Asian multiracial population? These pressing questions deserve further inquiry as the fastest-growing population evolves and becomes an ever-increasing share of the U.S. population.

In conclusion, we reiterate that while we recognize the value and function of the success frame, we must not ignore the costs of embracing it too tightly or the potential of broadening it. In fact, that broadening has already begun as the second generation comes of age, and it is likely to continue if the incorporation experiences of second- and later-generation European ethnics (especially Jews) are a precursor of what lies ahead for later-generation Asians. Some second-generation Asians have carved out names for themselves as celebrated chefs, restaurant owners, journalists, actors, and professional athletes—all of whom are paving the way for a broader, more diverse, and more inclusive success frame for Asian Americans.

For example, a new cadre of Asian American chefs has taken the culinary scene by storm, including Christina Ha (the first blind contestant and winner of the *MasterChef* competition), Hung Huynh (winner on the third season of *Top Chef*, Bravo's reality cooking competition show), Hooni Kim (chef of Danji and Hanjan in New York), and Ming Tsai (owner and chef of Boston's Blue Ginger). Bridging ethnoracial and cultural divides with their cuisine, these chefs have garnered a following that extends far beyond ethnic niches, ethnic taste buds, and coethnic circles.

Hung Huynh, a 1.5-generation Vietnamese American, worked in his parents' restaurants as a young boy and received a degree from the Culinary Institute of America. He later cooked for some of the country's most acclaimed restaurants, including Per Se in New York City and the Guy Savoy in Las Vegas. Hooni Kim, a 1.5-generation Korean American who grew up in New York, went west to pursue his medical degree at the University of California at Berkeley but ended up back east in the French Culinary Institute to be trained as a chef. His restaurant, Danji, is the first Korean restaurant to earn a Michelin star and has garnered praise from ethnic and mainstream media alike, from the *Korea Times* and *Donga Ilbo* to the *New York Times* and the *Wall Street Journal*.

Ming Tsai is a second-generation Chinese with a bachelor's degree in mechanical engineering from Yale as well as a master's degree in hotel administration and hospitality marketing from Cornell. Despite his educational pathway, Chef Tsai has pursued his passion in cooking and opened Blue Ginger, a restaurant in Boston. He has also garnered fame as the celebrity chef of fusion cuisine and host of the television cooking show *East Meets West*. Christina Ha's educational profile is similar to Ming Tsai's in that both attained master's degrees. A second-generation Vietnamese, Christina Ha earned a bachelor's degree in business from the University of Texas at Austin and a master's degree in fine art from the University of Houston. The host of a cooking show, she maintains a popular food blog.

Perhaps the most notorious chef is Eddie Huang, the son of Taiwanese immigrants who grew up in Orlando, Florida. Huang turned to hip-hop culture as a refuge from the abuse, bullying, and violent racism that he experienced growing up as a second-generation Asian American in Orlando. Chef and co-owner of the popular Taiwanese bun shop, BaoHaus, in the East Village, Huang is also a popular blogger, television personality, and author of a best-selling memoir *Fresh Off the Boat,* which has become the basis of a new ABC television series with the same name. But even Huang—whose uncensored, ardent criticism of the model minority stereotype and success frame permeates his public persona and writing—earned a JD from Cardozo School of Law. He worked as an associate practicing corporate law at Chadborne & Parke before launching his culinary and writing career.[38]

Even these accomplished chefs have admitted that their road to culinary stardom was not one that their immigrant parents initially supported. Like the Chinese and Vietnamese immigrant parents in our study, their parents wanted their children to become doctors or lawyers. Writers like Wesley Yang, who wrote the thought-provoking piece "Paper Tigers" for *New York* magazine, and Jeff Yang, a *Wall Street Journal* columnist whose weekly column, Tao Jones, focuses on Asian American popular culture, are other examples of Asian Americans who bucked the traditional success frame and charted an alternative path to success.[39] Film directors like Justin Lin, and actors like Lucy Liu and Jonathan Luke Huy Quan—members of the 1.5 or second generation—have paved their own way in Hollywood and broken barriers along the way. And how could we fail to mention Jeremy Lin, who defies the traditional stereotypes of Asian Americans, not mention the stereotypes of National Basketball Association players?

That Asian Americans are departing from the success frame, choosing alternative pathways, and achieving success on their own terms should reassure Asian immigrant parents and their children that broadening the success frame is not a route to failure. Instead, loosening their grip on the success frame and commitment to success at all costs may lead to uncharted pathways that expand opportunity horizons for Asian Americans and lead to unanticipated but even more successful, more fulfilling outcomes. But this process is a two-way street. For Asian immigrant parents to loosen their grip on the success frame, or for them to break free of it, the children of immigrants must see alternative frames within their reach that fit their aspirations and pay off. If Asian Americans continue to encounter roadblocks when they pursue different pathways or if they hit a bamboo ceiling when they are poised for leadership positions, they may find little incentive to change their success frame. If, however, more Asian Americans attain success through unchartered pathways, then more Asian immigrant parents will feel confident that broadening the success frame is not tantamount to failure. Both the success frame and the achievement paradox are born out of Asian immigration and the Asian American experience; neither are intrinsic to Chinese, Vietnamese, or Asian culture. How much the success frame will change and how long the achievement paradox will endure will depend on both the pursuits of Asian Americans—who are becoming increasingly diverse in ethnicity, class, and generational status—and on the opportunities and challenges presented to them by the U.S. society they call home.

~ Notes ~

Chapter 1

1. Hereafter referred to as the Pew Report.
2. See Pew Research Center (2012), appendix 2. Min Zhou was one of the external advisers for the study.
3. Sakamoto, Goyette, and Kim (2009), 260.
4. See Khan (2013). Admission to these highly competitive and prestigious magnet high schools is based solely on a student's score on a single city-wide exam, the Specialized High School Admissions Test (SHSAT).
5. Associated Press (2009).
6. See also Ramakrishnan (2012).
7. Wu (2013).
8. Goyette and Xie (1999), Laurence Steinberg (1981), Sue and Okazaki (1990), Wilson (1996), and Zhou (1997). We use "ethnoracial" to denote America's racial and ethnic groups. We recognize that both race and ethnicity are socially constructed, and that racial and ethnic boundaries have changed over time and will continue to evolve. Our 1.5- and second-generation Chinese and Vietnamese interviewees often used racial and ethnic categories interchangeably, although in the several instances when they drew clear boundaries around race and ethnicity, the terms we use reflect these distinctions. We also recognize that Asian American is a broad, heterogeneous category that encompasses more than twenty national-origin groups. However, given the racialization that occurs in the United States, ethnic distinctiveness is less salient and apparent to most non-Asian Americans compared to racial differences. Again, we are cautious in our usage of ethnic and racial categories and distinguish between the two when relevant.
9. Goyette and Xie (1999) and Portes and Hao (2004).
10. Hsin and Xie (2014).
11. Patterson (2014, 2015).
12. Chua and Rubenfeld (2014), Fukuyama (1993), Ogbu (1974), Sowell (1981), and Stephen Steinberg (1996b).

13. See David Brooks, "The Party of Work," *New York Times,* November 8, 2012; and Murray (2012).
14. Banks, Eberhardt, and Ross (2006), Eberhardt et al. (2004), Solórzano, Ceja, and Yosso (2000), Steele (1997), Steele and Aronson (1995), and Sue et al. (2007).
15. See Carter (2005), Lamont (2000), McKee (2012), Simmel (1968), Small (2004), and Small, Harding, and Lamont (2010).
16. Harding (2007, 2010) and Small (2004, 2009).
17. Rumbaut et al. (2004).
18. Lee and Zhou (2009). The data are drawn from the study "Becoming 'Ethnic,' Becoming 'Angeleno,' and/or Becoming 'American': The Multifaceted Experiences of Immigrant Children and the Children of Immigrants in Los Angeles" by Jennifer Lee and Min Zhou (principal investigators). The qualitative study focuses on how members of today's 1.5 and second generation define "success," how their prospects and outcomes of success are affected by national origin, class, and immigration status, and how they come to identify themselves. Supported by the Russell Sage Foundation (#88-06-04), the study draws on a sample of 162 1.5- or second-generation Chinese (41), Vietnamese (41), and Mexicans (56) and also includes native-born blacks (12) and native-born whites (12) from the larger IIMMLA survey sample. The data collection began in the fall of 2006 and was completed in 2009. Lasting between 60 and 150 minutes, the interviews were taped and transcribed verbatim. Following institutional review board guidelines, we use pseudonyms throughout the book to protect the privacy of our respondents.
19. We employ Ann Swidler's (1986) concept of culture as a "toolkit" that people draw on to construct strategies of action.
20. Feliciano (2005).
21. On ethnic capital, see Borjas (1992).
22. Harding (2007).
23. Kasinitz et al. (2008), Lareau and Calarco (2012), Zhou and Bankston (1998), and Zhou and Cho (2010).
24. Ridgeway (2011) and Ridgeway and Fisk (2012).
25. On stereotypes, see Krueger (1996).
26. Steele and Aronson (1995).
27. Jennifer Lee (2014a).
28. Chao (1994), Dweck (2006), and Goffman (1974).
29. Swidler (1986).
30. See Hing (2014).
31. Duncan (2012a).
32. Moynihan (1965), 218–19.
33. Lewis (1959).
34. Gans (2011).

35. Wu (2013).
36. See Patterson (2014, 2015).
37. Holzer (1996), Massey and Denton (1993), and Wilson (1978, 1987).
38. Zhou (2004).
39. Hein (2006) and Skrentny (2008).
40. Carter (2005, 2012), Gould (2011), Harding (2007, 2010), Lamont (2000), Lareau (2003), Skrentny (2008), Small (2004, 2009), Small, Harding, and Lamont (2010), Sandra Smith (2007), Vaisey (2010), and Young (2010).
41. Binder et al. (2008), Carter (2005, 2012), DiMaggio (1997), Goffman (1974), Harding (2007), Polletta (2006), Small (2004), Swidler (1986), and Van Hook and Bean (2009).
42. Caplan, Whitmore, and Choy (1989).
43. Zhou (1997, 2006) and Zhou and Bankston (1998).
44. Alba and Nee (2003), Bean and Stevens (2003), FitzGerald and Cook-Martin (2014); Foner and Frederickson (2004), Kasinitz et al. (2008), Lee (2005), Lee and Bean (2010, 2014), Massey, Durand, and Malone (2002), Portes and Rumbaut (2001), Portes and Zhou (1993), and Waldinger and Lee (2001).
45. On the changes to the U.S. ethnoracial profile, see Frey (2014).
46. Gordon (1964), Park (1950), and Warner and Srole (1945).
47. Huntington (2004).
48. Kasinitz et al. (2008), Massey et al. (2002), Portes and Rumbaut (2001), and Telles and Ortiz (2008).
49. Alba and Waters (2011), Bean et al. (2011), Brown (2007), Lee and Zhou (2013), and Zhou and Lee (2007).
50. Jennifer Lee (2014b). We are grateful to Mark Vanlandingham for providing us with this illustrative baseball analogy.
51. Portes and Zhou (1993).
52. Alba and Nee (2003), Bean et al. (2011), Brown (2007), Jiménez (2010), and Zhou and Bankston (1998).
53. Portes and Zhou (1993).
54. Zhou (1997) and Zhou and Bankston (1998).
55. See also Fernández-Kelly and Konczal (2005), Foner (2010), Modood (2011), and Skrentny (2008).
56. Neckerman, Carter, and Lee (1999), Smith (2014), and Vallejo (2012).
57. Bourdieu (1984).
58. A notable exception is the Russell Sage Foundation's Working Group in Cultural Contact and Immigration, which brings together leading social psychologists with sociologists, political scientists, and geographers to design and undertake research projects that use multidisciplinary and interdisciplinary perspectives.

Chapter 2

1. Based on the 2010 U.S. census, Chinese are the largest Asian subgroup (4,010,114) and Vietnamese the fourth-largest group (1,737,433). Other groups with populations exceeding 1 million are Filipinos (3,416,840), Indians (3,183,063), Koreans (1,706,822), and Japanese (1,304,286) (Pew Research Center 2012, 19). Except for the Japanese, all Asian subgroups, including more than twenty national-origin groups from Asia east of Afghanistan, are fast-growing owing to contemporary immigration.
2. Neckerman, Carter, and Lee (1999).
3. Trieu (2008) and Whitmore (1985).
4. Wang (2002).
5. U.S. Census Bureau (2012).
6. Pew Research Center (2012).
7. BICS was formerly the Immigration and Naturalization Service. The total number of mainland China-born, Hong Kong-born, or Taiwan-born persons admitted was 2,124,402 between 1970 and 2011 (and 96,764 between 1960 and 1969); for Vietnam-born persons, the total number admitted during this period was 950,894 (and 2,949 from 1960 to 1969), according to the U.S. Bureau of Immigration and Citizenship (U.S. Department of Homeland Security 2012).
8. Barth (1964) and Zhou (1992). Under the credit-ticket system, potential emigrants could enter into labor contracts with their brokers, who then arranged the journey with Western sailing vessels. The migrants were expected to repay a certain proportion of their wages or to work a certain length of time once they were in the United States. This form of contract labor was often described by the Cantonese as the "selling of pigs" or the "pig trade."
9. Saxton (1971).
10. Chan (1986), FitzGerald and Cook-Martin (2014), Lee (2007), Lee and Bean (2010), Okihiro (1994), Saxton (1971), Sayler (1995), and Takaki (1979, 1989).
11. Saxton (1971) and Lee (1960).
12. Zhou (1992).
13. Rose Hum Lee (1960) and Lyman (1974).
14. Zhou (1992).
15. The "paper son" phenomenon was a strategy employed by the Chinese immigrant community as a way to circumvent the Chinese Exclusion Act. It refers to a phenomenon in which a U.S.-born Chinese or a Chinese merchant living in the United States would falsely report to the government the birth of a son in the United States and then sell the slot to a boy in the migrant-sending village in China to enable the boy to immigrate

into the United States. Sons who entered the United States in this fashion were dubbed "paper sons." For details, see Lau (2007).

16. Zhou (2009a).
17. Skeldon (1996).
18. USCIS (2012).
19. Li (1997), Logan and Zhang (2013), and Zhou, Chin, and Kim (2013).
20. Li (1997), Logan and Zhang (2013), Tseng (1994), and Zhou et al. (2013).
21. Tseng (1994), Zhou, Tseng, and Kim (2008), and Zhou et al. (2013).
22. Zhou et al. (2013).
23. U.S. Census Bureau (2012).
24. Rumbaut (2005) and Trieu (2008).
25. Freeman (1995) and Rumbaut (2005).
26. Zhou and Bankston (1998).
27. Freeman (1995).
28. Caplan et al. (1989), Freeman (1995), and Zhou and Bankston (1998).
29. Freeman (1995), Rumbaut (2005), Trieu (2008), and Zhou and Bankston (2008).
30. The 1965 Hart-Cellar Act was further amended by the 1990 Immigration and Nationality Act. The act expanded the limits on legal immigration to the United States and continued to favor family-based and employment-based migration.
31. Zhou and Bankston (1998) and Bloemraad (2006).
32. The total Vietnamese population in the United States in 2010 was 1,548,449 (U.S. Census Bureau 2012).
33. Borjas (1987), Chiswick (1978), Feliciano (2005), Gans (2000), Massey (1987), and Portes and Rumbaut (2001).
34. Feliciano (2005). The net difference index (NDI) is calculated by the percentage differences at different levels of education between immigrants and non-immigrants (Feliciano 2005; Lieberson 1976). An NDI of 0.220 indicates that the Mexican immigrants are more educated than Mexican non-immigrants 20 percent more often than is true of the converse (Feliciano 2005).
35. Feliciano (2005).
36. OECD (2011) and UNFPA (2012).
37. U.S. Census Bureau (2009).
38. Feliciano (2005).
39. Lanphier (1983) and Montero (1979). VOLAGs were working mainly under government contracts to oversee refugee resettlement and, in most cases, to decide on refugee destinations. The largest VOLAG was the U.S. Catholic Conference, which had the task of finding sponsors—individuals or groups that would assume financial and personal responsibility for refugee families for up to two years.
40. Zhou and Bankston (1998) and Zhou, Bankston, and Kim (2002).

41. Borjas (1992).
42. Fong (1994), Zhou (2009a), and Zhou, Chin, and Kim (2013).
43. U.S. Census Bureau (2007).
44. These findings come from the U.S. Census Bureau's 2007 Survey of Business Owners and were collected as part of the 2007 Economic Census. There were 163,217 Filipino-owned firms in 2007 and 192,465 Korean-owned firms.
45. Jennifer Lee (2002), Zhou and Cho (2010), and Zhou and Lee (2014).
46. Louie (2004), Lu (2013), Zhou (2008, 2009b), Zhou and Cho (2010), Zhou and Kim (2006), and Zhou and Li (2003).
47. Zhou (2009b), Zhou and Cho (2010), and Zhou and Li (2003).
48. Lee and Zhou (2013, 2014a) and Zhou and Bankston (1998).
49. The survey was conducted by a team of researchers that included the authors and was funded by the Russell Sage Foundation. For details, see Rumbaut, Rubén G., Frank D. Bean, Leo R. Chávez, Jennifer Lee, Susan K. Brown, Louis DeSipio, and Min Zhou (2004).
50. Kasinitz et al. (2008).
51. Blau and Duncan (1967), Duncan, Featherman, and Duncan (1972), and Haller and Portes (1973).
52. See also Smith (2006) and Bean et al. (2011).
53. Lee (2014b).
54. Bean et al. (2011).
55. Ibid.; Brown et al. (2011).
56. Telles and Ortiz (2008).
57. The IIMMLA data also show that, among 1.5- and second-generation Chinese whose parents both had little English proficiency, the college educational attainment rate (63 percent) was significantly higher than it was for native-born whites (46 percent). The rate for the Vietnamese whose parents both had little English proficiency was 37 percent—lower than that of native-born whites but still significantly higher than that of native-born blacks (24 percent) and Mexican immigrants or natives (18 percent).
58. Kim (2014), Lee and Zhou (2013, 2014a), Zhou (2014), and Zhou and Lee (2014).
59. Hereafter Lee and Zhou, L.A. Qualitative Study.
60. We also include data from our interviews with fifty-six 1.5- and second-generation Mexicans, twelve native-born blacks, and twelve native-born whites for reference in our analysis.

Chapter 3

1. Blau and Duncan (1978).
2. Bourdieu (1967, 1987), Haller and Portes (1973), Lareau (2003), Sewell, Haller, and Portes (1969), and Sewell, Haller, and Ohlendorf (1970).

3. Carter (2005, 2006), Reardon (2011), and Telles and Ortiz (2008).
4. Bean et al. (2011), Brown et al. (2011), Leach et al. (2011), and Van Hook and Bean (2009).
5. Goyette and Xie (1999), Hsin and Xie (2014), Kasinitz et al. (2008), Portes and Hao (2004), Xie and Goyette (2003), Zhou (2008, 2009a), and Zhou and Bankston (1998).
6. Goffman (1974).
7. Skrentny (2008).
8. Borjas (1995), Portes and Zhou (1993), and Zhou and Kim (2006).
9. See also Zhou (2009b).
10. Neckerman, Carter, and Lee (1999).
11. GPAs are based on a scale in which a 4.0 is the equivalent of an A grade (excellent). A 3.0 is a B (above average), a 2.0 is a C (average), and a 1.0 is a D (well below average). A GPA that exceeds 4.0 denotes that a student has taken AP or honors classes, which are weighted more highly because they are more difficult.
12. Steinberg, Dornbusch, and Brown (1992).
13. Huabin Chen (2011), and Shiang Chen (2006).
14. Hanson and Meng (2008), Kao and Tienda (1998), and Xie and Goyette (2003).
15. Zhou (2009b), Zhou and Kim (2006), and Zhou and Li (2003).
16. Fordham and Ogbu (1986).
17. Ibid.
18. See, for example, Carter (2005, 2006).
19. Carter (2005).
20. See also Carter (2005, 2006), O'Connor, Horvat, and Lewis (2006), and Warikoo (2011).
21. Vallejo (2012).
22. Smith (2014).
23. Ibid.
24. Jiménez and Horowitz (2013).
25. Lee (2013) and Lee and Zhou (2014b).
26. Okihiro (1994), Sayler (1995), Takaki (1979, 1989), and Volpp (2003).
27. Chua and Rubenfeld (2014); Petersen (1996), and *U.S. News & World Report* (1966).
28. Charles (2003), Lee and Bean (2010, 2014), Massey and Denton (1993), Pew Research Center (2012), and Sakamoto, Goyette, and Kim (2009).
29. Jiménez and Horowitz (2013).
30. Neckerman, Carter, and Lee (1999), Smith (2014), and Vallejo (2012).

Chapter 4

1. On "Tiger Mother" parenting, see Chua (2011) and Fu and Markus (2014).
2. Patterson (2015) and Tran (2015).

3. Zhou (1997).
4. Zuckerman (1988).
5. Borjas (1992) and Bourdieu (1984).
6. Lee and Zhou (2013, 2014a), Zhou and Kim (2006), and Zhou and Lee (2014).
7. The motivation to move to a better neighborhood in order to provide stronger educational opportunities for one's child is a theme in the traditional Chinese *Three-Character Classic,* which tells an inspirational story about Mencius's mother, who moves three times in order to provide a better education for her son. (The famous line "xi Meng mu, ze lin chu" translates as "past Meng mother, chose a neighborhood.") The story is inspiring and resonates among the Chinese because moving is extraordinarily difficult in a nonmobile traditional society.
8. There have been cases of African American parents who tried to place their children in more competitive schools, with penal consequences. For example, Kelley Williams-Bolar was convicted of lying about her address and falsifying records so that her children could attend a public school in another Ohio school district. The school officials asked her to pay $30,000 in back tuition, and when she refused, she was indicted and convicted of falsifying her residency records. Williams-Bolar was sentenced to ten days in county jail and placed on probation for three years. For more details, see Canning and Tanglao (2011).
9. Espenshade and Radford (2009), Massey et al. (2003), Sacerdote (2011), and Sidanius et al. (2011).
10. Gordon, Bridglall, and Meroe (2004).
11. Lareau (2003).
12. Jenny Anderson, "Push for A's at Private Schools Is Keeping Costly Tutors Busy," *New York Times,* June 7, 2011.
13. Reardon (2011).
14. Zhou and Kim (2006) and Lu (2013).
15. Bray (2013), Marimuthu et al. (1991), Stevenson and Baker (1992), Stigler, Lee, and Stevenson (1987), and Zhou and Kim (2006).
16. Ramstad (2011).
17. For more information about hagwon in South Korea, see Ripley (2011).
18. Zhou and Cho (2010).
19. Louie (2004) and Zhou (2008).
20. Kaplan, Inc. (http://portal.kaplan.edu), founded in 1938 and headquartered in New York City, and the Princeton Review (http://www.princetonreview.com/), founded in 1981, are some of the best-known and largest academies in the United States that have international partners and offer test preparation and tutoring services.
21. Byun and Park (2012), Lu (2013), Sun (1998), Zhou (2008), and Zhou and Cho (2010).

22. See also Chin and Phillips (2004).
23. Skrentny (2008).
24. Stevenson and Lee (1990).
25. Chao (1994), Hsin and Xie (2014), and Kao (1995).
26. Luo and Holden (2014).
27. Pew Research Center (2012).
28. Hsin and Xie (2014).
29. Fuligni (1997) and Stevenson and Lee (1990).
30. Stevenson and Lee (1990).
31. See also Fuligni (1997), Vallejo (2012), and Vallejo and Lee (2009).
32. Kao (2001), Massey et al. (2003), Sacerdote (2011), Sewell, Haller, and Portes (1969), and Sidanius et al. (2010).
33. Steinberg (1996b).
34. Lareau and Calarco (2012), Ridgeway and Fisk (2012), and Small (2009).
35. DiMaggio (1982), Lareau and Calarco (2012), Ridgeway and Fiske (2012), and Small (2004, 2009).
36. Small (2009).
37. Lareau and Calarco (2012).
38. Louie (2004) and Zhou and Kim (2006).
39. Zhou and Kim (2006) and Zhou and Cho (2010).

Chapter 5

1. Borjas (1995).
2. Lee (2014b).
3. Crul et al. (2012).
4. Huntington (2004).
5. Harding (2007).
6. Desmond and López Turley (2009).
7. IRCA granted a path toward legalization for certain immigrants who had been continuously and illegally residing in the United States since January 1, 1982.
8. Lareau (2003).
9. Tavis Smiley, who was born in Gulfport, Mississippi, and grew up in Bunker Hill, Indiana, is a well-known African American talk show host, author, liberal political commentator, and philanthropist.
10. On "linked fate," see Dawson (1995), Hochschild (1995), and Pattillo-McCoy (1999).
11. See Hochschild (1995), Lamont (2000), Lee (2002), and Newman (1999).
12. Dawson (1995), Hochschild (1995), Lee (2002), Vallejo (2012), and Vallejo and Lee (2009).

Chapter 6

1. Lee (2014a).
2. Duncan (2012b).
3. Lee (2007), Okihiro (1994), Sayler (1995), and Takaki (1979).
4. Lee and Zhou (2014b).
5. Lee (2014a).
6. On stereotype threat, see Deaux et al. (2007), Massey and Fischer (2005), Spencer, Steele, and Quinn (1999), and Steele and Aronson (1995).
7. Bourdieu (1984); see also Bourdieu (1987) and Wacquant (2013).
8. Okamoto (2014) and Omi and Winant (1994).
9. Hsin and Xie (2014).
10. See also Hibel, Penn, and Morris (manuscript).
11. Jiménez and Horowitz (2013).
12. Drake (2014).
13. Carter (2005, 2006) and Warikoo (2011).
14. Merton (1948), p. 200.
15. Krueger (1996) and Shih et al. (2007).
16. Spencer et al. (1998), Steele (1998), and Steele and Aronson (1995).
17. Aronson et al. (1999), Deaux et al. (2007), Inzlicht and Schmader (2012), Massey and Fischer (2005), Steele (1997), Steele and Aronson (1995), Stone et al. (1999), and Yopyk and Prentice (2005).
18. Spencer, Steele, and Quinn (1999), Steele (1997), and Steele and Aronson (1995).
19. Cheryan and Bodenhausen (2000), Dijksterhuis et al. (1998), Kray, Thompson, and Galinsky (2001), Levy (1996), Shih, Pittinsky, and Ambady (1999), and Shih, Pittinsky, and Ho (2012).
20. Shih, Pittinsky, and Ambady (1999).
21. Cheryan and Bodenhausen (2000) and Shih et al. (2002).
22. Shih, Pittinsky, and Ho (2012) and Walton and Cohen (2003).
23. Lee (2014a).
24. Cheryan and Bodenhausen (2000), Shih, Pittinsky, and Ambady (1999), Shih, Pittinsky, and Ho (2012), and Shih et al. (2002).
25. Steele (1997).
26. Böhme (2012), Kozlowski (2014), Rist (1970), and Rosenthal and Jacobson (1968).
27. Rosenthal and Jacobsen (1968).
28. Yang (2011).
29. Ridgeway (2011), Shih et al. (1999), Spencer, Steele, and Quinn (1999), and Steele and Aronson (1995).
30. On being "marked" with a criminal record, see Pager (2003, 2007).
31. See Lee and Fiske (2006) and Lin et al. (2005).
32. See Williams, Phillips, and Hall (2014).

33. Yang (2011).
34. Gee, Hom, and Anand (2014).
35. Yang (2011).
36. Hyun (2005), Woo (1999), and Yang (2011).
37. Yang (2011) and Wan (2013).
38. Gee, Hom, and Anand (2014).
39. Alon and Tienda (2007), Karabel (2005), Rivera (2012), Samson (2013), Skrentny (2014), and Uhlmann and Cohen (2005).
40. Samson (2013).
41. Karabel (2005).
42. Fernandez (1998) and Tang (1993).
43. Palepu et al. (1995).
44. Fryer, Levitt, and List (2008), Nguyen, O'Neal, and Ryan (2003), and Sackett and Ryan (2011).
45. Espenshade and Radford (2009).
46. Karabel (2005).
47. Ibid.; see also Samson (2013) and Uhlmann and Cohen (2005).
48. On the question of Asian American admissions to Harvard, see Mounk (2014).

Chapter 7

1. Dweck (1999).
2. Ibid., and Mueller and Dweck (1998).
3. Ibid.
4. Mueller and Dweck (1998).
5. Dweck (1999), 120.
6. Chao (1994), Hsin and Xie (2014), Kao (1995), and Stevenson and Lee (1990).
7. Dweck (1999).
8. Alon and Tienda (2007), Karabel (2005), Samson (2013), and Uhlmann and Cohen (2005).
9. Dweck (1999), 150.
10. Massey et al. (2003) and Sidanius et al. (2010).
11. Fuligni (1997) and Lee and Zhou (2014a).

Chapter 8

1. Dweck (1999).
2. Min (1984).
3. Jennifer Lee (2002).
4. Zhou (2008) and Zhou and Cai (2002).
5. Dweck (1999).
6. Mueller and Dweck (1998) and Hong et al. (1999).

7. Dweck (1999).
8. Lee (2006).
9. Guendelman, Cheryan, and Monin (2011), Kibria (2003), Siy and Cheryan (2013), and Devos and Banaji (2005).
10. On optional and symbolic ethnic identification, see Gans (1979), Okamura (1981), Waters (1990), and Yancey, Ericksen, and Juliani (1976). On ethnic identification for nonwhite Americans, see Waters (1999).
11. Lee (2006).
12. Fiske, Lin, and Neuberg (1999).
13. Ridgeway (2011).
14. Ibid.
15. Ibid., 162.
16. Hochschild (1995), Lamont (2000), and Jennifer Lee (2002).
17. Carter (2005, 2006) and Warikoo (2011).

Chapter 9

1. See also Smith (2014) and Vallejo (2012).
2. See Cheryan and Bodenhausen (2000) and Siy and Cheryan (2013).
3. Bourgois (1991), Gibson (1988), and Fordham and Ogbu (1986).
4. Fordham (1996), 39.
5. Kohl (1994), 2.
6. Carter (2005), Horvat and O'Connor (2006), and O'Connor, Horvat, and Lewis (2006).
7. Carter (2005).
8. See also Drake (2014) and Jiménez and Horowitz (2013).
9. Gibson and Ogbu (1991) and Ogbu and Simons (1998).
10. Yiu (2013).
11. Lee and Zhou (2014b), Lee (2015), and Saperstein (2015).
12. Ramakrishnan and Ahmad (2014).
13. Massey et al. (2003) and Sidanius et al. (2010).
14. Jiménez and Horowitz (2013).
15. Bourdieu (1967, 1984) and Portes and Hao (2004).
16. Carter (2005, 2006) and Lareau (2003).
17. Portes and Zhou (1993).
18. Neckerman, Carter, and Lee (1999).
19. Ibid.
20. Drake (2014), Liu, Miller, and Wang (2014), Zhou (2009b), and Zhou and Li (2003).
21. Lareau (2003), Putman (2015), and Reardon (2011).
22. Zhou and Cho (2010).
23. Our point about intergenerational mobility is vividly captured by Mark Borigini's (2014) ingenious use of this mathematical analogy.

24. For detailed analysis of role of resources on long-term and intergenerational outcomes, see Johnson (2014) and Johnson, Jackson, and Persico (2015).
25. Jennifer Lee (2002) and Zhou (2009).
26. Liu et al. (2014) and Zhou and Cho (2010).
27. CDC (2013).
28. Williams, Phillips, and Hall (2014).
29. Lee, Carling, and Orrenius (2014) and Noam (2014).
30. Yiu (2013).
31. Ceccagno and Gruppi (2009), Marsden (2014), and Pedone (2011).
32. Foner (2011) and Noam (2014).
33. Alba (1985, 1990), Alba and Nee (2003), Gans (1979, 2015), and Waters (1990).
34. Noam (2014).
35. Frey (2014).
36. Lee and Bean (2010, 2014).
37. Lee and Bean (2010).
38. Huang (2013).
39. Yang (2011).

~ References ~

Alba, Richard. 1985. *Italian Americans: Into the Twilight of Ethnicity.* Englewood Cliffs, N.J.: Prentice-Hall.

————. 1990. *Ethnic Identity: The Transformation of White America.* New Haven, Conn.: Yale University Press.

————. 1999. "Immigration and the American Realities of Assimilation and Multiculturalism." *Sociological Forum* 14(1): 3–25.

Alba, Richard, and Victor Nee. 2003. *Remaking the American Mainstream: Assimilation and Contemporary Immigration.* Cambridge, Mass.: Harvard University Press.

Alba, Richard, and Mary C. Waters. 2011. *The Next Generation: Immigrant Youth in a Comparative Perspective.* New York: New York University Press.

Alon, Sigal, and Marta Tienda. 2007. "Diversity, Opportunity, and the Shifting Meritocracy in Higher Education." *American Sociological Review* 72: 487–511.

Anderson, Jenny. 2011. "Push for A's at Private Schools Is Keeping Costly Tutors Busy." *New York Times*, June 7.

Aronson, Joshua, Michael J. Lustina, Catherine Good, Kelli Keough, Claude M. Steele, and Joseph Brown. 1999. "When White Men Can't Do Math: Necessary and Sufficient Factors in Stereotype Threat." *Journal of Experimental Social Psychology* 35: 29–46.

Associated Press. 2009. "Asian-Americans Blast UC Admissions Policy," April 24. Available at: http://www.nbcnews.com/id/30393117/ns/us_news-life/t/asian-americans-blast-uc-admissions-policy/#.UzGMytNOWM9 (accessed March 27, 2015).

Banks, Richard, Jennifer L. Eberhardt, and Lee Ross. 2006. "Discrimination and Implicit Bias in a Racially Unequal Society." *California Law Review* 94(4): 1169–90.

Barth, Gunther. 1964. *Bitter Strength: A History of the Chinese in the United States, 1850–1870.* Cambridge, Mass.: Harvard University Press.

Bean, Frank D., Mark A. Leach, Susan K. Brown, James D. Bachmeier, and John Hipp. 2011. "The Educational Legacy of Unauthorized Migration:

Comparisons Across U.S.-Immigrant Groups in How Parents' Status Affects Their Offspring." *International Migration Review* 45(2): 348–85.

Bean, Frank D., and Gillian Stevens. 2003. *America's Newcomers and the Dynamics of Diversity.* New York: Russell Sage Foundation.

Binder, Amy, Mary Blair-Loy, John Evans, Kwai Ng, and Michael Schudson. 2008. "Introduction: The Diversity of Culture." *Annals of the American Academy of Political and Social Science* 619: 6–14.

Blau, Peter, and Otis Dudley Duncan. 1967. *American Occupational Structure.* New York: Wiley.

Bloemraad, Irene. 2006. *Becoming a Citizen: Incorporating Immigrants and Refugees in the United States and Canada.* Berkeley: University of California Press.

Böhme, Marcus. 2012. "Migration and Educational Aspirations – Another Channel of Brain Gain?" *Kiel* working paper no. 1811. Paper presented at the Kiel Institute for the World Economy, Kiel, Germany (November).

Borigini, Mark. 2014. "Why Mexican-Americans Do Better Than Others Academically: Tiger Mom Versus Taco Mom." *Psychology Today,* September 7. Available at: http://www.psychologytoday.com/blog/overcoming-pain/201409/why-mexican-americans-do-better-others-academically-9 (accessed March 27, 2015).

Borjas, George J. 1987. "Self-Selection and the Earnings of Immigrants." *American Economic Review* 77: 531–53.

———. 1992. "Ethnic Capital and Intergenerational Mobility." *Quarterly Journal of Economics* 107(1): 123–50.

Bourdieu, Pierre. 1967. "Systems of Education and Systems of Thought." *International Social Science Journal* 19(3): 367–88.

———. 1984. *Distinction: A Social Critique of the Judgment of Taste.* Cambridge, Mass.: Harvard University Press.

———. 1987. "What Makes a Social Class?" *Berkeley Journal of Sociology* 32: 1–17.

Bourgois, Philippe. 1995. *In Search of Respect: Selling Crack in El Barrio.* New York: Cambridge University Press.

Bray, Mark. 2013. "Benefits and Tensions of Shadow Education: Comparative Perspectives on the Roles and Impact of Private Supplementary Tutoring in the Lives of Hong Kong Students." *Journal of International and Comparative Education* 2(1): 18–30.

Brown, Susan K. 2007. "Delayed Spatial Assimilation: Multigenerational Incorporation of the Mexican-Origin Population in Los Angeles." *City & Community* 6: 193–209.

Brown, Susan K., Frank D. Bean, Mark Leach, and Rubén Rumbaut. 2011. "Legalization and Naturalization Trajectories Among Mexican Immigrants and Their Implications for the Second Generation." In *The Next Generation: Immigrant Youth in a Comparative Perspective,* edited by Richard Alba and Mary C. Waters. New York: New York University Press.

Byun, Soo-yong, and Hyunjoon Park. 2012. "The Academic Success of East Asian American Youth: The Role of Shadow Education." *Sociology of Education* 85(1): 40–60.

Canning, Andrea, and Leezel Tanglao, 2011. "Ohio Mom Kelley Williams-Bolar Jailed for Sending Kids to Better School District." *ABC News,* January 26. Available at: http://abcnews.go.com/US/ohio-mom-jailed-sending-kids-schooldistrict/story?id=12763654 (accessed December 7, 2014).

Caplan, Nathan, John K. Whitmore, and Marcella H. Choy. 1989. *The Boat People and Achievement in America: A Study of Family Life, Hard Work, and Cultural Values.* Ann Arbor: University of Michigan Press.

Carter, Prudence L. 2005. *Keepin' It Real: School Success Beyond Black and White.* New York: Oxford University Press.

———. 2006. "Straddling Boundaries: Identity, Culture, and School." *Sociology of Education* 79: 304–28.

———. 2012. *Stubborn Roots: Race, Culture, and Inequality in U.S. and South African Schools.* New York: Oxford University Press.

Ceccagno, Antonella, and Valentina Gruppi. 2009. "Does Modernity Resist the International Crisis? Notion(s) of Modernity Among Young People of Chinese Origin and Chinese Students in Italy." Paper presented at the Fourth International Conference of Institutes and Libraries for Overseas Chinese Studies. Jinan University, Guangzhou, China (May 9–11).

Centers for Disease Control and Prevention (CDC). 1991–2013. High School Youth Risk Behavior Survey Data. Available at: http://nccd.cdc.gov/youthonline/ (accessed January 16, 2015).

Chan, Sucheng. 1986. *This Bitter Sweet Soil: The Chinese in California Agriculture, 1860–1910.* Berkeley: University of California Press.

Chao, Ruth K. 1994. "Beyond Parental Control and Authoritarian Parenting Style: Understanding Chinese Parenting Through the Cultural Notion of Training." *Child Development* 56(4): 1111–19.

Charles, Camille Zubrinsky. 2003. "The Dynamics of Racial Residential Segregation." *Annual Review of Sociology* 29: 167–207.

Chen, Huabin. 2011. "Parents' Attitudes and Expectations Regarding Science Education: Comparison Among American, Chinese-American, and Chinese Families." *Adolescence* 36: 305–13.

Chen, Shiang Jiun. 2006. *The Impact of Parental Expectations on the Career Decisions of Academically Successful and Multi-Talented Asian American Students.* New York: Teachers College, Columbia University.

Cheryan, Sapna, and Galen V. Bodenhausen. 2000. "When Positive Stereotypes Threaten Intellectual Performance: The Psychological Hazards of 'Model Minority' Status." *Psychological Science* 11(5): 399–402.

Chin, Tiffani, and Meredith Phillips. 2004. "Social Reproduction and Child-Rearing Practices: Social Class, Children's Agency, and the Summer Activity Gap." *Sociology of Education* 77: 185–210.

Chiswick, Barry R. 1978. "The Effect of Americanization on the Earnings of Foreign-Born Men." *Journal of Political Economy* 86: 897–921.

Chua, Amy. 2011. *Battle Hymn of the Tiger Mother.* New York: Penguin.

Chua, Amy, and Jed Rubenfeld. 2014. *The Triple Package: How Three Unlikely Traits Explain the Rise and Fall of Cultural Groups in America.* New York: Penguin.

Crul, Maurice, Min Zhou, Jennifer Lee, Philipp Schnell, and Elif Keskiner. 2012. "Success Against the Odds: Second-Generation Mexicans in Los Angeles and Second-Generation Turks in Western European Cities." In *The Changing Face of World Cities: The Second Generation in Europe and the United States,* edited by Maurice Crul and John Mollenkopf. New York: Russell Sage Foundation.

Dawson, Michael C. 1995. *Behind the Mule: Race and Class in African-American Politics.* Princeton, N.J.: Princeton University Press.

Deaux, Kay, Nida Bikmen, Alwyn Gilkes, Ana Ventuceac, Yvanne Joseph, Yasser A. Payne, and Claude M. Steele. 2007. "Becoming American: Stereotype Threat Effects in Afro-Caribbean Immigrant Groups." *Social Psychology Quarterly* 70(4): 384–404.

Desmond, Matthew, and Ruth N. López Turley. 2009. "The Role of Familism in Explaining the Hispanic-White College Application Gap." *Social Problems* 56(2): 311–34.

Devos, Thierry, and Mahzarin R. Banaji. 2005. "American = White?" *Journal of Personality and Social Psychology* 88(3): 447–66.

DiMaggio, Paul. 1982. "Cultural Capital and School Success: The Impact of Status Culture Participation on the Grades of U.S. High School Students." *American Sociological Review* 47: 189–201.

———. 1997. "Culture and Cognition." *Annual Review of Sociology* 23: 263–87.

Dijksterhuis, Ap, Russell Spears, Tom Postmes, Diederik A. Stapel, Willem Koomen, Ad van Knippenberg, and Daan Scheepers. 1998. "Seeing One Thing and Doing Another: Contrast Effects in Automatic Behavior." *Journal of Personality and Social Psychology* 75: 862–71.

Drake, Sean J. 2014. "The Model Majority: How Achievement and Ethnoracial Diversity in High Schools Destabilize the Racial Order." Presentation at the Yale Urban Ethnography Project Conference. Yale University, New Haven, Conn. (April).

Duncan, Arne. 2012a. "Jeremy Lin, Point Guard," *Time,* April 18, 2012. Available at: http://content.time.com/time/specials/packages/article/0,28804,2111975_2111976_2111945,00.html (accessed March 27, 2015).

———. 2012b. "Time 100: The List: Jeremy Lin: Point Guard," *Time,* April 18. Available at: http://www.time.com/time/specials/packages/article/0,28804,2111975_2111976,00.html/ (accessed May 26, 2014).

Duncan, Otis Dudley, David L. Featherman, and Beverly Duncan. 1972. *Socioeconomic Background and Achievement.* New York: Seminar Press.

Dweck, Carol S. 1999. *Self-Theories: Their Role in Motivation, Personality, and Development.* New York: Psychology Press.

———. 2006. *Mindset: The New Psychology of Success.* New York: Ballantine Books.

Eberhardt, Jennifer L., Phillip Atiba Goff, Valerie J. Purdie, and Paul G. Davies. 2004. "Seeing Black: Race, Crime, and Visual Processing." *Journal of Personality and Social Psychology* 87(6): 876–93.

Espenshade, Thomas J., and Alexandria Walton Radford. 2009. *No Longer Separate, Not Yet Equal: Race and Class in Elite College Admission and Campus Life.* Princeton, N.J.: Princeton University Press.

Feliciano, Cynthia. 2005. "Educational Selectivity in U.S. Immigration: How Do Immigrants Compare to Those Left Behind?" *Demography* 42(1): 131–52.

Fernandez, Marilyn. 1998. "Asian Indian Americans in the Bay Area and the Glass Ceiling." *Sociological Perspectives* 41(1): 119–49.

Fernández-Kelly, Patricia, and Lisa Konczal. 2005. "'Murdering the Alphabet': Identity and Entrepreneurship Among Second-Generation Cubans, West Indians, and Central Americans." *Ethnic and Racial Studies* 28(6): 1153–81.

Fiske, Susan T., Monica Lin, and Stephen Neuberg. 1999. "The Continuum Model: Ten Years Later." In *Dual-Process Theories in Social Psychology,* edited by Shelly Chaiken and Yaacov Trope. New York: Guilford.

FitzGerald, David Scott, and David Cook-Martin. 2014. *Culling the Masses: The Democratic Origins of Racist Immigration Policy in the Americas.* Cambridge, Mass.: Harvard University Press.

Foner, Nancy. 2010. "Questions of Success: Lessons from the Last Great Immigration." In *Helping Young Refugees and Immigrants Succeed: Public Policy, Aid, and Education,* edited by Gerhard Sonnert and Gerald Holton. New York: Palgrave.

———. 2011. "Black Identities and the Second Generation: Afro-Caribbeans in Britain and the United States." In *The Next Generation: Immigrant Youth in a Comparative Perspective,* edited by Richard D. Alba and Mary C. Waters. New York: New York University Press.

Foner, Nancy, and George M. Fredrickson. 2004. *Not Just Black and White: Historical and Contemporary Perspectives on Immigration, Race, and Ethnicity in the United States.* New York: Russell Sage Foundation.

Fong, Timothy P. 1994. *The First Suburban Chinatown: The Remaking of Monterey Park, California.* Philadelphia: Temple University Press.

Fordham, Signithia. 1996 *Blacked Out: Dilemmas of Race, Identity, and Success at Capital High.* Chicago: University of Chicago Press.

Fordham, Signithia, and John U. Ogbu. 1986. "Black Students' School Success: Coping with the Burden of 'Acting White.'" *Urban Review* 18: 176–206.

Freeman, James M. 1995. *Changing Identities: Vietnamese Americans, 1975–1990.* Boston, Mass.: Allyn and Bacon.

Frey, William H. 2014. *Diversity Explosion: How New Racial Demographics Are Remaking America.* Washington, D.C.: Brookings Institution Press.

Fryer, Roland G., Steven D. Levitt, and John A. List. 2008. "Exploring the Impact of Financial Incentives on Stereotype Threat: Evidence from a Pilot Study." *American Economic Review* 98(2): 370–75.

Fu, Alyssa S., and Hazel Rose Markus. 2014. "My Mother and Me: Why Tiger Mothers Motivate Asian Americans But Not European Americans." *Personality and Social Psychology Bulletin* 40(6): 739–49. Available at: http://dx.doi.org/10.1177/0146167214524992 (accessed February 12, 2015).

Fukuyama, Francis. 1993. "Immigrants and Family Values." *Commentary* 95(5): 26–32.

Fuligni, Andrew J. 1997. "The Academic Achievement of Adolescents from Immigrant Families: The Roles of Family Background, Attitudes and Behavior." *Child Development* 68: 351–63.

Gans, Herbert J. 1979. "Symbolic Ethnicity." *Ethnic and Racial Studies* 2: 1–20.

———. 2000. "Filling in Some Holes: Six Areas of Needed Immigration Research." In *Immigration Research for a New Century,* edited by Nancy Foner, Rubén G. Rumbaut, and Steven J. Gold. New York: Russell Sage Foundation.

———. 2011. "The Moynihan Report and Its Aftermath: A Critical Analysis." *Du Bois Review* 8(2): 315–27.

———. 2015. "The End of Late-Generation European Ethnicity in America?" *Ethnic and Racial Studies* 38(3): 418–29. Available at: 10.1080/01419870.2015.967707 (accessed March 27, 2015).

Gee, Buck, Wes Hom, and Ajay Anand. 2014. "The Failure of Asian Success – Five Years Later." Research Report, February 9. Available at: http://c.ymcdn.com/sites/ascendleadership.site-ym.com/resource/resmgr/Research_NEW/The_Failure_of_Asian_Success.pdf (accessed February 12, 2015).

Gibson, Margaret A. 1988. *Accommodation Without Assimilation: Sikh Immigrants in an American High School.* Ithaca, NY: Cornell University Press.

Gibson, Margaret A., and John U. Ogbu. 1991. *Minority Status and Schooling: A Comparative Study of Immigrant and Involuntary Minorities.* New York: Garland.

Goffman, Erving. 1974. *Frame Analysis.* Cambridge, Mass.: Harvard University Press.

Gordon, Edmund W., Beatrice L. Bridglall, and Aundra Saa Meroe, eds. 2004. *Supplementary Education: The Hidden Curriculum of High Academic Achievement.* Lanham, Md.: Rowman & Littlefield.

Gordon, Milton M. 1964. *Assimilation in American Life: The Role of Race, Religion, and National Origins.* New York: Oxford University Press.

Gould, Mark. 2011. "More Than Just Social Structure: The Poverty of Cultur(al) Analysis." *Du Bois Review* 8(2): 10–22.

Goyette, Kimberly, and Xie Yu. 1999. "Educational Expectations of Asian American Youths: Determinants and Ethnic Differences." *Sociology of Education* 72(1): 22–36.

Guendelman, Maya D., Sapna Cheryan, and Benoît Monin. 2011. "Fitting In but Getting Fat: Identity Threat and Dietary Choices Among U.S. Immigrant Groups." *Psychological Science* 22(7): 959–67.

Haller, Archibald O., and Alejandro Portes. 1973. "Status Attainment Processes." *Sociology of Education* 46(1): 51–91.

Hanson, Sandra L., and Yu Meng. 2008. "Science Majors and Degrees Among Asian American Students: Influences of Race and Sex in 'Model Minority' Experiences." *Journal of Women and Minorities in Science and Engineering* 14: 225–52.

Harding, David J. 2007. "Cultural Context, Sexual Behavior, and Romantic Relationships in Disadvantaged Neighborhoods." *American Sociological Review* 72: 341–64.

———. 2010. *Living the Drama: Community, Conflict, and Culture Among Inner-City Boys.* Chicago: University of Chicago Press.

Hein, Jeremy. 2006. *Ethnic Origins: The Adaptation of Cambodian and Hmong Refugees in Four American Cities.* New York: Russell Sage Foundation.

Hibel, Jacob, Daphne M. Penn, and R. C. Morris. Unpublished Manuscript. "Racial/Ethnic Concordance in the Associations Among Academic Self-Efficacy, Achievement, and Global Self-Esteem During Elementary and Middle School."

Hing, Julianne. 2014. "The Chinese-American Community Grapples with Affirmative Action, and Itself," Colorlines, March 18. Available at: http://colorlines.com/archives/2014/03/the_chinese-american_community_grapples_with_affirmative_action_and_itself.html (accessed March 27, 2014).

Hochschild, Jennifer L. 1995. *Facing Up to the American Dream.* Princeton, N.J.: Princeton University Press.

Holzer, Harry J. 1996. *What Employers Want: Job Prospects for Less-Educated Workers.* New York: Russell Sage Foundation.

Hong, Ying-yi, Chi-yue Chiu, Carol S. Dweck, Derrick M.-S. Lin, and Wendy Wan. 1999. "Implicit Theories, Attributions, and Coping: A Meaning System Approach." *Journal of Personality and Social Psychology* 77(3): 588–99.

Horvat, Erin McNamara, and Carla O'Connor. 2006. *Beyond Acting White: Reframing the Debate on Black Student Achievement.* Lanham, Md.: Rowman & Littlefield.

Hsin, Amy, and Xu Xie. 2014. "Explaining Asian Americans' Academic Advantage over Whites." *Proceedings of the National Academy of Sciences of the United States of America* 111(23): 8416–21.

Huang, Eddie, 2013. *Fresh Off the Boat: A Memoir.* New York: Spiegel & Grau.

Huntington, Samuel P. 2004. *Who Are We? The Challenges to America's National Identity.* New York: Simon & Schuster.

Hyun, Jane. 2005. *Breaking the Bamboo Ceiling: Career Strategies for Asians.* New York: HarperCollins.

Inzlicht, Michael, and Toni Schmader. 2012. *Stereotype Threat: Theory, Process, and Application.* New York: Oxford University Press.

Jiménez, Tomás R. 2010. *Replenished Ethnicity: Mexican Americans, Immigration, and Identity.* Berkeley: University of California Press.

Jiménez, Tomás R., and Adam L. Horowitz. 2013. "When White Is Just Alright: How Immigrants Redefine Achievement and Reconfigure the Ethnoracial Hierarchy." *American Sociological Review* 78(5): 849–71.

Johnson, Rucker C. 2014. "Long-Term Impacts of School Desegregation and School Quality on Adult Attainments." *NBER* working paper no. 16664. Cambridge, Mass.: National Bureau of Economic Research.

Johnson, Rucker C., C. Kirabo Jackson, and Claudia Persico. 2015. "The Effects of School Spending on Educational & Economic Outcomes: Evidence from School Finance Reforms." *NBER* working paper no. 20847. Cambridge, Mass.: National Bureau of Economic Research.

Kao, Grace. 1995. "Asian Americans as Model Minorities? A Look at Their Academic Performance." *American Journal of Education* 103: 121–59.

———. 2001. "Race and Ethnic Differences in Peer Influences on Educational Achievement." In *The Problem of the Century: Racial Stratification in the U.S. at the Millennium,* edited by Douglas Massey and Elijah Anderson. New York: Russell Sage Foundation.

Kao, Grace, and Marta Tienda. 1998. "Educational Aspirations of Minority Youth." *American Journal of Education* 106: 349–84.

Karabel, Jerome. 2005. *The Chosen: The Hidden History of Admission and Exclusion at Harvard, Yale, and Princeton.* New York: Houghton Mifflin.

Kasinitz, Philip, John H. Mollenkopf, Mary C. Waters, and Jennifer Holdaway. 2008. *Inheriting the City.* New York: Russell Sage Foundation.

Khan, Yasmeen. 2013. "Most Eighth Graders Matched to a High School of Their Choice," WNYC Schoolbook, March 15, 2013. Available at: http://www.schoolbook.org/2013/03/15/high-school-admissions (accessed March 27, 2015).

Kibria, Nazli. 2003. *Becoming Asian American: Second-Generation Chinese and Korean American Identities.* Baltimore Md.: Johns Hopkins University Press.

Kim, Eunyoung. 2014. "When Social Class Meets Ethnicity: College-Going Experiences of Chinese and Korean Immigrant Students." *Review of Higher Education* 37(3): 321–48.

Kohl, Herbert R. 1994. *"I Won't Learn from You" and Other Thoughts on Creative Maladjustment.* New York: New Press.

Kozlowski, Karen Phelan. 2014. "Culture or Teacher Bias? Racial and Ethnic Variation in Student-Teacher Effort Assessment Match/Mismatch." *Race and Social Problems* (December). Available at: http://link.springer.com/article/10.1007/s12552-014-9138-x#page-1 (accessed March 27, 2015).

Kray, Laura J., Leigh Thompson, and Adam Galinsky. 2001. "Battle of the Sexes: Gender Stereotype Confirmation and Reaction in Negotiations." *Journal of Personality and Social Psychology* 80(6): 942–58.

Krueger, Joachim. 1996. "Personal Beliefs and Cultural Stereotypes About Racial Characteristics." *Journal of Personality and Social Psychology* 71(3): 536–48.

Lamont, Michèle. 2000. *The Dignity of Working Men.* Cambridge, Mass., and New York: Harvard University Press and Russell Sage Foundation.

Lanphier, C. Michael. 1983. "Dilemmas of Decentralization: Refugee Sponsorship and Service in Canada and the United States." In *The Southeast Asian Environment,* edited by Douglas R. Webster. Ottawa: University of Ottawa Press.

Lareau, Annette. 2003. *Unequal Childhoods.* Berkeley: University of California Press.

Lareau, Annette, and Jessica McCrory Calarco. 2012. "Class, Cultural Capital, and Institutions: The Case of Families and Schools." In *Facing Social Class: How Societal Rank Influences Interaction,* edited by Susan T. Fisk and Hazel Rose Marcus. New York: Russell Sage Foundation.

Lau, Estelle T. 2007. *Paper Families: Identity, Immigration Administration, and Chinese Exclusion.* Durham, N.C.: Duke University Press.

Leach, Mark A., Frank D. Bean, Susan K. Brown, and Jennifer Van Hook. 2011. "Unauthorized Immigrant Parents: Do Their Migration Histories Limit Their Children's Education?" US2010: Discover America in a New Century (October). Available at: http://www.s4.brown.edu/us2010/Data/Report/report101811.pdf (accessed March 31, 2015).

Lee, Erika. 2007. "The 'Yellow Peril' and Asian Exclusion in the Americas." *Pacific Historical Review* 76(4): 537–62.

Lee, Jennifer. 2002. *Civility in the City: Blacks, Jews, and Koreans in Urban America.* Cambridge, Mass.: Harvard University Press.

———. 2005. "Who We Are: America Becoming and Becoming American." *Du Bois Review* 2(2): 287–302.

———. 2013. "From Unassimilable to Exceptional." The Society Pages: Social Science That Matters, August 27. Available at: http://thesocietypages.org/specials/from-unassimilable-to-exceptional/ (accessed March 27, 2015).

———. 2014a. "Asian American Exceptionalism and Stereotype Promise." In *Color Lines and Racial Angles,* edited by Douglas Hartmann and Christopher Uggen. New York: W. W. Norton.

———. 2014b. "Don't Tell Amy Chua: Mexicans Are the Most Successful Immigrants." *Time,* February 25, 2014. Available at: http://ideas.time.com/2014/02/25/dont-tell-amy-chua-mexicans-are-the-most-successful-immigrants/ (accessed February 12, 2015).

Lee, Jennifer, and Frank D. Bean. 2010. *The Diversity Paradox: Immigration and the Color Line in Twenty-First-Century America.* New York: Russell Sage Foundation.

———. 2014. "America's New Racial/Ethnic Diversity: Immigration, Intermarriage, and Multiracial Identification in the 21st Century." In *Oxford Handbook on Racial and Ethnic Politics,* edited by Taeku Lee and Mark Sawyer. New York: Oxford University Press.

————. 2015. "Immigration and the Changing Status of Asian Americans." In *Emerging Trends in the Social and Behavioral Sciences*, edited by Robert Scott and Stephen Kosslyn. New York: Wiley & Sons, Inc.

Lee, Jennifer, Jørgen Carling, and Pia Orrenius. 2014. "The International Migration Review at 50: Reflecting on Half a Century of International Migration Research and Looking Ahead." *International Migration Review* 48(suppl. 1): S3–36.

Lee, Jennifer, and Min Zhou. 2009. "Becoming 'Ethnic,' Becoming 'Angeleno,' and/or Becoming 'American': The Multifaceted Experiences of Immigrant Children and the Children of Immigrants in Los Angeles." New York: Russell Sage Foundation.

————. 2013. "Frames of Achievement and Opportunity Horizons: Second-Generation Chinese, Vietnamese, and Mexicans in Los Angeles." In *Immigration, Poverty, and Socioeconomic Inequality*, edited by David Card and Steven Raphael. New York: Russell Sage Foundation.

————. 2014a. "The Success Frame and Achievement Paradox: The Costs and Consequences for Asian Americans." *Race and Social Problems* 6(1): 38–55.

————. 2014b. "From Unassimilable to Exceptional: The Rise of Asian Americans and 'Stereotype Promise.'" *New Diversities* 16(1): 7–22.

Lee, Rose Hum. 1960. *The Chinese in the United States of America.* Hong Kong: Hong Kong University Press.

Lee, Sara S. 2006. "Class Matters: Racial and Ethnic Identities of Working- and Middle-Class Second-Generation Korean Americans in New York City." In *Becoming New Yorkers: Ethnographies of the New Second Generation*, edited by Philip Kasinitz, John H. Mollenkopf, and Mary C. Waters. New York: Russell Sage Foundation.

Lee, Sharon M. 2002. "Do Asian American Faculty Face a Glass Ceiling in Higher Education?" *American Education Research Journal* 39(3): 695–724.

Lee, Tiane L., and Susan T. Fiske. 2006. "Not an Outgroup, Not Yet an Ingroup: Immigrants in the Stereotype Content Model." *International Journal of Intercultural Relations* 30: 751–68.

Levy, Becca. 1996. "Improving Memory in Old Age Through Implicit Self-Stereotyping." *Journal of Personality and Social Psychology* 71: 1092–107.

Lewis, Oscar. 1959. *Five Families: Mexican Case Studies in the Culture of Poverty.* New York: Basic Books.

Li, Wei. 1997. "Spatial Transformation of an Urban Ethnic Community from Chinatown to Chinese Ethnoburb in Los Angeles." PhD diss., Department of Geography, University of Southern California.

Lieberson, Stanley. 1976. "Rank-Sum Comparisons Between Groups." *Sociological Methodology* 7: 276–91.

Lin, Monica H., Virginia S. Y. Kwan, Anna Cheung, and Susan T. Fiske. 2005. "Stereotype Content Model Explains Prejudice for an Envied Outgroup: Scale of Anti-Asian American Stereotypes." *Personality and Social Psychology Bulletin* 31(1): 34–47.

Liu, Cathy Yang, Jonathan Miller, and Qingfang Wang. 2014. "Ethnic Enterprises and Community Development." *GeoJournal* 79(5): 565–76.

Logan, John R., and Weiwei Zhang. 2013. "Separate but Equal: Asian Nationalities in the U.S." US2010: Discover America in a New Century (June). Available at: http://www.s4.brown.edu/us2010/Data/Report/report06112013.pdf (accessed March 27, 2015).

Louie, Vivian. 2004. *Compelled to Excel: Immigration, Education, and Opportunity Among Chinese Americans.* Stanford, Calif.: Stanford University Press.

Lu, Wei-Ting. 2013. "Confucius or Mozart: Community Cultural Wealth and Upward Mobility Among Children of Chinese Immigrants." *Qualitative Sociology* 36: 303–21.

Luo, Tian, and Richard J. Holden. 2014. "Do Different Groups Invest Differently in Higher Education?" *Beyond the Numbers* 3(June 13). Available at: http://www.bls.gov/opub/btn/volume-3/do-different-groups-invest-differently-in-higher-education.htm (accessed March 27, 2015).

Lyman, Stanford M. 1974. *Chinese Americans.* New York: Random House.

Marimuthu, T., J. S. Singh, K. Ahmad, H. K. Lim, H. Mukherjee, S. Osman, T. Chelliah, J. R. Sharma, N. M. Salleh, L. Yong, T. L. Lim, S. Sukumaran, L. K. Thong, and W. Jamaluddin. 1991. *Extra-School Instruction, Social Equity, and Educational Quality* [in Malaysian]. Singapore: International Development Research Centre.

Marsden, Anna. 2014. "Chinese Descendants in Italy: Emergence, Role and Uncertain Identity." *Ethnic and Racial Studies* 37(7): 1239–52.

Massey, Douglas S. 1987. "Do Undocumented Immigrants Earn Lower Wages Than Legal Immigrants?" *International Migration Review* 21: 236–74.

Massey, Douglas S., Camille Z. Charles, Garvey Lundy, and Mary J. Fischer. 2003. *The Source of the River: The Social Origins of Freshmen at America's Selective Colleges and Universities.* Princeton, N.J.: Princeton University Press.

Massey, Douglas S., and Nancy A. Denton. 1993. *American Apartheid: Segregation and the Making of the Underclass.* Cambridge, Mass.: Harvard University Press.

Massey, Douglas, Jorge Durand, and Nolan J. Malone. 2002. *Beyond Smoke and Mirrors: Mexican Immigration in an Era of Economic Integration.* New York: Russell Sage Foundation.

Massey, Douglas S., and Mary J. Fischer. 2005. "Stereotype Threat and Academic Performance: New Findings from a Racially Diverse Sample of College Freshmen." *Du Bois Review* 2(1): 45–67.

McKee, Robert J. 2012. "In Response to Gans: The Culture-Structure Binary." *Identities: Global Studies in Culture and Power* 19(5): 632–38.

Merton, Robert K. 1948. "The Self-Fulfilling Prophecy." *Antioch Review* 8(2): 193–210.

Min, Pyong Gap. 1984. "From White-Collar Occupations to Small Business: Korean Immigrants' Occupational Adjustment." *Sociological Quarterly* 25(3): 333–52.

Modood, Tariq. 2011. "Capitals, Ethnic Identity, and Educational Qualifications." In *The Next Generation: Immigrant Youth in a Comparative Perspective,* edited by Richard Alba and Mary C. Waters. New York: New York University Press.

Montero, Darrel. 1979. *Vietnamese Americans: Patterns of Resettlement and Socioeconomic Adaptation in the United States.* Washington, D.C.: Economic Policy Institute.

Mounk, Yascha. 2014. "Is Harvard Unfair to Asian-Americans?" *New York Times,* November 24.

Moynihan, Daniel Patrick. 1965. *The Negro Family: The Case for National Action.* Washington: U.S. Department of Labor, Office of Policy Planning and Research.

Mueller, Claudia M., and Carol S. Dweck. 1998. "Intelligence Praise Can Undermine Motivation and Performance." *Journal of Personality and Social Psychology* 75: 33–52.

Murray, Charles. 2012. "Why Aren't Asians Republicans?" AEI Ideas, November 26. Available at: http://www.aei-ideas.org/2012/11/why-arent-asians-republicans/ (accessed March 27, 2015).

Neckerman, Kathryn M., Prudence Carter, and Jennifer Lee. 1999. "Segmented Assimilation and Minority Cultures of Mobility." *Ethnic and Racial Studies* 22(6): 945–65.

Newman, Katherine S. 1999. *Falling from Grace: Downward Mobility in the Age of Affluence.* Berkeley, Calif.: University of California Press.

Nguyen, Hannah-Hanh D., Alisha O'Neal, and Ann Marie Ryan. 2003. "Relating Test-Taking Attitudes and Skills and Stereotype Threat Effects to the Racial Gap in Cognitive Ability Test Performance." *Human Performance* 16: 261–93.

Noam, Kris R. 2014. "How National Context Influences the Childrearing Practices of Second-Generation Chinese Tiger Parents." *New Diversities* 16(1): 44–55.

O'Connor, Carla, Erin McNamara Horvat, and Amanda E. Lewis. 2006. "Introduction: Framing the Field: Past and Future Research on the Historic Underachievement of Black Students." In *Beyond Acting White: Reframing the Debate on Black Student Achievement,* edited by Erin McNamara Horvat and Carla O'Connor. Lanham, Md.: Rowman & Littlefield.

Ogbu, John U. 1974. *The Next Generation: An Ethnography of Education in an Urban Neighborhood.* New York: Academic Press.

Ogbu, John U., and Herbert D. Simons. 1998. "Voluntary and Involuntary Minorities: A Cultural-Ecological Theory of School Performance with Some Implications for Education." *Anthropology and Education Quarterly* 29(2): 155–88.

Okamoto, Dina G. 2014. *Redefining Race: Asian American Panethnicity and Shifting Ethnic Boundaries.* New York: Russell Sage Foundation.

Okamura, Jonathan. 1981. "Situational Ethnicity." *Ethnic and Racial Studies* 4: 452–65.

Okihiro, Gary Y. 1994. *Margins and Mainstreams: Asians in American History and Culture.* Seattle: University of Washington Press.

Omi, Michael, and Howard Winant, 1994. *Racial Formation in the United States: From the 1960s to the 1990s.* 2nd ed. New York: Routledge.

Organization for Economic Cooperation and Development (OECD). Centre for Educational Research and Innovation. 2011. "Education at a Glance 2011: OECD Indicators." OECD iLibrary (September 13). Available at: http://dx.doi.org/10.1787/eag-2011-en (accessed March 27, 2015).

Pager, Devah. 2003. "The Mark of a Criminal Record." *American Journal of Sociology* 108(5): 937–75.

———. 2007. *Marked: Race, Crime, and Finding Work in an Era of Mass Incarceration.* Chicago: University of Chicago Press.

Palepu, Anita, Phyllis L. Carr, Robert H. Friedman, Harold Amos, Arlene S. Ash, and Mark A. Moskowitz. 1995. "Minority Faculty and Academic Rank in Medicine." *Journal of the American Medical Association* 250: 767–71.

Park, Robert. 1950. *Race and Culture.* Glencoe, Ill.: Free Press.

Patterson, Orlando. 2014. "How Sociologists Made Themselves Irrelevant." *Chronicle of Higher Education,* December 1. Available at: http://chronicle.com/article/How-Sociologists-Made/150249/ (accessed December 4, 2014).

———. 2015. *The Cultural Matrix: Understanding Black Youth.* Cambridge, Mass: Harvard University Press.

Pattillo-McCoy, Mary. 1999. *Black Picket Fences: Privilege and Peril Among the Black Middle Class.* Chicago: University of Chicago Press.

Pedone, Valentina. 2011. " 'As a Rice Plant in a Wheat Field': Identity Negotiation Among Children of Chinese Immigrants." *Journal of Modern Italian Studies* 16: 492–503.

Petersen, Williams. 1966. "Success Story, Japanese-American Style." *The New York Times Magazine,* January 9: 21.

Pew Research Center. 2012. *The Rise of Asian Americans.* Washington, D.C.: Pew Research Center.

Polletta, Francesca. 2006. *It Was Like a Fever: Storytelling in Protest and Politics.* Chicago: University of Chicago Press.

Portes, Alejandro, and Lingxin Hao. 2004. "The Schooling of Children of Immigrants." *Proceedings of the National Academy of Sciences of the United States of America* 101: 11920–27.

Portes, Alejandro, and Rubén G. Rumbaut. 2001. *Legacies: The Story of the Immigrant Second Generation.* New York: Russell Sage Foundation.

Portes, Alejandro, and Min Zhou. 1993. "The New Second Generation: Segmented Assimilation and Its Variants." *Annals of the American Academy of Political and Social Science* 530: 74–96.

Ramakrishnan, Karthick. 2012. "When Words Fail: Careful Framing Needed in Research on Asian Americans." *Hyphen: Asian America Unabridged*, June 27. Available at: http://www.hyphenmagazine.com/blog/archive/2012/06/when-words-fail-careful-framing-needed-research-asian-americans#sthash.zwBleJ6i.dpuf (accessed May 1, 2013).

Ramakrishnan, Karthick, and Farah Z. Ahmad. 2014. "Education." State of Asian Americans and Pacific Islanders Series. Center for American Progress, April 23. Available at: http://www.americanprogress.org/wp-content/uploads/2014/04/AAPI-Education.pdf (accessed May 1, 2014).

Ramstad, Evan. 2011. "Studying Too Hard Is a No-No in Upwardly Mobile South Korea." *Wall Street Journal*, October 6.

Reardon, Sean F. 2011. "The Widening Academic Achievement Gap Between the Rich and the Poor: New Evidence and Possible Explanations." In *Whither Opportunity: Rising Inequality, Schools, and Children's Life Chances*, edited by Greg J. Duncan and Richard N. Murnane. New York: Russell Sage Foundation.

Ridgeway, Cecilia L. 2011. *Framed by Gender: How Gender Inequality Persists in the Modern World*. New York: Oxford University Press.

Ridgeway, Cecilia, and Susan R. Fisk. 2012. "Class Rules, Status Dynamics, and 'Gateway' Interactions." In *Facing Social Class: How Societal Rank Influences Interaction*, edited by Susan T. Fisk and Hazel Rose Marcus. New York: Russell Sage Foundation.

Ripley, Amanda. 2011. "Teacher, Leave Those Kids Alone." *Time*, September 25. Available at: http://www.time.com/time/magazine/article/0,9171,2094427,00.html (accessed March 27, 2015).

Rist, Ray C. 1970. "Student Social Class and Teacher Expectations: The Self-Fulfilling Prophecy in Ghetto Education." *Harvard Educational Review* 40(3): 411–51.

Rivera, Lauren A. 2012. "Hiring as Cultural Matching: The Case of Elite Professional Service Firms." *American Sociological Review* 77(6): 999–1022.

Rosenthal, Robert, and Lenore Jacobson. 1968. *Pygmalion in the Classroom: Teacher Expectation and Pupils' Intellectual Development*. New York: Holt, Rinehart, and Winston.

Rumbaut, Rubén G. 2005. "Vietnamese, Laotian, and Cambodian Americans." In *Asian Americans: Contemporary Trends and Issues*, edited by Pyong Gap Min. Thousand Oaks, Calif.: Sage Publications.

Rumbaut, Rubén G., Frank D. Bean, Leo R. Chávez, Jennifer Lee, Susan K. Brown, Louis DeSipio, and Min Zhou. 2004. Immigration and Inter-generational Mobility in Metropolitan Los Angeles (IIMMLA), 2004. ICPSR22627-v1. Ann Arbor, Mich.: Inter-university Consortium for Political and Social Research [distributor], 2008-07-01. Available at: http://www.icpsr.umich.edu/icpsrweb/DSDR/studies/22627 (accessed March 31, 2015).

Sacerdote, Bruce. 2011. "Peer Effects in Education: How Might They Work, How Big Are They, and How Much Do We Know Thus Far?" *Handbook of the Economics of Education* 3: 249–77.

Sackett, Paul R., and Ann Marie Ryan. 2011. "Concern About Generalizing Stereotype Threat Research Findings to Operational High Stake Testing." In *Stereotype Threat: Theory, Process, and Application,* edited by Michael Inzlicht and Tony Schmader. New York: Oxford University Press.

Sakamoto, Arthur, Kimberly A. Goyette, and Chang Hwan Kim. 2009. "Socioeconomic Attainments of Asian Americans." *Annual Review of Sociology* 35: 255–76.

Samson, Frank L. 2013. "Multiple Group Threat and Malleable White Attitudes towards Academic Merit." *Du Bois Review* 10(1): 233–60.

Saperstein, Aliya. 2015. "Developing a Racial Mobility Perspective for the Social Sciences." RSF Review: Research from the Russell Sage Foundation. Available at: http://www.russellsage.org/blog/developing-racial-mobility-perspective-social-sciences (accessed March 27, 2015).

Saxton, Alexander. 1971. *The Indispensable Enemy: Labor and the Anti-Chinese Movement in California.* Berkeley: University of California Press.

Sayler, Lucy E. 1995. *Laws Harsh as Tigers: Chinese Immigrants and the Shaping of Modern Immigration Law.* Chapel Hill: University of North Carolina Press.

Sewell, William H., Archibald O. Haller, and George W. Ohlendorf. 1970. "The Educational and Early Occupational Status Attainment Process: Replication and Revision." *American Sociological Review* 35(6): 1014–27.

Sewell, William H., Archibald O. Haller, and Alejandro Portes. 1969. "The Educational and Early Occupational Attainment Process." *American Sociological Review* 34(1): 82–92.

Shih, Margaret, Nalini Ambady, Jennifer A. Richeson, Kentaro Fujita, and Heather M. Gray. 2002. "Stereotype Performance Boosts: The Impact of Self-Relevance and the Manner of Stereotype Activation." *Journal of Personality and Social Psychology* 83(3): 638–47.

Shih, Margaret, Courtney Bonam, Diana Sanchez, and Courtney Peck. 2007. "The Social Construction of Race: Biracial Identity and Vulnerability to Stereotypes." *Cultural Diversity and Ethnic Minority Psychology* 13: 125–33.

Shih, Margaret, Todd L. Pittinsky, and Nalini Ambady. 1999. "Stereotype Susceptibility: Identity Salience and Shifts in Quantitative Performance." *Psychological Science* 10(1): 80–83.

Shih, Margaret J., Todd L. Pittinsky, and Geoffrey C. Ho. 2012. "Stereotype Boost: Positive Outcomes from the Activation of Positive Stereotypes." In *Stereotype Threat: Theory, Process, and Application,* edited by Michael Inzlicht and Toni Schmader. New York: Oxford University Press.

Sidanius, Jim, Shana Levin, Colette Van Laar, and David O. Sears. 2010. *The Diversity Challenge: Social Identity and Intergroup Relations on the College Campus.* New York: Russell Sage Foundation.

Simmel, Georg. 1968. *The Conflict of Modern Culture and Other Essays.* New York: Teachers College Press.

Siy, John Oliver, and Sapna Cheryan. 2013. "When Compliments Fail to Flatter: American Individualism and Responses to Positive Stereotypes." *Journal of Personality and Social Psychology* 104(1): 87–102.

Skeldon, Ronald. 1996. "Migration from China." *Journal of International Affairs* 49(2): 434–55.

Skrentny, John D. 2008. "Culture and Race/Ethnicity: Bolder, Deeper, and Broader." *Annals of the American Academy of Political and Social Science* 619: 59–77.

———. 2014. *After Civil Rights: Racial Discrimination in the New American Workplace.* Princeton, N.J.: Princeton University Press.

Small, Mario Luis. 2004. *Villa Victoria: The Transformations of Social Capital in a Boston Barrio.* Chicago: University of Chicago Press.

———. 2009. *Unanticipated Gains: Origins of Network Inequality in Everyday Life.* New York: Oxford University Press.

Small, Mario L., David J. Harding, and Michèle Lamont. 2010. "Reconsidering Culture and Poverty." *Annals of the American Academy of Political and Social Science* 629: 6–27.

Smith, Robert C. 2006. *Mexican New York: Transnational Lives of New Immigrants.* Berkeley: University of California Press.

———. 2014. "Black Mexicans, Conjunctural Ethnicity, and Operating Identities—Long-Term Ethnographic Analysis." *American Sociological Review* 79(3): 517–48.

Smith, Sandra S. 2007. *Lone Pursuit: Distrust and Defensive Individualism Among the Black Poor.* New York: Russell Sage Foundation.

Solórzano, Daniel, Miguel Ceja, and Tara Yosso. 2000. "Critical Race Theory, Racial Microaggressions, and Campus Racial Climate: The Experiences of African American College Students." *Journal of Negro Education* 69: 60–73.

Sowell, Thomas. 1981. *Ethnic America: A History.* New York: Basic Books.

Spencer, Steven J., Claude M. Steele, and Diane M. Quinn. 1999. "Stereotype Threat and Women's Math Performance." *Journal of Experimental Social Psychology* 35: 4–28.

Steele, Claude M. 1997. "A Threat in the Air: How Stereotypes Shape Intellectual Identity and Performance." *American Psychologist* 52: 613–29.

———. 1998. "Stereotyping and Its Threat Are Real." *American Psychologist* 53: 680–81.

Steele, Claude M., and Joshua Aronson. 1995. "Stereotype Threat and the Intellectual Test Performance of African Americans." *Journal of Personality and Social Psychology* 69(5): 797–811.

Steinberg, Laurence. 1996a. *Beyond the Classroom: Why School Reform Has Failed and What Parents Need to Do.* New York: Simon & Schuster.

————. 1996b. "Ethnicity and Adolescent Achievement." *American Educator* 20(2, Summer): 44–48.

Steinberg, Laurence, Sanford M. Dornbusch, and B. Bradford Brown. 1992. "Ethnic Differences in Adolescent Achievement." *American Psychologist* 47(6): 723–29.

Steinberg, Stephen. 1981. *The Ethnic Myth: Race, Ethnicity, and Class in America.* Boston, Mass.: Beacon Press.

Stevenson, David L., and David P. Baker. 1992. "Shadow Education and Allocation in Formal Schooling: Transition to University in Japan." *American Journal of Sociology* 97(6): 1639–57.

Stevenson, Harold W., and Shin-ying Lee. 1990. "Contexts of Achievement: A Study of American, Chinese, and Japanese Children." *Monographs of the Society for Research in Child Development* 55(12, Serial no. 221): 1–119.

Stigler, James W., Shin-ying Lee, and Harold W. Stevenson. 1987. "Mathematics Classrooms in Japan, Taiwan, and the United States." *Child Development* 58(5): 1272–85.

Stone, Jeff, Christian I. Lynch, Mike Sjomeling, and John M. Darley. 1999. "Stereotype Threat Effects on Black and White Athletic Performance." *Journal of Personality and Social Psychology* 77: 1213–27.

Sue, Derald Wing, Jennifer Bucceri, Annie I. Lin, Kevin L. Nadal, and Gina C. Torino. 2007. "Racial Microaggressions and the Asian American Experience." *Cultural Diversity and Ethnic Minority Psychology* 13: 72–81.

Sue, Stanley, and Sumie Okazaki. 1990. "Asian-American Educational Achievements: A Phenomenon in Search of an Explanation." *American Psychologist* 45(8): 913–20.

Sun, Yongmin. 1998. "The Academic Success of East-Asian-American Students: An Investment Model." *Social Science Research* 27: 432–56.

Swidler, Ann. 1986. "Culture in Action: Symbols and Strategies." *American Sociological Review* 51(2): 273–86.

Takaki, Ronald T. 1979. *Iron Cages: Race and Culture in Nineteenth-Century America.* Seattle: University of Washington Press.

————. 1989. *Strangers from a Different Shore: A History of Asian Americans.* Boston, Mass.: Little, Brown.

Tang, Joyce. 1993. "The Career Attainment of Caucasian and Asian Engineers." *Sociological Quarterly* 34: 467–96.

Telles, Edward E., and Vilma Ortiz. 2008. *Generations of Exclusion: Mexican Americans, Assimilation, and Race.* New York: Russell Sage Foundation.

Tran, Van C. 2015. "More Than Just Black: Cultural Perils and Opportunities in Inner-City Neighborhoods." In *The Cultural Matrix: Understanding Black Youth,* edited by Orlando Patterson. Cambridge, Mass.: Harvard University Press.

Trieu, Monica Mong. 2008. "Ethnic Chameleons and the Contexts of Identity: A Comparative Look at the Dynamics of Intra-national Identity Construction Between 1.5 and Second Generation Chinese-Vietnamese and

Vietnamese Americans." PhD diss., Department of Sociology, University of California–Irvine.

Tseng, Yen-fen. 1994. "Chinese Ethnic Economy: San Gabriel Valley, Los Angeles County." *Journal of Urban Affairs* 16(2): 169–89.

Uhlmann, Eric Luis, and Geoffrey L. Cohen. 2005. "Constructed Criteria: Redefining Merit to Justify Discrimination." *Psychological Science* 16(6): 474–80.

United Nations Population Fund (UNFPA). 2012. "Fact Sheet: Education in Viet Nam: Evidence from the 2009 Census." Available at: http://vietnam.unfpa.org/webdav/site/vietnam/shared/Factsheet/FINAL_Factsheet_Education_ENG.pdf (accessed March 7, 2015).

U.S. Census Bureau. 2007. Survey of Business Owners: Asian-Owned Businesses. Available at: www.census.gov/econ/sbo/about.html (accessed March 27, 2015)

———. 2009. "S0201, Selected Population Profile in the United States" (data set: 2009 American Community Survey one-year estimates). Available at: http://www.ohadatabook.com/ACS_2009_US_Combo.pdf (accessed February 12, 2015).

———. 2010a. "General Population and Housing Characteristics, Selected Population Profile of the United States (S0201)," Available at: http://factfinder.census.gov/faces/nav/jsf/pages/searchresults.xhtml?refresh=t (accessed July 15, 2013).

———. 2010b. "Public-Use Microdata Samples (PUMS): 2010 Tracts." Available at: https://www.census.gov/geo/maps-data/maps/2010tract.html (accessed September 1, 2012).

———. 2012. *The Asian Population: 2010.* March (C2010BR-11). Washington: U.S. Department of Commerce, Economics and Statistics Administration.

U.S. Citizenship and Immigration Services (USCIS). 2012. "Persons Obtaining Legal Permanent Resident Status by Region and Selected Country of Last Residence: Fiscal Years 1820–1912." Table 2 in *Yearbook of Immigration Statistics, 2012.* Available at: http://www.dhs.gov/yearbook-immigration-statistics-2012-legal-permanent-residents (accessed February 12, 2015).

U.S. Department of Homeland Security. 2012. *Yearbook of Immigration Statistics: 2011.* Washington: U.S. Department of Homeland Security, Office of Immigration Statistics.

U.S. News & World Report. 1966. "Success of One Minority Group in U.S.," December 26.

Vaisey, Stephen. 2010. "What People Want: Rethinking Poverty, Culture, and Educational Attainment." *Annals of the American Academy of Political and Social Science* 629: 75–101.

Vallejo, Jody Agius. 2012. *Barrios to Burbs: The Making of the Mexican American Middle Class.* Stanford, Calif.: Stanford University Press.

Vallejo, Jody Agius, and Jennifer Lee. 2009. "Brown Picket Fences: The Immigrant Narrative and 'Giving Back' Among the Mexican Middle-Class." *Ethnicities* 9(1): 5–31.

Van Hook, Jennifer, and Frank D. Bean. 2009. "Explaining Mexican-Immigrant Welfare Behaviors: The Importance of Employment-Related Cultural Repertoires." *American Sociological Review* 74(3): 423–44.

Volpp, Leti. 2003. "American Mestizo: Filipinos and Anti-Miscegenation Laws in California." In *Mixed Race in America and the Law,* edited by Kevin R. Johnson. New York: New York University Press.

Wacquant, Loïc. 2013. "Symbolic Power and Group-Making: On Pierre Bourdieu's Reframing of Class." *Journal of Classical Sociology* 13(2): 274–91.

Waldinger, Roger, and Jennifer Lee. 2001. "New Immigrants in Urban America." In *Strangers at the Gates: New Immigrants in Urban America,* edited by Roger Waldinger. Berkeley: University of California Press.

Walton, Gregory M., and Geoffrey L. Cohen. 2003. "Stereotype Lift." *Journal of Experimental Social Psychology* 39: 456–67.

Wan, Helen. 2013. *The Partner Track: A Novel.* New York: St. Martin's Press.

Wang, Hui. 2002. "'Modernity' and 'Asia' in the Study of Chinese History." In *Across Cultural Borders: Historiography in Global Perspective,* edited by Eckhardt Fuchs and Benedikt Stuchtey. Lanham, Md.: Rowman & Littlefield.

Warikoo, Natasha Kumar. 2011. *Balancing Acts: Youth Culture in the Global City.* Berkeley: University of California Press.

Warner, W. Lloyd, and Leo Srole. 1945. *The Social System of American Ethnic Groups.* New Haven, Conn.: Yale University Press.

Waters, Mary C. 1990. *Ethnic Options: Choosing Identities in America.* Berkeley: University of California Press.

———. 1999. *Black Identities: West Indian Immigrant Dreams and American Realities.* Cambridge, Mass.: Harvard University Press.

Whitmore, John K. 1985. "Chinese from Southeast Asia." In *Refugees in the United States: A Reference Handbook,* edited by David W. Haines. Westport, Conn.: Greenwood Press.

Williams, Joan C., Katherine W. Phillips, and Erika V. Hall. 2014. "Double-Jeopardy? Gender Bias Against Women of Color in Science." Research Report. UC Hastings College of Law, University of California, San Francisco. Available at: http://www.worklifelaw.org (accessed February 12, 2015).

———. 1987. *The Truly Disadvantaged: The Inner City, the Underclass, and Public Policy.* Chicago: University of Chicago Press.

———. 1996. *When Work Disappears: The World of the New Urban Poor.* New York: Vintage Books.

Wilson, William Julius. 1978. *The Declining Significance of Race.* Chicago: University of Chicago Press.

Woo, Deborah. 1999. *Glass Ceilings and Asian Americans: The New Face of Workplace Barriers.* Walnut Creek, Calif.: Alta Mira Press.

Wu, Ellen D. 2013. *The Color of Success: Asian Americans and the Origins of the Model Minority.* Princeton, N.J.: Princeton University Press.

Xie, Yu, and Kimberly Goyette. 2003. "Social Mobility and the Educational Choices of Asian Americans." *Social Science Research* 32: 467–98.

Yancey, William L., Eugene P. Ericksen, and Richard N. Juliani. 1976. "Emergent Ethnicity: A Review and Reformulation." *American Sociological Review* 41: 391–402.

Yang, Wesley. 2011. "Paper Tigers." *New York,* May 8. Available at: http://nymag.com/news/features/asian-americans-2011-5/ (accessed March 27, 2015).

Yiu, Jessica. 2013. "Calibrated Ambitions: Low Educational Ambition as a Form of Strategic Adaptation Among Chinese Youth in Spain." *International Migration Review* 47(3): 573–611.

Yopyk, Darren J.A., and Deborah A. Prentice. 2005. "Am I an Athlete or a Student? Identity Salience and Stereotype Threat in Student-Athletes." *Basic and Applied Social Psychology* 27: 329–36.

Young, Alford A. 2010. "New Life for an Old Concept: Frame Analysis and the Reinvigoration of Studies in Culture and Poverty." *Annals of the American Academy of Political and Social Science* 629: 53–74.

Zhou, Min. 1992. *Chinatown: The Socioeconomic Potential of an Urban Enclave.* Philadelphia Pa.: Temple University Press.

———. 1997. "Segmented Assimilation: Issues, Controversies, and Recent Research on the New Second Generation." *International Migration Review* 31(4): 825–58.

———. 2004. "Are Asian Americans Becoming White?" *Contexts* 3(1): 29–37.

———. 2006. "Negotiating Culture and Ethnicity: Intergenerational Relations in Chinese Immigrant Families in the United States." In *Cultural Psychology of Immigrants,* edited by Ram Mahalingam. Mahwah, N.J.: Lawrence Erlbaum.

———. 2008. "The Ethnic System of Supplementary Education: Non-Profit and For-Profit Institutions in Los Angeles' Chinese Immigrant Community." In *Toward Positive Youth Development: Transforming Schools and Community Programs,* edited by Beth Shinn and Hirokazu Yoshikawa. New York: Oxford University Press.

———. 2009a. *Contemporary Chinese America: Immigration, Ethnicity, and Community Transformation.* Philadelphia Pa.: Temple University Press.

———. 2009b. "How Neighborhoods Matter for Immigrant Children: The Formation of Educational Resources in Chinatown, Koreatown, and Pico Union, Los Angeles." *Journal of Ethnic and Migration Studies* 35(7): 1153–79.

———. 2014. "Segmented Assimilation and Socioeconomic Integration of Chinese Immigrant Children in the United States." *Ethnic and Racial Studies* 37(7): 1172–83.

Zhou, Min, and Carl Bankston III. 1998. *Growing Up American: How Vietnamese Children Adapt to Life in the United States.* New York: Russell Sage Foundation.

Zhou, Min, Carl L. Bankston III, and Rebecca Kim. 2002. "Rebuilding Spiritual Lives in the New Land: Religious Practices Among Southeast Asian Refugees in the United States." In *Religions in Asian America: Building Faith*

Communities, edited by Pyong Gap Min and Jung Ha Kim. Walnut Creek, Calif.: AltaMira Press.

Zhou, Min, and Guoxuan Cai. 2002. "The Chinese Language Media in the United States: Immigration and Assimilation in American Life." *Qualitative Sociology* 25(3): 419–40.

Zhou, Min, Margaret M. Chin, and Rebecca Y. Kim. 2013. "The Transformation of Chinese America: New York vs. Los Angeles." In *New York and Los Angeles: The Uncertain Future,* edited by David Halle and Andrew Beveridge. New York: Oxford University Press.

Zhou, Min, and Myungduk Cho. 2010. "Noneconomic Effects of Ethnic Entrepreneurship: Evidence from Chinatown and Koreatown in Los Angeles, USA." *Thunderbird International Business Review* 52(2): 83–96.

Zhou, Min, and Susan S. Kim. 2006. "Community Forces, Social Capital, and Educational Achievement: The Case of Supplementary Education in the Chinese and Korean Immigrant Communities." *Harvard Educational Review* 76(1): 1–29.

Zhou, Min, and Jennifer Lee. 2007. "Becoming Ethnic or Becoming American? Reflecting on the Divergent Pathways to Social Mobility and Assimilation Among the New Second Generation." *Du Bois Review* 4(1): 1–17.

———. 2014. "Assessing What Is Cultural About Asian Americans' Academic Advantage" (a commentary). *Proceedings of the National Academy of Sciences* 111(23): 8321–22.

Zhou, Min, Jennifer Lee, Jody Agius Vallejo, Rosaura Tafoya-Estrada, and Yang Sao Xiong. 2008. "Success Attained, Deterred, and Denied: Divergent Pathways to Social Mobility Among the New Second Generation in Los Angeles." *Annals of the American Academy of Political and Social Science* 620: 37–61.

Zhou, Min, and Xiyuan Li. 2003. "Ethnic Language Schools and the Development of Supplementary Education in the Immigrant Chinese Community in the United States." *New Directions for Youth Development* 100(Winter): 57–73.

Zhou, Min, Yen-fen Tseng, and Rebecca Y. Kim. 2008. "Rethinking Residential Assimilation Through the Case of Chinese Ethnoburbs in the San Gabriel Valley, California." *Amerasia Journal* 34(3): 55–83.

Zuckerman, Harriet. 1988. "The Role of the Role Model: The Other Side of a Sociological Coinage." In *Surveying Social Life,* edited by Hubert J. O'Gorman, 119–44. Middletown, Conn.: Wesleyan University Press.

~ Index ~